WOMEN
America's Last Best Hope

Kimberly Fletcher

Copyright © 2010 by Kimberly Fletcher. All rights reserved. No part of this publication may be reproduced, stored in a retrieval system, or transmitted in any form or by any means, electronic, mechanical, photocopying, recording or otherwise, without prior written permission of Kimberly Fletcher. International rights and foreign translations available only through permission of Kimberly Fletcher.

Because of the dynamic nature of the Internet, any Web addresses or links contained in this book may have changed since publication and may no longer be valid.

www.kimberlyfletcher.com

Printed in the United States of America.

ISBN: 978-1-938772-31-3

To my parents who raised me well,
the man who loves me well,
and our precious children—the reason for it all.

CONTENTS

Acknowledgments ix
In the Beginning 1
Two Sides of Women 10
Ladies First. 23
A Woman's Influence 33
Lest We Forget 50
White Wigs and Fat Cats 62
God Is Too Controversial 80
Warmongers. 95
Is There Truth Out There? 110
Fort Knox. 129
Stimulating Facts 153
Your Voice Counts 178
Rise Up, Ye Women!. 197
Ordinary Women Doing Extraordinary Things 223
The Angels Behind it All. 240

ACKNOWLEDGMENTS

I think all books begin with a moment of inspiration that leads to a journey, and that is exactly how this project came to be. There are so many people who shared this journey with me, and I have made some wonderful friends along the way. I couldn't possibly adequately express my gratitude to all those who contributed to this project and inspired me, but I hope that one day they will come to know just how much their support and encouragement meant to me. And I hope they will come to appreciate the journey as much as I have.

I want to first thank my parents for instilling in me the principles of freedom, hard work, and virtue, principles that established a firm foundation on which I could build. I want to thank my mother, especially, for her example, her devotion to her country, and her courage to stand up for what is right. My journey began with *her*, and it was her influence that led me to where I am.

I want to thank my husband, Derek, for his constant encouragement; for his unwavering dedication to God, our family, and our country; and, most of all, for his love. He has been my shoulder to cry on, my strength to lean on, and my cheerleader encouraging me onward. Knights in shining armor really do still exist in this world, and he is definitely mine.

Any mother can attest that without the support of her children, she can't get much of anything done. That is definitely the case with this book. Derek and I have been blessed with eight beautiful children, and they are the reason I do what I do. DJ, Cassiopeia, Jordan, Zachary, Adam, Amber,

Noah, and Ethan, I want you to know that your mother loves you, and someday I hope that you will come to realize just how great a role you each played in the completion of this work.

I want to thank all those who lent their eyes and ears to this project and those who made it possible: Lori for her amazing graphic design skills, Sheila for her keen eye in creating the picture that says it all, Kitty for her hours of dedicated editing—even through morning sickness—and Debi, my dear friend and kindred spirit, who understands that the best colors in the world are red, white, and blue. Without her, this book would not be possible. I owe a special debt of gratitude to my dear friend Misty, who inadvertently started this whole thing when she introduced me to the joy of home school; and to Herb Lux for introducing me to a world I never knew existed and teaching me what civic responsibility really means. I want to thank my friends for their tireless support—especially Kelli, my dearest friend, who was always there for me no matter what. And special thanks must go to all the wonderful women of Homemakers for America for their encouragement and dedication to liberty—they inspire me daily.

Most of all, I want to thank God. It was through His guidance and direction that this project evolved from what *I* thought it *should* be to what *He* knew it was *meant* to be. I'm glad I listened.

IN THE BEGINNING

Adore God.
Reverence and cherish your parents.
Love your neighbor as yourself, and your country more than yourself.
Thomas Jefferson

Two hundred thirty years ago, my ancestors were caught in the middle of a critical battle that would reshape their world and would leave a legacy of faith, hope, and freedom that would course through the blood of their descendents for generations to come. That blood flows through my veins and beats within my heart, for I am a living heir to their legacy. I am a daughter of liberty, and I have lived an amazing life because of all those remarkable men and women who forged this path of freedom for me. However, patriotism did not come from my bloodline alone. I had to experience it firsthand.

My mother was a patriot. It was her example and her love for our country that first instilled those principles of patriotism and liberty within me. However, it wasn't until I put that patriotism into practice that I truly understood and internalized just what freedom meant. Though there are many things that led me to where I am today, there was one event in particular that would significantly influence the direction my life would take.

In June of 1985, I said, "I do" to an officer in the United States Air Force. I have always loved my country, but being a military wife opens one's eyes and heart to a whole new understanding of freedom and the cost of preserving it. However, even I didn't completely understand that cost until September 11, 2001, when a group of terrorists flew a jet into the Pentagon, where my husband was stationed. It was a harrowing day, but through the grace of God, my husband's life was spared, and he came home to me. However, there is much more to the story.

Late in the evening of that tragic day, my husband Derek received a phone call from his commander. Derek came into our room to relay the news. "I'm going to work tomorrow," he said. "All personnel have been ordered to report to duty."

I was stunned. "Where?" I asked.

"The Pentagon."

"The Pentagon?" I repeated in utter disbelief.

"Yes, at the Pentagon."

"But the Pentagon is still burning," I said.

"I know," my husband responded, "but they contained the fire to one area. The rest of the Pentagon is secure." He paused and then looked at me and spoke with deep devotion in his voice, "This came straight from Secretary Rumsfeld. We are sending a message to the world—America stands strong … *we are still here!*" I was so proud to be an American at that moment. America *would* stand, and it would stand strong.

The next morning, my husband put on his uniform, kissed me good-bye, and reported for duty—in a burning building. As I watched him pull out of the driveway, I was torn. The unthinkable had happened, and all I wanted to do was stay home, close to my family. The last thing I wanted was to say good-bye to my husband. I was so proud, but my heart ached. Then, as he drove down the street, something caught my attention. On the house next to ours, I noticed the banner of freedom—our United States flag hanging high and blowing majestically in the morning breeze. My heart leaped with pride, and then as I looked down the street, I saw, to my utter amazement, house after house proudly displaying the Stars and Stripes of our beloved Old Glory.

Suddenly, I didn't feel so alone. I felt the love and support of every American hanging those flags, and I was infused with a new sense of hope. For a whole year, our nation stood united. Flags hung from homes, businesses, cars, and lapels. The spirit of America was strong, and we were united. Partisan politics disappeared when we watched our elected leaders stand side by side on the steps of the United States Capitol, singing "God Bless America" with tear-filled eyes. There was no left and right, no Democrats and Republicans. Race wasn't an issue. Politics were set aside. It was just American standing with American from sea to shining sea, and it was glorious. Then, on September 11, 2002, President Bush announced the end of the year of mourning. Almost overnight, the unity that we had enjoyed for a whole year ended as abruptly as it had begun.

Just a year and a half later, during the lead-up to the 2004 election, our nation was ripped into a great divide. All the brotherhood and patriotism we had shared for a whole year was gone. It was heart-wrenching. The people who stood united as Americans just a few months before were now strongly divided. My heart broke, and I felt such a deep loss.

As time has passed, our divisions have become deeper and more numerous. We have become a nation of divisions, not because we are dividing ourselves, but because we are standing by, *allowing others* to divide us. It is like there is some invisible hand that is separating us by race, ethnicity, religion, and income and an invisible voice telling us we can't get along. We are no longer Americans united as one nation, but fractured extensions of various groups that just happen to live in the same country. Why are we allowing this to happen? Why are we allowing ourselves to give in to the notion of a class system when our founding families sacrificed so much to stop that very thing? We are not *incapable* of standing united. We did it once before. Why does it have to take a national catastrophe to wake us up?

9/11 was a horrible tragedy, but there was one good thing that came from it—it united us as Americans. For a whole year, we put our petty differences and selfishness aside. For a whole year, America wasn't the enemy; this nation was our friend. For a whole year, Americans loved America and no one dared speak out against our country. It wasn't about what our country could do for us, but what we could do for our country and how we could help our fellow Americans. The spirit of brotherhood was everywhere. People smiled more. We were more patient at busy intersections. God was called on daily, churches were filled to capacity, and stores couldn't keep up with consumer demand for American flags and yellow ribbons.

That is what we lived with for a whole year. That is what I think America should be every day. *That* is what I miss. That is *my* America. And I want it back. I want to be "One Nation" once again, united "Under God." I don't expect euphoria and I don't expect everyone to agree on everything. Of course we will have differences. That's what America is about—expressing our own opinions and being free to do so. But I think we should all be able to agree that there is *one* thing we *should* all agree on—*we are all Americans*. We need to stand together in preserving those things that made our nation great. America is not our enemy. She is our home!

We have an incredible history and heritage. The blood of selfless patriots still covers the ground on which we walk today, and I for one will be eternally grateful for their sacrifices. But to my great regret, most Americans are completely unaware of their own history and heritage. The heroic stories of our founders are all but lost. Our history has been rewritten and America has been turned into the enemy—battered and bruised by its own citizens.

The United States of America is on perilous ground. Families are under attack. Our freedoms are being eroded. Our schools are breeding grounds for socialism. The media has evolved from an information source to a Hollywood sideshow. Values have been distorted and the Constitution has been misinterpreted, manipulated, and even ignored. Statesmen have been replaced with politicians. Accountability no longer exists. Religion is ridiculed and God is unconstitutional. Did you ever wonder how we got here? That is the big question I hear as I travel around the country today: How did we get here and what can we do about it? Believe it or not, our Founding Fathers already answered these questions over two hundred years ago.

In 1787 after a long hot summer of deep debates and negotiations, the Continental Congress signed the Constitution of the United States of America. Because the meetings were held in complete confidence, the American people were most curious about the outcome of the meeting. It was the topic of discussion in churches, markets, fields, dinner tables, and pubs. Anywhere people gathered, discussions ensued. So when Congress adjourned, there were many who waited in anticipation to find out what the result of the long months of meetings would be. As Benjamin Franklin left Independence Hall at the close of Congress, a woman approached him and asked, "Sir, what did you give us?" Mr. Franklin replied, "A republic, ma'am, if you can keep it."

What do you suppose Benjamin Franklin meant by "if you can keep it"? I often wonder what kind of inflection Mr. Franklin had in his voice when he spoke those words. Was he just simply answering a question or was he pleading to generations yet unborn, "please, keep it"? After reading so many writings and biographies of the Founding Fathers, I have come to realize just how incredibly insightful they were.

Benjamin Franklin *knew* how hard it would be to keep the Republic. He *knew* how easy it would be for men in power to usurp power and authority not granted them if we were not vigilantly watching. He knew how easy it would be for us to forget what the Republic was about and the ideas that made it strong if we were not constantly reminding ourselves. He knew how easy it would be for us to start looking to the government to solve our problems and save us from ourselves. He *knew* "keeping" the Republic would mean hard work, a firm understanding of the principles of liberty, and an unwavering commitment to preserve them. Benjamin Franklin knew what a challenge it would be to sustain a Republic but he fervently believed that if ever there were a people who could do it, it would be us.

After two centuries of freedom, we have certainly done better than any other nation, country, or empire, but we have definitely *not* done our due diligence in *keeping* the Republic. In fact, the Republic our Founders left to us is hardly recognizable anymore. All the things our Founding Fathers feared, warned us about, and tried so desperately to protect us against are the very things we are facing today. Just take a look at the Declaration of Independence to see proof of this. The grievances against the king are eerily similar to our grievances against our own Congress. We have actually come full circle—despite all of our Founders' efforts to prevent it.

Our Founders knew that to preserve liberty and sustain the Republic, we would have to be united—as *one* people, under *one* flag, sharing *one* spirit of allegiance with this *one* nation; but we are no longer united. Our Founders knew that if we did not study our history and heritage, we would eventually forget it—and we have. Our Founders knew that if we looked to the government for our welfare, they would soon hold our welfare in their hands—and they do. Our Founders knew that if we relied on the government to solve our problems, the government would soon become our biggest problem—and it is.

There is a lot of blame going around right now. We blame government, the president, Congress, and bureaucrats, but they are not the problem. The harsh reality is that if we don't like what's going on in our country, we only have ourselves to blame. We have heard a lot in the last several years about government "for" the people but we are also a government "of" the people and "by" people. Our government is what it is because we walked away from our civic responsibility. Our Founders sacrificed everything so we could live the American dream of freedom—and we have. It has been a wonderful blessing, but we have been so busy living it, we forgot to preserve and protect it. And now we are living with the consequences of our own actions. But there *is* good news. If we are the ones who got us here, we are also the ones who can get us out—and we are the only ones who can—and the women of America play a vital role in the direction our nation will go.

It was this realization, and the events of 9/11 that woke a passion within me. I became determined to do everything in my power to ensure that my children remained free. That determination led me to an intense study of American history, world history, and public policy. I started paying attention to what was going on around me, and it left me with an incredible thirst for knowledge and truth. I began reading books on history and current events. I watched the news more often, and I started listening to talk radio. (Yes, I listened to talk radio!) And I was thrilled to find like-minded individuals who actually had a microphone—as well as common sense. How refreshing!

Right around the same time, a series of events occurred that led my husband and me to make the decision to homeschool our children. And that has led me on an extraordinary journey that simply began with reading history stories to my children. As we read together, I learned right along with my children, and with each story we read, I became more and more fascinated with our history and heritage. Through these readings, I developed a deep respect for our Founding Fathers and their families.

We studied world history and civilizations, American history, United States government, the United States Constitution, and the Declaration of Independence and other writings from many of our Founding Fathers. Every day was a wondrous enlightenment, and the more I learned, the more I wanted to learn. When the children and I studied the American Revolution and Colonial era, I became so fascinated with that time period, I began reading everything I could find on it. I was very fortunate to come upon some reprints of old nineteenth-century school history books, and I immersed myself in them, absorbing every word. My passion for American history grew and the search for more information became a quest. Then one day, Herb Lux, a friend from church, invited me to attend a town hall meeting, and my eyes suddenly opened to a whole new world I didn't even know existed. It only took one meeting to get me really hooked and realize not only my rights, but also my *responsibilities* as a citizen of this country.

As I sat in the town hall meeting that day listening to city council members discuss issues and make decisions that directly impacted my family, I was stunned to realize just how much went on without me. Decisions were made every day that directly impacted my life, my family, and my wallet, and I had no say in the matter—because I wasn't taking the time to say anything.

Until I met Herb, I thought I was too "busy" to be involved. I told myself it wasn't my time in life, and when I got older, I would do more.

But now I realize just how detrimental that is and how much politicians count on our busy lives to keep our focus off of them. As the old adage goes—when the cat's away, the mice will play. If we aren't watching and holding their feet to the fire, they will run all over us. Our Founding Fathers knew this. Thomas Jefferson warned, "If once [the people] become inattentive to the public affairs, you and I, and Congress, and Assemblies, Judges, and Governors, shall all become wolves."

And now we see the results of us not paying attention—a whole pack of wolves fills not only Congress but statehouses and city administration buildings all over America. As I attended more community and government meetings, I became increasingly aware of this. Just attending one school board meeting is an eye-opening experience—an experience, I might add, that I highly recommend.

As time passed, I became increasingly involved in our community. I attended political meetings, citizenship seminars, and Constitution classes. I became involved with our local government, our neighborhood watch, and even ran for school board. Oh, I didn't do it all at once. I did what I could, when I could, and the more I learned, the more I realized just how great a role women have played in the process that has led us here—and how badly we need good women to rise up, take a stand, and get us back on track. "The hand that rocks the cradle rules the world," is not just a saying, it is the truth.

Women are the very roots of society—laying the foundation for the future. We have been at the rise and fall of thousands of years of civilizations. Even the Bible tells us of the far-reaching influence of women. Just as Esther saved an entire nation, Jezebel brought one down. Women provide a powerful influence. We always have been and we always will be.

In AD 431, when St. Patrick went to Ireland to teach Christianity to a violent and corrupt culture, he taught the women first because he believed if he could convert the women, he would convert Ireland. Thirty years, one hundred twenty thousand baptisms, and three hundred churches later, St. Patrick proved his theory was sound.

Women are the center of the home, and home is the center of society, so it only makes sense that women would play an integral role in any nation. And that is where we need to begin—with us.

The fate of our nation is in our hands. It is the women of America who will determine the direction in which our nation will go. Will it continue to increase in liberty, moral integrity, and freedom, or will it fall into socialism, communism, corruption, and slavery? That is the battle we face. And we are the ones who must decide. The future of America is in our hands!

If you are frustrated with the direction our nation is heading, tired of being ignored by our elected leaders, frustrated with the mounting debt being heaped on you, and exhausted with the daily battle you fight for morality in your effort to teach your children right and wrong, then you are not alone. I want to assure you that all is not lost because the women of America have the power to bring America back to her greatness. We have the power to influence the nation and we must start with truth.

George Orwell once said, "In a time of universal deceit, telling the truth is a revolutionary act." We live in a world of universal deceit, and we need a revolution of truth—a revolution that begins in our own hearts and our own homes.

It is time we seek for truth and embrace the principles and values that we hold dear and that our nation was founded upon. It will require some effort, and you may have to change your entire way of thinking to understand that what you have come to know as truth or have been taught is fact, probably isn't. If you are concerned with the direction our nation is heading and want to have your voice heard, then it is time to stand up and join the fight. But we can't fight for what we don't understand. We can't protect rights and preserve freedoms we don't even know we have. We must begin by embarking on a quest for truth and knowledge that will prepare us to take our place on the front lines of freedom. This book is the first step in that quest.

The book you now hold in your hands contains a priceless treasure: information. It is information that perhaps you have been denied, information you have forgotten, and information that has been lost. It is the beginning of a great awakening.

This is *not* a book of statistics, logistics, polling data, and scientific studies. It is simply a book about truth, common sense, and the voice of reason. It is about arming women with the power of knowledge and helping us to realize our intrinsic value and phenomenal influence. It is a book that will re-introduce hope into our lives. It is a revival of the American legacy and spirit, a celebration of our history and heritage and the principles which our beloved America was founded on—God, freedom, and family!

The women of America are the souls that breathe life into our country. *We* are the mothers of a nation. There *is* truth in this world and there *is* hope for a brighter future for our children, and it is *you*. The answers you desire and the truth you seek are written on the pages within this book. You *can* make the difference and you are now taking the first step. The power of information is in your hands. All you need to do is read.

> *"All that's needed for evil to triumph is for good men [and women] to do nothing."*
>
> –Edmund Burke

TWO SIDES OF WOMEN

The house does not rest upon the ground, but upon a woman.
~Mexican Proverb

"In my heart, I think a woman has two choices: either she's a feminist or a masochist." Those are the words of Gloria Steinem, a self-professed feminist and political activist. For those of you who don't know what masochism is, *Webster's Dictionary* defines it as "gratification gained from pain, deprivation, degradation, inflicted or imposed on oneself." If you agree with Ms. Steinem's statement then you are either a feminist or you have been deceived into believing that you are. I hope by the time you finish reading this chapter, you know which it is. And I hope you will realize just how powerful the influence of women is in any society—whether for good or bad.

I agree with Ms. Steinem that women have two choices, but I completely *disagree* with her options. I am not a feminist. I am a homemaker, and I am proud to be one. There are, in fact, two basic kinds of women in America, and both of them are influencing the future of our country. It is important that we as women understand this, because while we are making our homes, tending our children, working full-time jobs, and living our busy lives, Washington continues business as usual. And if we aren't taking the time to speak out and be heard, there are plenty of people and organizations who will—and we won't like what they are saying.

There are powerful forces at work in this country that have spent decades systematically unraveling the very foundation America is built on. And much to my dismay, I have discovered the secret to much of their success—women!

Several years ago, while living in the San Francisco Bay area, I heard

Patricia Ireland, the former president of the National Organization for Women, speak about women's rights. She talked at length on the plight of the American woman being forced to stay home doing menial chores and having babies when what they really wanted was to be in the workplace and be valued. I can't remember her words exactly, but that was pretty much the gist of it. I sure remember how I felt as I listened to her speak. I was almost thirty at the time, and the experience left a deep impression on me. It was my first experience with feminism. Until that time, I had no idea what the feminist movement was or what a prominent role it would play in my future. I had barely heard of NOW, and I had no idea who Patricia Ireland was, but on that crisp fall day in San Francisco, all that would change.

As Ms. Ireland finished her speech, I stood there completely dumbfounded. There I was—a stay-at-home mother with five children listening to this woman tell me what I was doing had no value—and what's worse, she said she was speaking on behalf of *me*. She was telling the audience, reporters, and anyone else who would listen that I didn't want to be home with my children. I wondered how she could possibly say that. She didn't know anything about me. And yet, there she was, speaking *for* me.

The next day, I wrote a letter to the editor of our local newspaper, titled, "NOW Doesn't Speak for Me!" But I soon realized that most women didn't even know what NOW was. And the definition of feminism for many women was completely skewed. So NOW kept talking. The world kept listening—and no one even heard me. After all, I was just a homemaker and NOW was a cause with a platform. They had the microphone and I had the dinner dishes to do.

Over the last forty years, feminists have slowly eased their way into our culture and our society, evolving into a force that is mind-boggling. While I completely disagree with everything NOW and the feminist ideology stands for, it would be carelessly irresponsible for me not to acknowledge their existence, because to do so allows them to continue their negative influence on our country and culture. Whether we recognize it or not, whether we choose to acknowledge it or not, the feminist presence in our society is deeply rooted—so deeply rooted that most of us don't even realize it's there.

Feminists have succeeded in politicizing things as self-evident as God, freedom, family, marriage, life, and public law. They have used our public schools to manipulate young minds to accept their agenda. They have used the media to redirect the priorities and passions of the American public. And they have infiltrated our court system to secure their agenda into law—and the National Organization for Women was the vehicle they used to do it.

As years passed, NOW has been joined by an entourage of anti-God, freedom, and family groups that I refer to as their "cohorts of destruction." You will recognize the names of many of these groups—American Civil Liberties Union (ACLU); Gay, Lesbian, and Straight Education Network (GLSEN); National Education Association (NEA); and Planned Parenthood, just to name a few. Their cohorts also include hundreds of smaller organizations that are lesser known. And then there are the specifically designated and/or recognized feminist organizations such as The Feminist Majority, National Council of Women's Organizations, National Abortion and Reproductive Rights Action League (NARAL), and even the League of Women Voters.

Today, we witness the fruits of their labors. We now live in a nation where our very foundation—the Constitution of the United States—hangs by a thread. The very things that our founding families sacrificed everything for are now under attack.

Our Founding Fathers have been turned into self-centered, male chauvinist bigots. Families have been redefined. College campuses have become feminist breeding grounds. Marriage no longer means anything. Men are the enemy. God is controversial. Religion is a neurological disorder. Prayer is a crime. Consequences are unfair. And hundreds of thousands of American citizens have been murdered in the name of "women's rights." The most tragic thing about all of this is that NOW has done it all in *my* name … and *yours*.

So in 2004, I decided we needed a new organization for women—one that would represent the *real* women of America—those of us who like men, love our country, put our family first, know how to be happy, and don't have a problem with smart, pretty women. And since 22 million American women define themselves as homemakers, the organization would fittingly be called Homemakers for America. The National Organization for Women has been promoting their radical agenda for more than four decades, but with Homemakers for America, *we* would now have a platform. *We* would have the microphone—and *still* get the dinner dishes done. It was absolutely liberating.

However, even after forming Homemakers for America, it became apparent to me that most women still have no idea what feminism really stands for. And since the National Organization for Women claims that they are the largest organization for feminist women in America, it seems only fitting that we use them to discover what feminism is all about.

NOW has been perceived as the voice of women in America for four decades. They speak for us all the time. They lobby in our name in Washington. They speak in our name to the media and their ideology is promoted in our schools. If NOW is spending this much time speaking for *us*—the women of America—don't you think it's about time we know what they are saying on our behalf? After all, they claim to be speaking for *you*.

The fastest way to find out about NOW is to visit their Web site. The first thing you will notice when you visit NOW's Web page is a list of articles that are updated several times a week. If you want to know what NOW is saying on your behalf at any given time, that's a good place to go. The buttons on the right side of the Web site will give you a glimpse of what is beyond, but if you want a quick and clear picture of who NOW is, hit the "about us" button and prepare to be dazzled. It states:

> *The National Organization for Women (NOW) is the largest organization of feminist activists in the United States. NOW has 500,000 contributing members and 550 chapters in all 50 states and the District of Columbia.*
>
> *Since its founding in 1966, NOW's goal has been to take action to bring about equality for all women ...*

Okay, that's the dazzle. If you stopped there, I can see why you might think NOW might be a good thing. But read on ...

> NOW *works to eliminate discrimination and harassment in the workplace, schools, the justice system, and all other sectors of society; secure abortion, birth control, and reproductive rights for all women; end all forms of violence against women; eradicate racism, sexism, and homophobia; and promote equality and justice in our society.*

That pretty much sums them up right there, but it is just the beginning. To get a more in-depth view of their agenda, here is just a sampling of the things NOW supports, endorses, and/or lobbies for:

- Abortion rights
- Partial-birth abortion
- Same-sex marriage
- Promote a proactive media campaign promoting marriage equality (same-sex marriage)
- Birth control in secondary schools
- "Fight the Right" electoral campaign
- U.N. oversight of United States presidential elections
- Increase number of feminists elected to public office
- Defeat the Promise Keepers agenda
- Facilitate removal of biased judges who support father's rights
- Oppose the diversion of public resources to religious organizations and their affiliates for public health care and social service
- Full equality for lesbian, gay, bisexual, transgendered, and intersex people

I didn't even know what transgendered and intersex people were. I had to look it up in the dictionary. I guess that makes me "unenlightened." Whatever you do, don't do this research on the Internet. You might be shocked and appalled at what pops up.

One of NOW's ongoing campaigns is called "Stop the Right," and it pretty much means just that. They jump on any issue that the "right" (which basically means conservatives who support family values and/or fiscal responsibility) are supporting and immediately take the opposite stand. When you start delving deeper into NOW's Web site and research their issues further, it gets downright creepy.

NOW opposes any ban or even restrictions on partial-birth abortion. They promote worldwide legalization of prostitution, and they defend unrestricted access to pornography (including pornography on the Internet), as well as opposing any legislation to restrict access to pornography in public libraries.

As if this wasn't enough, according to the Capital Research Center's Guide to Feminist Organizations, NOW has an affiliated project called S/M NOW that teaches "local chapters that sadomasochistic acts are manifestations of love and benefit the women who practice them."[1]

I warned you it was creepy.

NOW has captivated our culture with powerful words and phrases that on the surface sound great, but in action, they are very hollow. Lacy Peterson is the perfect example.

Lacy Peterson was a woman who was violently killed by her own husband when she was eight months pregnant. And since NOW states they are against violence being perpetrated on women, it only made sense they would comment on the case. And they did, but not to condemn Lacy's killer. Instead, NOW launched a PR campaign against the court system for trying Lacy's case as a double homicide. Her baby, according to NOW, wasn't a person, so you can't accuse anyone of his death. NOW paid no attention to the fact that an entire family was ripped apart and grieving over the death of their daughter and grandson. NOW had to protect their precious "reproductive rights." Lacy would just have to die alone. Her baby didn't exist.

Is that who you want speaking for you?

We can no longer ignore this group of radicals, and we can no longer roll our eyes when we hear them speak, because too many people are listening and too many people are falling prey to their propaganda.

A few years ago, I had the opportunity to get an up-close and personal look at the power and influence of NOW and their feminist agenda. It was in Virginia, where our family was living at the time and where I had the pleasure of meeting Gary Jackson—a man who served as an elected member of the county board of supervisors.

I met Gary at a community meeting at a difficult time in his life. That meeting, the events that led up to it, and the events that would follow taught me some valuable lessons. It also gave me firsthand experience on how feminists operate when someone chooses to question, or heaven forbid, *oppose* their agenda. I will always remember Gary Jackson for his commitment to the people he represented, and his courageous stand for what was right.

One of Mr. Jackson's duties as a county supervisor was to serve on the board of the central library system. During his service, he became aware of the fact that there were no filters on the library computers to block out pornography. He brought it to the attention of the library board. The board told him they wouldn't filter the computers because that would be censorship. Mr. Jackson expressed his concern for the children who would be using the computers and unintentionally happen on a porn site. The board remained immovable on the issue. They reiterated their stand and adamantly stated there would be *no* filters on the public library computers because it would be censoring content to the public—a popular claim promoted by NOW and their cohorts.

As Mr. Jackson explored further, he realized that our county taxpayers were covering a huge portion of the funds for the library system but only had one representative from our county on the board. So while we were paying the greatest amount of money, we had the least amount of input. Mr. Jackson took issue with this, especially after learning of their deep opposition to filters. The more he expressed his concerns, the more the library board (run by feminists) let him know, in no uncertain terms, just how little clout he and the residents of Spotsylvania County had. Mr. Jackson then told the board his constituents would have a serious problem with the central library system's policy on pornography. They basically said, "So what?"

It was at that time that Mr. Jackson decided to look into the necessity of a central library system and wondered why our county didn't just pull our money out and start our own library system—after all, we were already paying for it. So Mr. Jackson started asking questions and began researching the cost effectiveness of the central library system.

The feminists on the library board found out about Mr. Jackson's probing and decided he needed to be stopped. The library board then launched a personal smear campaign on Mr. Jackson the likes of which I had never seen before.

The feminists on the library board sent emails and letters out to all the libraries in the system stating that Mr. Jackson was trying to shut down our libraries. The Central Library Board claimed that since all the books, materials, equipment, and reference materials were purchased under the name of the Central Library System, our county would lose everything if they pulled out. Our county essentially *was* the system. That didn't matter. Neither did the fact that it was county residents who paid for the materials. According to the feminist library board, we owned nothing.

Mr. Jackson was aghast at their blatant arrogance. He just knew the residents of the county would be up in arms over this. Unfortunately, he greatly underestimated the power of feminists when crossed. Virtually overnight, the library board launched a "Save Our Library" campaign that would turn Mr. Jackson into public enemy number one.

The newspaper ran article after article attacking Mr. Jackson's proposal to shut down the library. Posters, flyers, and petitions appeared in each and every branch of the library system: "Save Our Library!"; "Stop the Funding Cuts!"; "Your children are worth it!" It was absolutely astounding. I too fell prey to the campaign's agenda. I jumped right on the "Save the Library" bandwagon.

As a homeschooler, the public library is a valuable and necessary resource for our family. *I* didn't want a funding cut. *I* didn't want the library closed. And *my* children were definitely worth it. Our homeschool support group meetings became campaign headquarters to "Save Our Library!" While circulating "Save the Library" petitions at one of our monthly homeschool meetings, one woman in the crowd had the insight to suggest that we be careful what we sign and suggested that maybe we should look into this further. But we paid no attention. We were on a mission.

Mr. Jackson's colleagues on the county board of advisors buckled under the mounting pressure. Those who thought he had legitimate concerns suddenly had a change of heart. Those who weren't sure to begin with joined the campaign mounted against him. The newspaper articles ridiculing him intensified, and I was proud to be a part of the army calling this renegade politician to the carpet.

About halfway into the media blitz, I attended a community meeting where I was able to meet "Public Enemy Number One" in person. Mr. Jackson came to the front of the room to address those in attendance. As my eyes followed him through the assembled crowd, I thought *he doesn't look much like a criminal.* He had a kind, sincere face and walked with confidence, but the campaign had obviously taken its toll on him. *Good,* I thought, *he's come to apologize for his wrongdoing.*

As he reached the front of the room, he smiled warmly and thanked us for allowing him to speak. He then told us all about the filters, the money issues, and his genuine concerns on the matter. My mouth dropped to the floor. I had been duped! I looked at Mr. Jackson again. Suddenly before me, there stood a mountain of a man. Now I saw him for what he really was—a simple, humble public servant who had the courage to stand up for what was right—even if it meant losing the election. How often do we see that nowadays?

Mr. Jackson continued to address the assembled crowd. He told us how he'd spent the last two weeks going from one forum to another, speaking to the citizens directly so they would know what was really going on. He stated he was committed to do whatever it took to get the truth out. Then he said we shouldn't take his word for it. He suggested we do our own homework and find out for ourselves. This really impressed me. So, I took Mr. Jackson up on his challenge.

I looked through the research he presented. I studied charts, graphs, and memos. I visited the library system headquarters and asked questions.

After a week and a half of researching the subject, I realized, not only was Mr. Jackson right, but the situation was even worse than he let on. There was a complete lack of accountability. Our county was paying a huge amount of money into a system we had no control over. A whole county was being held hostage by a handful of arrogant, power-hungry, feminist board members who dominated the whole library system. *They* ruled supreme and we were the insignificant nothings who foot the bill.

I spent the next few months feverishly trying to undo the damage I had caused. I was very ashamed. If only I had taken the time to look into the matter for myself. But our newspaper was reporting on the side of the library. If it's in the newspaper, it's true, right? Wrong! The newspaper never did print the facts in the case. It was just one agenda promoting story after another. In fact, when I suggested to Mr. Jackson that we take out an ad in the paper giving the full information and offered to help pay for it, he said, "Money isn't the issue. I would pay for it myself if I thought the paper would run it. But they have made it clear they don't want the truth out." Mr. Jackson was facing Goliath, and Goliath won.

The whole thing eventually died down and gradually went away. A few weeks later, the library board proudly announced to the region how the people had spoken and won. But the reality is, the people were duped. And as far as I know, the citizens of Spotsylvania County, Virginia are still footing the bill for a system they have no say in.

As I said, I learned several valuable lessons from the experience. I learned I can't count on the media to report the facts. I learned I shouldn't jump on every bandwagon that sounds like a worthy cause. I learned the importance of information and the value and power of *the people*. I learned that the bigger a government organization gets, the less the people have a say in it. And the most valuable lesson of all: I learned how easy it is to deceive the people. That is why it is so important that we seek truth and stay informed—so we are not so easily deceived. And believe me, there are plenty of groups and individuals in our world who are masters of deceit. We therefore must be detectors of truth. This is the challenge we face in our day.

Ronald Reagan said, "The ultimate determinant in the struggle now going on for the world will not be bombs and rockets but a test of wills and ideas—a trial of spiritual resolve: the values we hold, the beliefs we cherish and the ideals to which we are dedicated."

It is very important that we as women realize the critical role we play in this battle. Home is the center of society and women are the center of the home. That is a huge influence, and with it comes enormous responsibility. If we want a moral society, we need to be raising moral children. If we don't like the way our culture is going, then we need to stand up and speak out, because believe me, if we aren't taking the time to be heard, the feminists sure are. And they have worked hard to make sure they are the only voice being heard, by convincing us that our voice doesn't matter because we don't have a title. One of NOW's most effective tools has been their ability to devalue and demean us by convincing us and the world that homemaker is a ridiculous profession and stay-home moms are wasting their lives away—all in an effort to distract us from that thing that matters most to us—our family.

NOW has deceived us into thinking that what we do is menial and of little value. But the reality is—they know just how valuable and influential we are. They know the great impact homemakers can have on a nation. That is why they work so hard to deceive, distract, and discredit us. The bottom line is, NOW is trying to push their poisonous agenda through our culture and the homemakers and mothers of America are standing in their way. They can't have us speaking for ourselves, because they don't want the world to hear what we have to say. They can't have us teaching and instilling values in our children, because they want our children to embrace *their* values. They can't have us respecting God, because they are trying to remove Him from society. They can't have us promoting liberty and the Constitution, because that limits their control and influence.

Yes, they know full well just how powerful we are.

Oprah Winfrey said, "To play down mothering as small is to crack the very foundation on which greatness stands … We should no longer allow a mother to be defined as 'just a mom.' It is on her back that great nations are built."[2]

The majority of homemakers are, have been, or will be mothers. The skills we learn and tasks we accomplish as homemakers are the very things that facilitate our *role* as mothers. Motherhood isn't a downgrade or a fallback, and neither is being a homemaker. It is the greatest, most challenging, and most critical thing we will ever do.

We need to stop running from our roles as mothers and homemakers. We need to embrace them.

For centuries, homemakers have been honored and revered. The role of a homemaker is a time-honored profession. It has only been in the last few decades, with the negative influence of NOW, that this has changed. Homemakers played a vital role in the building of our nation. They were instrumental in the abolitionist movement, the civil rights movement, and one of the foremost leaders of women's suffrage, Elizabeth Cady Stanton, was a homemaker as well as a stay-at-home mom. Even today, many of America's greatest leaders and most influential citizens are self-proclaimed homemakers. We seem to be the only ones that *don't* realize how important we are.

Notice I said Elizabeth Cady Stanton was a homemaker *and* a stay-home mom. We need to get the idea out of our heads that "homemaker" is synonymous with stay-home mom. Homemaker is not a status, it is our divine nature. All women are homemakers. It is our birthright. We are, by design, the nurturers, the teachers, the constructors of the environment, and determiners of the tone in our homes.

Women are a very diverse group. Some of us have children at home. Some of us have children who are grown and have their own homes and families. And some of us have never had children. No matter what our status, however, we are all making homes. We share a variety of religions, races, incomes, and ethnicities. We live in small towns, suburbs, and big cities. We hold high school diplomas, college degrees, and doctorates. We are educated, motivated, and highly industrious. We are CEOs, administrators, college students, community volunteers, teachers, business owners, and line workers; but first and foremost—we are homemakers. Homemaker is the one name that recognizes our diversity and celebrates our unity. We *are* a diverse group, but it is the homemaker within us that unites us.

There is no shame in being a homemaker. It is the greatest celebration of a woman, and we should embrace it. Feminism is dying, and I think we need to speed up the process. It is time to take back our glory as women and celebrate the God-given, time-honored tradition that is our greatest legacy.

America needs us. The women of America have a vital role in the preservation of our country. And it is the women who will ultimately determine the direction our nation will go. NOW knows this. We literally stand in their way of completely destroying our nation. We are the biggest obstacle they face, because we are the real women of America. We respect God, love our country, and are devoted to our families. We are concerned for the moral welfare of our nation. We are deeply concerned for our children's safety and for their future. We know what kind of world we want our children to live in, and what NOW is shoving down our throats just isn't it.

For years, NOW has had a platform, and they have been heard on a multitude of issues despite the fact that they represent less than 1 percent of the women in America. It's time the other 99 percent were heard. It is time we—as women, mothers, and homemakers—were given back our due respect in society. We have been called housewives, Kool-Aid moms, soccer moms, and security moms. Retailers pursue us, politicians need us, and America will not survive without us. We are the mothers of our future leaders. The fate of America is in our very hands. We *must* take a stand—for God, for our families—and yes, for our beloved America!

From Our Founders

God grants liberty only to those who love it, and are always ready to guard and defend it.
-Daniel Webster

No country upon earth ever had it more in its power to attain these blessings than United America. Wondrously strange, then, and much to be regretted indeed would it be, were we to neglect the means and to depart from the road which Providence has pointed us to so plainly; I cannot believe it will ever come to pass.
-George Washington

We have the wolf by the ears, and we can neither hold him, nor safely let him go. Justice is in one scale, and self-preservation in the other.
-Thomas Jefferson

Liberty exists in proportion to wholesome restraint.
-Daniel Webster

The issue today is the same as it has been throughout all history, whether man shall be allowed to govern himself or be ruled by a small elite.
-Thomas Jefferson

Suggested Books & Resources:
It Takes a Mother to Raise a Village by Colleen Down

Web sites
Homemakers for America *www.homemakersforamerica.com*
Homemakers by Choice *www.homemakersbychoice.com*

LADIES FIRST

To put the world right in order, we must first put the nation in order; to put the nation in order, we must first put the family in order; to put the family in order, we must first cultivate our personal life; we must first set our hearts right.
~Confucius

I am not a fan of flying. In fact, the more I fly, the more I realize I thoroughly despise flying. I am obviously not alone, but the mode of travel is just too expedient to avoid. So we all come up with our own way of dealing with it. Some people drink themselves through their in-air experience. I go the Dramamine route.

A few years ago, I had the opportunity to fly with my daughter Amber, who at the time was just over a week old. I had flown to Arizona to witness the miracle of her birth. Amber was a very exciting, unexpected addition to our family through the miracle of adoption.

As I settled into our seat, the flight attendant came to the front of the plane to go over the usual flight procedure information. This time, however, her words caught my attention. "If the oxygen masks are released and you are traveling with young children, put the mask on yourself first and then your child."

I suddenly looked up at the attendant. *Put myself first?* I thought. *How could I do* that?

I looked down at the precious little bundle who lay cradled in my arms. I couldn't stand the thought of anything happening to her. *Surely that isn't what the attendant meant,* I rationalized in my mind. Of course, I had no intention of taking care of myself before my helpless baby.

As if to read my thoughts, the flight attendant looked at me and said,

"It is imperative that you first place the oxygen mask on yourself and then your child. If you don't do so," she continued, "you may lose consciousness due to lack of oxygen yourself, and you will not be able to care for your infant." She was looking right at me when she said the last few words. Suddenly it made perfect sense. I wasn't being selfish putting myself first. I was being responsible. My sweet little baby relied completely on me. What if I wasn't there? I *needed* to take care of myself first, so I could be there to care for her.

It goes completely against our nature as women to put ourselves first, but sometimes we have to. If we don't put our health first, we may not be around to care for our children. If we don't take the time to exercise and eat healthy foods, we won't have the stamina we need to fulfill our responsibilities. And if we do not take the time to educate ourselves on our heritage, we can't possibly expect to share it with our children. We can't teach our children how great America is if we don't even know ourselves.

For years, I have been frustrated and deeply concerned about the distorted history our children are being taught in public schools. However, I had a very enlightening experience a few years ago when, after reading a book titled *Treason,* I suddenly realized that I too had been deceived. The author of the book went to great lengths to collect data and provide detailed references based on historical fact, instead of the media fiction we often get in our history books. The book was extremely well referenced and thoroughly captivating, but it was the fifth chapter that really caught my attention.

Chapter five goes into great detail about Senator Joe McCarthy. For those of you who have somehow slipped by that indoctrination, Senator McCarthy has been blamed for single-handedly creating the Hollywood Blacklist in the 1950s when so many Hollywood actors, writers, and producers were accused of being Communist sympathizers and as a result, were blacklisted from working. Even Lucille Ball was accused based simply on the fact that her husband was from Cuba. But she handled the matter with her usual class and flair and escaped the ax. (There is a great movie with Jim Carrey in an uncharacteristically serious role called *The Majestic* that deals with this subject.)

Now, I want to pause here and make it clear that I am adamantly opposed to members of Congress acting like God and using their political muscle and scare tactics to intimidate American citizens for any reason—kind of like they are doing today with the IRS or American sports figures, but the fact is, that is not what Senator McCarthy did. I am, by the way, still trying to figure out why Congress has anything to do with sports franchises and why they are wasting taxpayers' time and money interrogating baseball players. I am not at all pleased that national sports figures (whom children look up to) are using drugs to enhance their performance, but I just can't understand why Congress thinks they have anything to do with it and why we should be letting them. But, that's a discussion for another day. Back to the point at hand.

When I was in school, the term "McCarthyism" was taught as a synonym for anyone who didn't believe in a person's right to free speech because, as I was taught, Senator McCarthy blacklisted hundreds of Hollywood actors for supporting Communism. The thing is, that never happened. Joseph McCarthy had nothing to do with the Hollywood Blacklist. Don't get me wrong, the Hollywood Blacklist did happen, but it was members of the House who launched that fiasco. Though Senator McCarthy has been blamed for the whole thing in our history books, he had nothing to do with it. What he *did* do, however, was launch an investigation on Communist sympathizers he stated were helping to shape our foreign policy in our own State Department. Surely you can see the danger of this. Having members of our own government helping the Communists in the 1950s was not in the best interest of our national security. Kind of like when Jimmy Carter flies to the Middle East and cavorts with known terrorists. As a private citizen, former president Carter is just an annoying distraction when he does such anti-American things, but if he was a member of the State Department, I would consider that an act of treason and would expect Congress to do something about it. After all, the defense of our nation, unlike counting the steroid content in Roger Clemens's bloodstream, *is* the job of Congress.

In the cold war, we couldn't afford to have members of the State Department sympathizing with the communist agenda and having secret talks about American policy behind closed doors. Senator McCarthy knew this and he knew the danger of Communism. He was well within his rights to call an investigation. It was his *responsibility,* and I would expect any member of Congress to do the same. I have read a lot more about Joseph McCarthy since reading *Treason,* and I have come to admire and respect the man. He reminds me a lot of that courageous, humble servant in Spotsylvania, Virginia, who stood up for what he knew was right and was persecuted because of it. Joe McCarthy was made out to be a dunce, a boy crying wolf, and even worse—an enemy of the state. But he wasn't any of those things. He was an American hero.

When I finished reading *Treason*, I'll admit, I was steamed. All this time, I had been angry about the lies my children were learning in history class and then I find out I was lied to as well? I suddenly started questioning everything I had been taught. I wasn't sure what was true and what wasn't. I thought about all those true and false tests I took in school and wondered if true was really true and false was really false. I had no idea. All I knew is what I was told but I wanted to know for myself. That is when I began to research, study, and read in earnest to find the answers.

From 2000 to 2004, I read everything I could get my hands on that had anything to do with American history. I also watched documentaries, read historical fiction, and talked to people who were firsthand witnesses. Our older generations are a wealth of knowledge and information, and they love to talk. In 2001, after making the decision to homeschool our children, I began an intense, in-depth study of the Constitution and the Declaration of Independence. I marveled at the things our Founding Fathers wrote in those remarkable documents. I kept searching and reading, hungering for more. It was absolutely astounding to me how much I learned in such a short time. But the more I learned, the more I realized how much I didn't know and that was very eye-opening.

I think the greatest lesson I learned was that I still had so much to learn. Our Founding Fathers were very inspired. I understand that much better after reading their words, letters, and documents. They knew what would happen to our nation if we did not remain vigilant. They knew that ignorance and apathy would be our downfall.

It has become much too easy for Congress to legislate and regulate our lives. It has become much too easy for the judiciary to completely disregard our rights. And it has become much too easy for us to ignore it all. If we took the time to search our history and learn what our Founding Fathers had learned by studying thousands of years of governments that failed, you would know just how wise they really were. If you knew what they knew, you would never allow our elected leaders to rule over you, and you certainly wouldn't give your rights away.

Benjamin Franklin said, "A nation of well-informed men [and women] who have been taught to know and prize the rights which God has given them cannot be enslaved. It is in the region of ignorance that tyranny begins."

Today, we are surrounded by tyranny. The very things our ancestors sacrificed so much to fight against are the very things we are tolerating and even accepting today. Just take a few minutes and read the Declaration of

Independence. Read the grievances against King George. It will amaze you to see the similarities between Congress and King George. Our Founding Fathers and their families would never have tolerated what we have come to accept and even embrace as "progress." We are not *pro*gressing. We are *re*gressing. But how can we know this when so many Americans have never even read the Declaration of Independence? Even more troubling, way too many Americans have never read the United States Constitution. And that is how so many usurpations of power can take place today. The government has the power to rule over us because we don't hold it accountable to its very limited powers, which are clearly outlined in the United States Constitution. When we study the Constitution, we suddenly realize just how simple the answers are to our complex problems.

The perfect example of this is the Seventeenth Amendment. Millions of Americans are up in arms over the government healthcare bill and scrambling to figure out how to stop it. The simple answer is—repeal the Seventeenth Amendment.

When our Founding Fathers constructed the Constitution, they created something completely unique. Not only were the people represented in the new government, but so were the states themselves. The most heated battle of the convention was fought over the rights of the states. The smaller states felt if representatives to Congress were chosen by population, their voice would be overshadowed and even crushed by the states with higher population. That is where the great compromise came in that created a form of government that even the Founders were in awe of.

Under the compromise, each state would be represented in the House by population and voted on by the people. But in the Senate, each state would receive the same representation—two senators, two equal votes, and the senators would be appointed by the legislature because they were to represent the states in Congress. And that is how our government operated until 1913, when Congress decided to let the people vote on the senators instead of state legislators, and that was the beginning of the end of states' rights. Today, with the government-mandated healthcare bill, we see the consequences of thinking we know better than the Founding Fathers.

Within days of the federal healthcare amendment passing, twelve states filed lawsuits to stop the forced government-run program in their state. They filed these lawsuits against the government, but in actually they were filing them against their own senators who were supposed to be representing their interests in Congress and instead, voted *against* their states!

So let's think about this for a minute: If senators were still appointed by the state legislatures, then if they acted against the states, the state legislature could remove them from office. So instead of those twelve states filing lawsuits to stop healthcare, they would have just made twenty-four phone calls to the senators from their states and told them if they voted for that bill they would be fired, and—voila—no government healthcare bill.

Allowing the people to vote for their senator may sound like a great idea, but the fact is, it has actually limited the voice of the people in each state, not added to it. Our protection as citizens from an oppressive federal government *was* our state sovereignty. I mean seriously, how many of us feel like we can call our senators on the phone and actually speak to them, let alone get them to listen to us? We already know they aren't listening. We've gone to D.C. how many times? We've attended how many town halls, written how many letters, sent how many e-mails, made how many phone calls? It is obvious they are not listening to us, but what about our state representative or state senator? How easy is it for us to reach them?

That is the beauty of the Constitution. It keeps all government local. Our state representatives live and work in our communities. They are our neighbors. So, if our United States senator suddenly decides he loves the healthcare bill, we just call up our state representative and tell him it's time to rein in Senator So-and-so, and our state representative makes a call to the senator—who takes the call because he knows his job in the hands of the state legislature, and suddenly Senator So-and-so decides he isn't for national healthcare after all. Do you see how simple it is? If we don't know the Constitution, if we don't know those limited powers contained in it, it is very easy for the government to step in and extend those powers beyond their limits. That is exactly what has happened in our country. We have forgotten who we are. We have forgotten the power of *We the People*. And that is what power-hungry officials count on.

Our elected leaders—the Supreme Court, the judiciary—*have* become wolves, just as Thomas Jefferson predicted. But it is *not* too late. We can still stop the wolves. And our greatest tool is information. For as Thomas Jefferson stated, "Enlighten the people, generally, and tyranny and oppressions of body and mind will vanish like spirits at the dawn of day." He further stated, "Whenever the people are well-informed, they can be trusted with their own government." Feminists, their many cohorts, and the myriad of power-hungry, elitist officials running this country are desperately fighting to keep their control over our society. The last thing they want is an educated, well-informed citizenry. Ignorance is what keeps them in power and so far, it has worked.

I know most of you are just like me—women who are focused on our homes, our families, and often, a part-time or full-time job. It is an incredibly demanding life that keeps us extremely occupied. Even those of us who are stay-at-home moms don't just stay home all day. We are community volunteers, business owners, teachers, and full-time students. We are intelligent, patriotic, and concerned citizens of this country, but let's be honest, many of us are completely unaware of what goes on in Washington, D.C. or even in our local communities.

How many of us know who won *American Idol* or *Dancing with the Stars* last year but cannot name our congressman or senator? You see what I mean? I think more of us know more about the life of Britney Spears than what goes on in our own city council meetings. But it isn't Britney Spears who will make the decision to convert your neighborhood into an industrial park, so maybe we should pay attention to the city council now and then—attend a meeting every once in a while.

James Madison said, "A popular Government, without popular information, or the means of acquiring it, is but a Prologue to a Farce or a Tragedy; or, perhaps both. Knowledge will forever govern ignorance: And a people who mean to be their own Governors, must arm themselves with the power which knowledge gives."

And that, ladies, is why I started Homemakers for America. That is what it is all about—helping women arm themselves with the power of knowledge. It is so important that we take the time to be informed. We must know what the Constitution says. If we don't, then tyranny will surely prevail. It is okay to put ourselves first every now and then. We need to educate ourselves first. We need to be informed. If we don't, what kind of world will we be leaving our children? What kind of freedoms will be left to them? How much more corrupt will things become if we do not act now? We need to do this for our children.

So where do we start? We need to start at the beginning. The first thing I recommend is that you get a copy of the Declaration of Independence and the U.S. Constitution. You can find them both on the Internet. You can get a free copy of a pocket Constitution through the Heritage Foundation, and the National Center for Constitutional Studies offers them in bulk at a great price.

We *must* read our freedom documents. The Declaration of Independence is our founding document. The Constitution is the document that all our laws and our very form of government are based on. We, as citizens, must read these documents if we are to remain free. Thomas Jefferson stated, "If a nation expects to be ignorant—and free—in a state of civilization, it expects what never was and never will be."

We must begin with our freedom documents. We must study and understand them. There are so many amazing resources to help you in your study. The National Center for Constitutional Studies puts on some amazing one-day seminars on the Constitution called The Making of America Seminar. I highly recommend these seminars. You can get on their Web site to see where there is a seminar near you.

Brad Daccus, president of the Pacific Justice Institute, told me that if I could get women to read the Constitution of the United States, they would already be more knowledgeable than most of the lawyers in this country. And I don't doubt for a minute that is true, since they don't teach the Constitution in law school anymore—they teach you how to get around it using "case law." So, please start with the basics—start with the Constitution.

The next thing I highly recommend is getting a copy of *The 5000 Year Leap.* by Cleon Skousen. It is an excellent book that simply and easily outlines the twenty-eight Principles of Liberty on which our nation was founded. It is a great place to start. Then, I would start reading books to your children. I highly recommend the Libraries of Hope and Yesterday's Classics, which are all reprints of books printed prior to 1930. They are great stories for the whole family and an excellent addition to your freedom library.

I have also compiled a Patriot's Reading List, which is included in the back of the book. It is full of excellent books and resources that will help you gain a better knowledge and understanding of our history, heritage, and the values and principles that made this nation great. They are books you can read yourself, books your children can read, and books you can read together with your children—my favorite kind.

These are things that will get you started on your quest for truth. But there is a price for this knowledge: you must be willing to leave all your preconceived notions and ideas behind and come in with an open mind. The truth is sometimes inconvenient, even painful, but if we are to make a difference, we must be armed with the truth. You may have to change your entire way of thinking, but in the end, I think you will find it was worth it and the knowledge you gain will be priceless.

Once you are equipped with this knowledge, you will gain a passion for this country and realize its divine greatness in a way you never have before. And that passion will spread through your home and influence your family. And that, ladies, is how we will take our country back—*one* woman and *one* family at a time. For as Abigail Adams so fittingly stated, "If we mean to have heroes, statesmen, and philosophers, we should have learned women."

So, ladies, put yourselves first. When you educate yourself, you will influence an entire nation. The power is within you. It really is. That is why the National Organization for Women and their myriad of elitist cohorts have tried so hard to discredit, devalue, and deceive you. They know full well how important you are. They are completely aware of your influence. They don't want you to know the truth. If you do, their deception is exposed and they lose their power. NOW and their cohorts have enslaved a nation of citizens with ignorance for forty years. It's time we break the chains, diminish their power, and disrupt the hold they have on this country. *We* are the only ones who can.

From Our Founders

He therefore is the truest friend to the liberty of this country who tries most to promote its virtue, and who, so far as his power and influence extend, will not suffer a man to be chosen into any office of power and trust who is not a wise and virtuous man....The sum of all is, if we would most truly enjoy this gift of Heaven, let us become a virtuous people.

~Samuel Adams

Hold on, my friends, to the Constitution and to the Republic for which it stands. Miracles do not cluster and what has happened once in 6,000 years, may not happen again. Hold on to the Constitution, for if the American Constitution should fail, there will be anarchy throughout the world.

~Daniel Webster

I know of no safe depository of the ultimate powers of society but the people themselves and if we think them not enlightened enough to exercise their control with a wholesome discretion, the remedy is not to take it from them, but to inform them.

~James Madison

Cherish, therefore, the spirit of our people, and keep alive their attention. Do not be too severe upon their errors, but reclaim them by enlightening them. If once they become inattentive to the public affairs, you and I, and Congress, and Assemblies, Judges, and Governors, shall all become wolves.

~Thomas Jefferson

Other Notable Quotes

Liberty is not a cruise ship of pampered passengers. Liberty is a man-of-war, and we are all crew.

~Kenneth W. Royce

The saddest epitaph which can be carved in memory of a vanquished liberty is that it was lost because its possessors failed to stretch forth a saving hand while yet there was time.

~Justice George Sutherland

Suggested Resources:

National Center for Constitutional Studies *www.nccs.net*
This is an excellent place to start. NCCS has several excellent resources. I suggest you start with the feature film *A More Perfect Union*, which chronicles the Constitutional Convention of 1787.

U.S. Constitution Course *http://constitutionday.cpms.osd.mil*
Thanks to Public Law 108-477, institutes of education that receive funds from the United States government are required to teach the Constitution during Constitution Week (September 17–23 of each year). Government officials are also required to take an annual citizenship/ constitution class. The DOD has set up the above Web site for that purpose.

Institute on the Constitution *www.instituteontheconstitution.com*
This is a great site that gives information and offers educational programs that anyone can grasp and understand.

A WOMAN'S INFLUENCE

A sufficient measure of civilization is the influence of good women.
~ Ralph Waldo Emerson

In April of 2004, I sat glued to the television as the network news stations reported one of the most inspiring stories I have ever seen presented in the media. It was about a twenty-seven-year-old Army Ranger named Pat Tillman who had been killed in Afghanistan. What made the story so riveting were the circumstances behind his service. I don't follow professional sports much, so the name Pat Tillman didn't mean anything to me until the day his story broke on national television.

Pat Tillman was a professional football player who gave up a three-year, $3.6 million contract with the Arizona Cardinals of the National Football League to enlist in the army. Pat and his brother Kevin both joined the Army Special Forces right after 9/11. Several media outlets approached the brothers, requesting to cover their basic training and deployments, but Pat and Kevin wanted no special treatment or attention. They told the army they wanted to be considered soldiers doing their duty, no more, no less. That in and of itself is remarkable, but Pat Tillman was a remarkable young man.

Pat's former coach, Dave McGinnis, said, "Pat knew his purpose in life. He proudly walked away from a career in football to a greater calling."[1]

Pat's agent, Frank Bauer, said he was a deep and clear thinker who never valued material things. In fact, in 2001, Pat turned down a $9 million, five-year offer sheet from the Super Bowl champions, the St. Louis Rams, out of loyalty to the Cardinals, and by joining the army, he passed on millions of dollars more.

Michael Bidwill, vice president of the Cardinals, said, "He was a brave man. There are very few people who have the courage to do what he did, the courage to walk away from a professional sports career and make the ultimate sacrifice."[2] He then stated, *"He is a hero."* I think America would agree. I was, like so many other Americans, completely inspired by Pat Tillman's story. And while the media continued to run the story and lauded Pat Tillman as a hero, one thought kept coming to my mind—he must have an amazing mother.

I guess everyone has heroes and people they admire. I'm sure Pat Tillman had many people in his life who influenced and inspired him, but I know his mother had to have been one of the greatest influences in his life. I know the power of a mother's love, and I know how much *my* mother influenced me.

When I was about seven, I came into the house after playing outside to get something from my room. As I reached my bedroom door, I heard someone talking softly in my mother's room down the hall. I went closer to see who it was, and there was my mother on her knees, beside her bed, praying. I will never forget that sight as long as I live.

We had prayed together often as a family, but I had never seen my mother praying alone before. Later that evening, I told my mom I had seen her praying and asked her if she does that a lot.

"Every day," she answered, "sometimes several times a day."

I remember thinking that seemed like a lot of praying and felt sure I would have run out of things to say. Then I looked up at my mom. "What do you pray about?" I asked.

"Well," she said, "I pray for you and your sisters. I pray for your dad. I pray for our neighbor who lives alone. I pray that God will help me be a better person. I pray for a lot of things."

"Wow," I said. "I didn't know there were that many things to pray about."

My mother smiled and hugged me, and then I went back outside to play with my friends. It was just a quick conversation but my mother's words left a lasting impression on me. "I pray for you." *My mother prayed for me.* Even at a young age, that meant a lot to me. And as I grew older, when I was in a tough spot, struggling on a test or faced with a difficult decision, I would remember my mother was praying for me and somehow, it gave me courage. It reminds me of something Abraham Lincoln once said about his mother: "I remember my mother's prayers and they have always followed me. They have clung to me all my life."

That's just how I feel. My mother's prayers have clung to me all my life.

They still carry me on. My mother was such an incredible influence in my life. A mother's influence is a powerful thing. George Washington said, "My mother was the most beautiful woman I ever saw. All I am I owe to my mother. I attribute all my success in life to the moral, intellectual, and physical education I received from her." What an endorsement that is!

Abraham Lincoln gives further credit to *his* mother's influence. "All that I am or ever hope to be, I owe to my angel mother."

Napoleon Bonaparte gave substantial credit to the influence of women when he proclaimed, "Let France have good mothers, and she will have good sons." And Oliver Wendell Holmes credited a woman's influence when he stated, "The real religion of the world comes from women much more than from men—from mothers most of all, who carry the key of our souls in their bosoms."

The greatest influence we have on this nation is through the rearing and nurturing of our own children. After all, who was it who taught George Washington? Who was it who inspired Abraham Lincoln? And who was it who raised Pat Tillman to have such pride in his country that he would give up so much to fight for it? It was their mothers. It is women who are the greatest influence in America and it has always been so from the very foundation of our nation.

Feminists have done a good job of convincing the people of America that the women who lived prior to the foundation of NOW were oppressed, downtrodden little weaklings who had absolutely no say in anything. They give you the impression that women during the American Revolution were just pathetic bystanders, abused by their husbands, the system, and a cruel, sexist world. This is how our history textbooks portray the women of the Revolution. We are told the women were purposely left out of the process, but I want to assure you that none of that is true. In fact, it couldn't be further from the truth.

The women of the Revolution were strong, committed, and resilient, not downtrodden weaklings. Our founding mothers have been completely misrepresented in the feminist version of American history. The sacrifices and selfless contributions of women in the founding of this great nation have been completely ignored.

Isabelle Katz Pinzler, special counsel for the National Organization for Women, writes, "Last week we celebrated the Declaration of Independence in which the Founding Fathers observed that 'all men are created equal.' Let's pray that we are not headed back to a time when that was understood to mean only men."[3]

Feminists consistently use statements like these to discredit our founders, but the truth is women were an incredible influence in the founding of America. It is said that behind every good man is a good woman. Well, our Founding Fathers were *great* men, and right beside them stood *outstanding* women! Within America's founders were some of the greatest women who ever lived on American soil. They were the mothers, the homemakers, the patriots who forged this nation with their sacrifices, their devotion, and their insurmountable influence—especially in their own homes.

The wives of the founders were in the fight for freedom just as much as their husbands. And since it was the mothers of the founders who instilled in them the idea of all men being created equal, they certainly wouldn't have written themselves right out of the process. In fact, if it were not for the women joining the fight for independence, the struggle would have been in vain.

The women of the Revolution were equal to their husbands in many ways. They were treated with utmost respect—honored and revered by their husbands and their children. Benjamin Rush, one of our Founding Fathers, attested to this when he stated, "The women of America have at last become principals in the glorious American controversy. Their opinions alone and their transcendent influence in society and families must lead us on to success and victory."[4]

The women of the Revolution weren't left out. They have never been left out. Women have been and always will be a prominent and significant part of our nation's history. The women of America played a vital role in the founding of this great country. The influence these women had in their homes alone was enough to move a nation. But their participation in the American Legacy didn't stop there. Their contributions had such a far-reaching impact that they influenced our nation for years to come. Abigail Adams is a perfect example. The influence she had in her home not only raised patriots, it led to the sixth president of the United States—John Quincy Adams.

In 1775, as war raged around her Boston home, Abigail courageously cared for her young family alone, while her husband was away, serving his country. Her son, John Quincy, later spoke of this time as "the space of twelve months [in which] my mother, with her infant children, dwelt, liable every hour of the day and the night, to be butchered in cold blood."[5]

You see, the Founding Fathers weren't the only ones who made sacrifices and suffered losses. When the signers of the Declaration of Independence put their names on that historic document, they pledged their lives, their fortunes, and their sacred honor, but their wives and children were just as vulnerable to British persecution as they were. These men wouldn't have made such a life-altering decision without consulting their wives and families. These women knew what signing that document meant. It was their lives, their fortunes, and their sacred honors on the line just as much as their husbands'. They knew the sacrifice and they stood by their husbands.

Revolution, freedom, independence—these were all common subjects of discussion in colonial America. It was discussed at the dinner table, in the fields, and in the churches. These men and women didn't walk into the war for independence lightly. They knew what they were up against and they knew what it would cost. The wives of the signers knew very well what they were getting into and they encouraged their husbands to do their duty, knowing the danger it would put them in and the sacrifices they would have to make.

Many of the women of that time were Quakers and Christians who were adamantly opposed to war. And yet, they realized this battle was not only inevitable, it was divinely directed. John Quincy Adams spoke of just such a situation in his own family. He recalled, "My mother was the daughter of a Christian clergyman, and therefore bred in the faith of deliberate detestation of War … Yet, in that same spring and summer of 1775, she taught me to repeat daily, after the Lord's Prayer, and before rising from bed, the *Ode of Collins* on the patriot warriors."[6]

Abigail instilled a love of God and country in her children. She stood courageously against the evils of her day and supported her husband all throughout his long life of public service. Abigail was a strong supporter of the battle for independence. She frequently opened her home as a headquarters for the Minutemen and even offered her own pewter spoons to the troops to convert into bullets. Her son spoke of this experience, saying there were "some dozen or two of pewter spoons; and I well recollect going into the kitchen and seeing some of the men engaged in running those spoons into bullets for the use of the troops! Do you wonder that a boy of seven years of age, who witnessed this scene, should be a patriot?"[7]

I certainly don't. Abigail had considerable influence on our nation in great part because of the effect she had in her own home. She is a perfect example of the far-reaching impact and influence of the American homemaker showing great courage through all her service and sacrifice. Abigail, like so many of the wives of the patriots, was left much of the time to care for her home and family on her own. From 1774 to 1778, Abigail rarely saw her husband due to his public service.

During that time, Abigail was faced with the mounting pressures of war and had to bear many difficult challenges without the comfort and support of her husband. Disease fell on the small town where Abigail's family lived, and she and her family became infected. While Abigail was still recovering from illness herself, she opened her home as a hospital for the sick. So many people had been infected with the disease that Abigail had a difficult time finding a well person to look after the sick. Her mother died from the illness, and her youngest son was on the edge of death himself. Abigail spent several days and nights tirelessly nursing him back to health. Her devoted care saved her son's life.

Abigail had a thirst for knowledge and was a fervent writer. She loved reading and was determined to educate herself by reading a multitude of books in poetry, drama, history, theology, and political theory. She also taught herself how to speak and read French, which came in very handy when her husband was asked to serve as ambassador to France.

Abigail Adams was a remarkable woman who lived an epic life in the most significant time in American history. The contributions she made to this nation were given in love and devotion for her husband, her home, her children, and her beloved America. But Abigail is just one example of the great American women who helped build this nation. There were so many remarkable women of that era. Martha Washington is another excellent example.

During the years of battle in the Revolutionary War, Martha spent each winter at her husband's encampment. She occupied much of her time repairing the soldiers' clothes, darning their socks and visiting with the soldiers, especially those who were sick or wounded. Each year, she remained at the camp until the spring battles began again. Martha was known for her cheerful nature and was a great comfort to her husband and his men, as well as an example to the wives of the other soldiers. She told them, "Whilst our husbands and brothers are examples of patriotism, we must be patterns of industry."[8]

One of the officers at the camp said of Martha, "She reminded me of the Roman matrons of whom I had read so much, I thought that she well deserved to be the companion and friend of the greatest man of the age."[9]

One of the high society ladies of the day said of Mrs. Washington, "She seems very wise in experience, kind-hearted, and winning in all her ways.

She talked much of the suffering of the poor soldiers, especially of the sick ones. Her heart seemed to be full of compassion for them."[10]

Edmund Pendleton had the privilege of meeting Mrs. Washington when he traveled with her husband to the Second Continental Congress. He later remarked of the meeting, "She seemed ready to make any sacrifice, and was very cheerful, though I know she felt very anxious. She talked like a Spartan mother to her son going to battle. 'I hope you stand firm—I know George will,' she said. When we set off in the morning, she stood in the door and cheered us with good words. 'God be with you, gentlemen.'"[11]

Martha stood by her husband through all his service, supporting him and often courageously cheering him on. She once said of her husband, "I cannot blame him for having acted according to his ideas of duty in obeying the voice of his country."[12]

Martha was not at all interested in public life, and yet, because of her husband's service, she was continuously thrust into it, and she handled each challenge with grace and flare. After becoming first lady, Mrs. Washington went to great lengths to assure that the receptions and events held in the Capitol were worthy of the highest European court. She wanted our new country to be respected, and she achieved her purpose.

Martha took little satisfaction in "formal compliments and empty ceremonies" and declared that "I am fond of only what comes from the heart." Abigail Adams, who sat at her right during parties and receptions, praised her as "one of those unassuming characters, which create Love and Esteem."[13]

Though Martha suffered much pain and disappointment, including the loss of every one of her children, she remained strong and kept a cheerful disposition. She once told a family member, "I am still determined to be cheerful and happy, in whatever situation I may be; for I have also learned from experience that the greater part of our happiness or misery depends upon our dispositions, and not upon our circumstances."[14]

That is the heart of a real woman. It is certainly not the kind of woman feminists have portrayed in their bleak stories of the sad, downtrodden women of the Revolution. All women would benefit from the examples of dedication, commitment, sacrifice, and good nature of women like Martha and Abigail. But Martha and Abigail are just two examples of the courageous women of the time. There are many more. Some of them may not be as prevalent in your mind, but their influence and contributions were immeasurable. They were the women who stood at the foundation of this nation and we could not have become a nation without them. Here are the stories of just a few of them.

Laura Collins Wolcott was the wife of Oliver Wolcott, a signer of the Declaration of Independence. Oliver was very much involved in public service, which left Laura to care for their home and family. During much of their married life, almost the entire burden of directing Oliver's home and affairs rested on the shoulders of his wife. Laura managed the family farm, educated their children, and governed the home so that Oliver could devote his energies to public service. In a letter to Laura, Oliver wrote, "I only wish that the cares which oppress you were less."[15]

Oliver loved his wife dearly and wrote her often, expressing his concerns for her and the family. It reminds me of all the e-mails of encouragement my husband sends me while he is away serving our country in Iraq. I have such admiration for women like Laura because I know what it is like to be left behind and carry the burden of the family, the home, and finances while your husband is away in service to his country. But I also understand her commitment and dedication to the cause because I feel as duty-bound as my husband to serve our country. As hard as the separation is, I proudly and humbly accept the responsibility because I love America and all she stands for, just as much as Laura Wolcott did. I make the sacrifice for the same reason she did: so that our children and our children's children can have the same blessings of liberty that we have and so they too can live in a nation where we are free. And with that hope, all the sacrifices are worth it. So the very thought that our textbooks make women like Laura out to be pathetic little house slaves, barefoot and pregnant, infuriates me. That's just not who these women were. And once you get to know them, you will realize just how capable, instrumental, and influential they were.

Eliza Adams was the second wife of Samuel Adams. Samuel devoted almost all his time to public affairs and left very little time for providing financially for his home and family. Eliza supported her husband in all his service, even when they lived with meager means. They were never wealthy as some founding families were, but they always seemed to have enough for their needs. In the book <u>Wives of the Signers</u> by Wallbuilders, Hosmer, Samuel Adams biographer stated, "For years now, Samuel Adams had laid aside all pretence of private business and was devoted simply and solely to public affairs. His wife, like himself, was contented with poverty; through good management, in spite of their narrow means, a comfortable home life was maintained in which the children grew up happy and in every way well trained and cared for."[16]

Sam and Elizabeth Adams and their children (including a son who was imprisoned) sacrificed and suffered much for the cause of freedom. Even the family dog, a big Newfoundland named Queue, got involved in the war. Queue was "cut and shot in several places" by British soldiers, because every time a red uniform passed by the Adams farm, Queue viciously attacked. As Eliza Adams's biographer wrote: "[Queue] had a vast antipathy for the British uniform … and bore to his grave honorable scars from his fierce encounters."[17]

In a time when many people spoke against slavery but were constrained by laws that forbade them from freeing slaves, Samuel and Eliza Adams courageously stood for what they knew was right. They urged everyone to free any and all slaves, and then set the example by promptly freeing all slaves the moment they came into possession of them. John Adams wrote of his cousin, "Samuel Adams … never planned, laid a scheme, or formed a design of laying up anything for himself … The case of Samuel Adams is almost without a parallel as an instance of enthusiastic, unswerving devotion to public service throughout a long life."[18] And Eliza, unwavering, stood with him. What an amazing woman!

Sarah Clark is another example. She was the wife of Abraham Clark, who was also known as "the poor man's lawyer" because of his habit of service without pay. (You don't see *that* much today.) Though he started out as a poor farmer, his reading and study made him prominent and he was elected to Congress and signed the Declaration of Independence with the New Jersey delegation. Each of the signers of the Declaration of Independence was threatened and hunted by the British, but Sarah and Abraham paid an especially cruel price for their commitment to freedom.

The British captured two of their sons who were serving under Washington: twenty-five-year-old Thomas and their young teenage son Isaac. The British threw the young men into a prison ship in the harbor. They then informed Abraham Clark that his sons would not be given food until he publicly recanted his signature on the Declaration of Independence.

Abraham gladly offered his life, his freedom, and all his possessions, but they were not accepted. The British demanded that he recant his allegiance and support for independence or his sons would slowly starve. Abraham and Sarah determined that they could give up their lives and their fortune, but they simply could not give away their sacred honor—even to save the lives of their dear sons. Abraham never signed the recantation. I can just envision Sarah Clark sitting in complete despair, utterly torn over the circumstances that lay before her. And Abraham, by her side—equally distraught, comforting her. We just have no idea of the sacrifices these women made.

When word came to Congress of the mistreatment of the Clark boys, they sent a notice to the British fleet, stating that if the mistreatment of American prisoners continued, British captives would start being treated in the same manner. The British treatment of prisoners improved after that, and Sarah's sons were eventually released alive and well.

Lydia Darrah was a homemaker and Quaker woman who single-handedly saved Washington's army from ambush.

Lydia's home was used by the British army to house its officers. One night, one of the British officers who was stationed in her house ordered Lydia to see that her family was in bed and asleep by a certain hour, and to admit General Howe very quietly. She was to show the general to the officer's apartment and then be ready to show him out just as quietly when he was ready to go.

Lydia was suspicious and felt there might be some treacherous act in place. So, after General Howe was safely in the officer's apartment, Lydia took off her shoes, crept softly upstairs, and listened at the keyhole. There she heard the two men plan to surprise Washington and take his whole army. Lydia slipped away from the door and went, trembling back to her room.

The next day, Lydia got a pass from General Howe to go to the mill and get some flour ground. The mill was outside the lines of the British army in Philadelphia. Lydia carried her bag for twenty-five miles, walking straight to the outposts of the patriot army, where she met an American officer and told him of General Howe's plans.

When General Howe's army reached White Marsh to surprise Washington's army, they found the American army so well prepared to receive them that they turned around and marched right back again without striking a blow. Lydia Darrah's heroic act may have saved the entire colonial army.

Sybil Ludington, known as the female Paul Revere, was the teenage daughter of a colonial officer. When the British invaded Danbury, Connecticut, unexpectedly, Sybil voluntarily rode deep into the night throughout Putnam County, New York, by horseback to warn her neighbors the British were coming. The colonists held back the British and they never did make it to Putnam County because of the alert that was sent out by Sybil's midnight ride.

Another remarkable woman of the time was Penelope Barker, who was famous—or infamous, depending on whose side you were on—for instigating the "Edenton Tea Party." At a time when afternoon tea was the standard, it was a huge statement to refuse it. Penelope and her friend Elizabeth King invited several of their lady friends to come to Elizabeth's home for an afternoon tea—without tea. Penelope told the fifty-one ladies present that she felt it was their duty to support the congressional ban on English imports by refusing to purchase them. She then encouraged the ladies to sign a document stating their support of the ban on English imports, and thereby refusing to purchase anything from England.

Each one of the fifty-one women present that day in October 1774 signed Penelope's document. When news of the Edenton Tea Party reached England, the reaction was immediate and intense. One Londoner jokingly asked, "Is there a *female* congress in Edenton too?"[19] There may not have been women in Congress at the time, but their impact on our nation was remarkably influential, regardless. The Edenton Tea Party became an international incident that nearly bankrupted British companies because the women refused to do business with them. And we all know, women are the purchasers. Penelope and her lady friends hit them where it hurts most—in their wallets. Don't tell me *that* didn't send a message.

Hannah Hendee is one of my favorite Revolutionary Era ladies. She was an extremely courageous woman and well deserving of the title of heroine. In 1780, a messenger from the neighboring Vermont town where Hannah and her husband lived with their two small children came to warn them that Indians were raiding the area under the leadership of the British army. Hannah's town was next in their path. Hannah's husband told her to take their young son and baby daughter to a neighbor's house and hide there until the raids were over. He then rode out to warn the next town. On the way to her neighbor's house, Hannah was overcome by a band of Indians who rode by and ripped her seven-year-old son Michael right from her hands.

Hannah, holding her daughter in her arms, immediately ran after the vicious mob that stole her son, but they were too fast for her. Resolute in her mission to rescue her son, Hannah followed the Indians' path of destruction and burning homes until she finally reached the British camp where they had originated. Hannah's son and several other boys were huddled together in the encampment, surrounded by several Indians.

Hannah, upon finding the British officer in charge, walked up to him and demanded the release of her son. The officer, Lieutenant Horton, explained that the boys were payment to the Indians and that they would not be killed but taken to Canada and trained to become Indian warriors.

"No child will be able to endure the long trek back to Canada!" Hannah cried. "They will die before you reach there! Have you no mercy? Have the British become such savages that they murder children?" Hannah then pleaded, "Give me my son. Don't let him die."[20]

Lt. Horton finally relinquished her son, but Hannah didn't stop there. She also demanded the release of every one of the boys who had been stolen from their families in the raids. Horton finally relented and allowed Hannah to take *all* the boys. Still holding her baby in her arms, Hannah pulled the small, scared, and crying boys in around her skirts and walked them back to the town, where they were reunited with their families. Such stories of amazing courage are absolutely awe-inspiring. But there are still more.

Rebecca Sherman was a gifted woman and the second wife of Roger Sherman—a signer of the Declaration. Rebecca came from a very patriotic family and supported her husband in his service to the cause of freedom. Roger frequently consulted Rebecca in his business affairs and public matters, and he greatly relied on her judgment.

Rebecca took care of and schooled her husband's seven children from his previous marriage, as well as the eight additional children she and Roger had together. Raising fifteen children alone is an amazing feat. But Rebecca was also a patriot, as much as her husband was, so when she found out that George Washington had commissioned a flag for the new nation, Rebecca didn't hesitate to take part. She went to witness the work firsthand, and subsequently had the privilege of sewing some of the stars on our nation's very first flag. And she did so with great pride and humility.

Roger Sherman adored his wife and valued her counsel. He used to say that he never liked to decide a perplexing question without submitting it for the opinion of some intelligent woman. And Rebecca was the woman whose opinion he desired most. Katharine Prescott Bennett, a descendant of Roger and Rebecca, wrote:

> We always have been a patriotic race, and this marriage brought Aunt Rebecca into still more active touch with all matters pertaining to the interests of the Colonies at this stirring period; and when at last the Declaration of Independence was promulgated, you can fancy the

excitement and enthusiasm of the wife of Roger Sherman, the man who had so much to do with the momentous document.[21]

It is no wonder we won the war, with women like Rebecca supporting the cause. Our Founding Fathers were American patriots, but that alone was not enough to win our independence. They were only able to accomplish what they did because of the support of their wives and families. They just couldn't have done it without them.

Another woman whose story greatly impressed me was Elizabeth Annesley Lewis. Elizabeth was the wife of Francis Lewis, another signer of the Declaration of Independence. Like the other signers, Francis Lewis was considered an outlaw by the British, and a price was set on his head, but the British did not limit their efforts to the capture of Francis alone.

Very soon after the British troops were in possession of Long Island, a British captain was sent with several soldiers to Francis Lewis's home. The captain was ordered to seize Lewis's wife and destroy their property.

As the soldiers advanced on one side of Elizabeth's home, a British warship from the other side fired upon her house. Mrs. Lewis looked calmly on. A shot from the vessel struck the board on which she stood. One of her servants cried, "Run, mistress, run." To which Mrs. Lewis replied, "Another shot is not likely to strike the same spot."[22]

Mrs. Lewis remained standing, immovable, as the British soldiers entered her house, destroying books, papers, and pictures, and ruthlessly breaking up furniture and anything else in their path. Then, after they finished pillaging the house, they took Mrs. Lewis with them.

Elizabeth was carried to New York and thrown into prison, where she was not allowed a bed or change of clothing and was given barely enough food to survive. She was eventually released when Congress was made aware of the situation and threatened retaliation. But Mrs. Lewis had become very ill from the experience, and soon after being released, she died from the mistreatment and illnesses she sustained in prison. Her husband Francis lived without her for twenty-four more years; he never remarried but lived to know the high and lonely price of an American patriot.

Mrs. Lewis's courageous story was passed on through her family for generations. Her powerful conviction and support for the cause of freedom inspired many of her descendents. One of Mrs. Lewis's granddaughters wrote:

> In the war of the Revolution, Mrs. Lewis had more than one opportunity of showing the steady purpose, the firmness of nerve that would have distinguished her … To Francis Lewis, she was Heaven's best gift. When his adventurous spirit led him to embark on long and perilous voyages, he knew that he left his children to the care of an able as well as a tender mother, who could train their characters as well as protect their interests. The conduct and careers of her children is the best eulogy of Mrs. Francis Lewis.[23]

And there it is—the best testament of a woman's life: "the conduct and careers of her children." And isn't that how we all want to be remembered? Isn't our influence apparent? The influence we have in our homes is greater than any evil our nation will ever face. It is stronger than any enemy and more powerful than any foe. All we have to do is take advantage of it. We have the power and ability to create goodness like no other force on this earth. *We* have the power to move a nation. It *is* within us. It always has been. We start first within our home and branch out from there—just as our founding mothers did. Sarah Franklin Bache is the perfect example of this.

Sarah was the daughter of Benjamin Franklin, and although her primary role was the caretaker of her family and home, Sarah played an active role in the Revolution through her relief work and as her father's political hostess.

In 1780, Sarah led a movement of patriotic ladies in a campaign to raise funds for the American soldiers. Washington's army was in desperate need of basic clothing necessities. So Sarah rallied the ladies in Philadelphia and raised the money to purchase fabric so they could make shirts for the soldiers. Sarah opened her home as a cutting house where these ladies spent several weeks cutting fabric and assembling shirts. This group of patriotic women made 2,200 shirts for Washington's soldiers just at the time when they were so desperately needed. These women made a difference. They used their own time and talents and they made a difference—from their own homes.

What I find most amazing about this story is that Congress couldn't provide the American army with the things they needed. The bank was broke. The men threw their hands in the air. Then the women stepped in and provided Washington's army with brand new shirts. It is marveling to see the miracles created at the hands of women. Women don't generally look at an enormous task and think it undoable. It is merely a greater challenge—an opportunity to send out the call to rally more troops together to get the job done. That is how this nation came to be. The women weren't "left out" of the American process ... they were knee-deep in it. And despite what you may have been led to believe, *we* haven't been pushed out of the American process either—we *walked* away. The problem is, NOW and their many cohorts didn't.

For generations, women took care of their homes and families as a first priority. But it wasn't their *only* priority. Just look at us today. When someone at church has a baby, what happens? The women get together and plan a shower. When a friend is sick or there is a death in the family, women rally with casseroles and Jell-O salads. We make quilts for the homeless shelter, bake cookies for the PTO, visit our elderly neighbors, and spend hours cutting, gluing, and decorating our children's homemade scrapbooks. Sarah Bache made shirts for the soldiers. We gather diaper wipes and deodorant to make care packages for the troops overseas. We are influencing this nation with our little gifts of love and compassion every day.

A great-grandson of Benjamin Rush stated, "I am afraid our forebears did not keep with accuracy the deeds of noble women in the days that truly tried the souls of both men and women."[24] It isn't that these women didn't contribute in the process of forming our nation; it is just that, for the most part, they did it behind closed doors—in the walls of their own homes. It wasn't out in the open. And more often than not, the courageous, selfless acts of these women were witnessed by their families alone. But that is not inconsequential. In fact, that is the greatest influence we have. It made a difference in George Washington's life, Abraham Lincoln's life, and Pat Tillman's life. And it will make a difference in your own children's lives.

We are moving a nation, just by being who we are. We, as women and mothers, are an incredible influence in so many ways. E.T. Sullivan expresses this quite beautifully: "We fancy that God can only manage his world with battalions, when all the while he is doing it by beautiful babies. When a wrong wants righting, or a truth needs preaching or a continent wants opening, God sends a baby into the world ... perhaps in a simple home and of some obscure mother. And then God puts the idea into the mother's heart, and she puts it into the baby's mind. And then God waits. The greatest forces in the world are not the earthquakes and thunderbolts. The greatest forces in the world are babies."[25]

You *are* influencing a nation! Tomorrow's leaders are in your care. Your deeds do not go unnoticed. They will be remembered for generations to come in the lives of your children, and their children. John W. Whitehead profoundly proclaimed, "Children are the living messages we send to a time we will not see."[26]

What message are *we* sending? Are we raising patriots as our founding mothers did? Are they witnessing from our own hands and from our own hearts how important this great nation is? *We are the hope of America. We have been from the beginning and we will be to the end.* Never underestimate your influence. Never undervalue your importance. God has put the idea in your heart. The future of America is in your hands. And now … God waits.

From Our Founders

The race is not to the swift, nor the battle to the strong; but the God of Israel is He that giveth strength and power unto His people. Trust in Him at all times, ye people, pour out your hearts before him; God is a refuge for us.

~Abigail Adams

Those who expect to reap the blessings of freedom must, like men, undergo the fatigue of supporting it.

~Thomas Paine

Your love of liberty—your respect for the laws—your habits of industry—and your practice of the moral and religious obligations, are the strongest claims to national and individual happiness.

~George Washington

It should be the highest ambition of every American to extend his views beyond himself, and to bear in mind that his conduct will not only affect himself, his country, and his immediate posterity; but that its influence may be co-extensive with the world, and stamp political happiness or misery on ages yet unborn.

~George Washington

Let me here bear testimony to the worth of this excellent woman. She fulfilled every duty as a wife, mother, and mistress with fidelity and integrity. To me she was always a sincere and honest friend.
                    ~Benjamin Rush, speaking of his wife Julia

---

Suggested Books & Resources:
Patriots in Petticoats by Patricia Edwards Clyne and Richard Lebenson
Women Patriots of the American Revolution by Charles E. Claghorn
Wives of the Signers (Reprint) by Walbuilders
Great Women in American History by Rebecca Price Janney

LEST WE FORGET

Freedom is never more than one generation away from extinction. We didn't pass it to our children in the bloodstream. It must be fought for, protected, and handed on for them to do the same, or one day we will spend our sunset years telling our children and our children's children what it was once like in the United States where men were free.
~Ronald Reagan

Those of us who grew up in the 1970s and 1980s probably remember the Saturday morning animated segments called *School House Rock*. They aired every weekend, in between our favorite Saturday morning cartoons. These little musical cartoons taught us everything from American government to the proper use of conjunctions. My favorite segment was how a congressional bill becomes a law. It had a cool, catchy song that went, "I'm just a bill; yes I'm only a bill, and I'm sitting here on Capitol Hill …" (You're singing it with me, aren't you?) We all remember those little musical sound bites and have probably passed a few tests in school because of them. I know I did. What you may *not* know is that they are now available on video and DVD.

I came across the DVD a year or so ago and purchased it so I could share it with my children. Okay, and so I could watch "Bill on the Hill." *School House Rock* quickly became one of our children's favorite DVDs. One afternoon, my daughter, then six years old, decided to watch the *School House Rock-America* DVD while I was making dinner. I was in the midst of peeling potatoes when the music from the TV suddenly caught my attention. A woman's voice was singing about the "Great American Melting Pot." Yes, I said the great American melting pot.

When I went to school, people talked a great deal about the American melting pot. Prior to being eradicated by today's political correctness, my elementary school teachers taught me all about this wonderful aspect of the American society. They proudly rehearsed various stories of how people from all over the world came to America to be free. Free from the horrific oppression of tyranny and the grips of appalling poverty. Free to live as they choose—able to be whatever they aspire to be. They came from every land and from various cultures and religions. Many of us were second- and third-generation immigrants at the time I was growing up. We vividly remembered the stories our grandparents told us of how they, their parents, or their grandparents came to America to begin their new life here. They were so proud to be called—and to *be*—Americans.

These immigrants brought their customs and languages with them, but once they landed on American soil, they became Americans. They learned to speak our language, learned our history, and became fully integrated members of our society. That doesn't mean they abandoned their customs and renounced their heritage. They shared them with us. We became a country filled with a variety of customs, food, stories and traditions from all over the world. We were a multicultural society but we were all Americans. We *were* the great American melting pot.

I know these things because when I was in school, it was part of our lessons. You won't find such information in today's textbooks, however. Today phrases like "American melting pot" are considered blasphemy. They have been replaced with phrases like African American, Latin American, Muslim American, Jewish American, Gay American … and on and on and on. We are no longer Americans, because we quit teaching our children about the great American melting pot. Watching that video clip was a major wake-up call for me.

My thoughts suddenly turned to my children. Did they know about the great American melting pot? Curiosity gripped me. I had to know. I approached each one of our children in turn, asking them if they knew what the term meant. I received a wide array of very interesting answers, yet none of them knew what I was talking about. Finally I asked my sixteen-year-old daughter. "Yes," she said, "I know what it is." She proceeded to accurately explain in detail what the great American melting pot was. I was very excited; I had a renewed hope in our decaying public school system. Then I asked my daughter in which grade she had learned this. "I didn't learn it at school," she said.

"Well, how do you know what it is?" I asked in earnest.

"I learned it in Sunday school."

Of course!

It was on that day that I fully realized just how important I am in the lives of my children. If they don't know something as simple and basic as the truth about the great American melting pot, then what else don't they know? Our children are living in the greatest country on earth and they don't even know it. They aren't being taught how great America is in our schools. So then, whose job is it? Well, the bottom line is, it's *our* job. It doesn't take a village to raise a child. It takes loving parents. The village is only there to *support* the parents as they fulfill their job. It is not there to do the job for them, and it is certainly not there to replace them. If the schools are not doing their job, the burden rests even greater upon our shoulders to teach our children the things they are lacking.

A few years ago, I had another enlightening experience while our family was studying the Declaration of Independence. I was in the process of reading, "We hold these truths to be self-evident: That all men are created equal …" when my daughter (then fourteen) interrupted me to explain that, "What they really meant was that these rights were for wealthy, white, land-owning men with a secondary education. They believed that equality was only for this exclusive group."

I was shocked. Did my daughter really just say what I thought she said? Did she really say our Founding Fathers were womanizing, male chauvinist bigots who oppressed the poor, believing that everyone outside of their "exclusive group" was beneath them? Where did this come from? I knew this wasn't true. But why didn't she?

Then, a few months ago while perusing the NOW Web site, I came across a very interesting statement that answered my question. *"The exclusion of women from the U.S. Constitution was not accidental. Equality has been deliberately denied."*[1]

In yet another statement, NOW declares, *"Last week, we celebrated the Declaration of Independence in which the Founding Fathers observed that 'all men are created equal.' Let's pray that we are not headed back to a time when that was understood to mean only men."*[2]

If you had any doubt before just how much influence NOW has had and continues to have on our society, this should clear up those doubts. Their doctrine, belief system, and philosophy permeate through our public school system. They couldn't win over our parents, so they have reverted to indoctrinating innocent, impressionable young children. And they are obviously succeeding. After all, my daughter pontificated NOW's propaganda. She didn't get it from their Web site. She learned it from her school textbook. It suddenly became clearly obvious to me that NOW and their feminist cohorts were a greater influence on my children than I was. I wasn't doing my job, and NOW was right there ready to fill in for me with all their anti-God, anti-freedom, and anti-family friends.

C. Bradley Thompson, a professor of history and political science at Ashland University, in Ashland, Ohio, has spent several years studying the history textbooks used in America's schools. He wrote, "The American pageant was a grand story of epic scale and heroic accomplishment. In short, the history of America was the history of freedom. Today, however, American history is something very different."[3] He went on to state that today our children are being taught that "the colonization of North America represents the greatest act of genocide in world history; that the Founding Fathers were racist, sexist, classist, homophobic, phallo-logo-Eurocentric bigots; that the winning of the American West was an act of capitalist pillage; that the so-called 'Robber Barons' forced widows and orphans into the streets; that the greatest consequence of World War II was the liberation of the American housewife; that the greatest threat to American freedom was Senator Joseph McCarthy; [and] that hidden in the closets of most white Americans is a robe and hood."[4]

I have read the textbooks. I assure you, he is not exaggerating. And NOW's feminist fingerprints are all over it. After all, who else would think the liberation of American housewives was the greatest achievement of WWII? Professor Thompson concluded his article by stating, "By debunking the principles and great deeds of the American past and by dethroning our most cherished heroes, today's college professors are destroying in our youth the natural reverence and patriotic attachment that is vital to the civic health of any regime … A nation that hates itself cannot last."[5]

Through my experiences I have realized that I, too, had failed to teach my children of the things that made our country so great. I neglected to teach them the importance of our heritage and the gift of our freedom. And yes, I neglected to teach them about the great American melting pot. Imagine if we all took the time to teach our children these things. How different our society would be! Instead of dividing into this group or that, our children would stand up and say, "Enough is enough! We are all Americans. We must stand together and stop trying to destroy each other."

We would have a nation of children who had pride in their heritage instead of a nation of children who refuse to stand when our national anthem is played. We would have a nation of adults who would stand up for our God-given and hard-earned freedom instead of condemning it as unfair and irrational. And we would have a nation of citizens who knew what our freedom documents said—and actually lived by them. If we lived in that reality, we would not live in a society where legislators institute various unconstitutional programs, nor where judges ignore the Constitution to legislate their personal agendas from the bench. We would be informed citizens and demand reform.

If we were teaching our children of our heritage and our freedom documents, we would be more moral, less selfish, and more patriotic. We would require ever-increasing integrity of our citizens as well as our government officials. And we would no longer accept, let alone promote, the "rob from the rich, give to the poor" mentality. We are doing our children a grave injustice, and it is not the fault of the schools alone. They are our children, after all.

We can't expect our children to be patriotic because they were born in America. Nor can we expect them to be patriotic just because we are (although it certainly helps). A baby isn't born knowing hot from cold. An infant doesn't just know the danger of putting scissors in an electrical outlet. We are not born knowing right from wrong. We have to be taught. We *must* teach our children about freedom. The preservation of our nation depends on it.

As president of Homemakers for America, I have had the great pleasure of meeting some amazing women. Violet Acanfara is one of them. Violet is an Iraqi-born United States citizen living in Ohio. Violet told me of her family's tragic experience as Christians in Iraq. When she was a child, her father was treacherously killed, strangled from behind, for his beliefs. Following his murder, Violet's mother vowed that the family would go to America someday, where they would have the freedom to live their faith in peace. Her mother never saw that day. She died when Violet was fourteen years old. As a young adult, Violet graduated from the University of Baghdad with a degree in education and foreign languages. However, she and her brother were determined to fulfill their parents' dream of going to America.

While still very young, the siblings were traveling outside Iraq. This provided them a window of opportunity to finally escape the persecution of their country. They eventually made the trip to America with the support of the World Council of Churches. Now, Violet is an American grandmother who has strong convictions of what makes America great.

I met Violet shortly after 9/11. After sharing her story with me, Violet looked up at me resolutely. "I know these terrorists," she said. "They are cowards. They are the same kind of cowards that killed my father. If we don't fight them now I am telling you, in one year, we will be fighting them in our own front yards."

I was moved by the emotion in her voice and her unwavering conviction. Violet, at just four feet ten inches tall, looked up at me and said, "America is my country. I would give my life for her."

I was amazed by this little powerhouse. She had a love for America like I had never seen before. The kind of love I think our founders shared. The kind of love that is rare today. Violet is a true American patriot.

I have another friend named Yuko, who was born and raised in Japan. Yuko met and married her husband (an American serviceman) while he was stationed in Japan several years ago. Then later, Yuko and her family moved to America. I met Yuko in 2004 when we attended the same church and we quickly became good friends because we had so much in common—especially our deep love for America. One day as we were talking she said, "I don't know why I was born in Japan when I feel so American." When I hear Yuko talk about her love for America, she absolutely takes my breath away. A couple of years ago, Yuko brought me a magazine article that greatly disturbed her. The article was about Americans' lack of knowledge for their country's history. Some very interesting statistics were referenced in the article, such as:

- 51 percent of American high school students think Germany, Japan, or Italy was an ally of the United States during World War II.
- 40 percent of seniors at America's top fifty-five colleges do not know that Abraham Lincoln was the president during the Civil War.
- 40 percent of seniors at America's top fifty-five colleges do not know that the document establishing the separation of powers in our government is the U.S. Constitution.
- 69 percent of voting-age Americans think that Karl Marx's principle of "from each according to his ability, to each according to his needs" either is or might be a quotation from the U.S. Constitution.

- 0 percent of America's top fifty-five colleges have an American history requirement.[6]

These statistics are absolutely staggering. I looked up at Yuko in utter disbelief and then my heart sank. Tears were streaming down her face. "Why don't they know?" she asked. "Why don't they know how wonderful America is? I would give my life to have what they were born with, and they don't even know what they have."

They don't know because we aren't teaching them. Yuko has taught her children. And I am ashamed to say her children are more versed in our American heritage than my own. Yuko's four children range in age from seven to twelve. The other day, while waiting for a meeting to begin, Yuko's children began passing the time by singing songs. They sang church songs, fun songs, patriotic songs, and just about every other song. Then, as I came down the hall, I heard them as they began singing the national anthem.

I stood in awe as they sang by heart, without any books or accompaniment and in perfect unison, four complete verses of the Star-Spangled Banner. A lump formed in my throat. I didn't even know there *were* four verses of our national anthem. It was absolutely magnificent. There was no music, no harmony; just the simple melodic voices of young children singing from their heart. Most American youth twice their age couldn't make it through the *first* verse without stumbling. And yet, here they were, four Japanese-born children singing without hesitation, four complete, flawless verses of our national anthem. If our nation's children were taught even a tenth of what Yuko's children have been taught, this truly would be a different country.

Recently both of my friends, Violet and Yuko, spoke at a women's meeting. The announcer gave them all the praise and recognition they so deserved as American patriots, and then introduced them as a Japanese American and an Iraqi American. Both women stood. Violet spoke first. "I am not an Iraqi American," she said. "I am an American. I was born in Iraq, but this is my country. I don't need or want to be called by any other name. My name is Violet Acanfara and I am an American."

Yuko then stood. "My blood may be Japanese," she added, "but my heart beats American." Everyone was touched by the devotion of these two women who were born in other lands but claim America as their home.

A few months ago, I was privileged to be present when Yuko raised her right hand and became a citizen of the United States of America. She knew what the words meant when she took the oath to uphold the Constitution of the United States. She knew how hard our founding families worked to give us these blessings. She knew our nation's greatness. And she knew the magnitude of the gift she received that day. Today, she is recognized as a citizen of our country, but long before it was established on paper, she was American in her heart. If only the people born in America would have this kind of passion for their county.

We have missed out on our nation's greatest stories. We have forgotten America's greatest heroes. Our schools have steadily and increasingly denied us this vital information. By revising, altering, and omitting America's history, they have deprived us of our own heritage.

There are so many groups vying for our attention. If you want to know who is winning the battle, go to your six-year-old child and show them a picture of George Washington and Ronald McDonald. Whom do they recognize? Carol is a friend of mine who has taught in the public school system in elementary schools throughout the country for more than twenty years. A few years ago, while teaching at a school rated top ten in our state, Carol quit her job. She said she could no longer stomach teaching from textbooks full of fabricated historical deceit. She has found pleasure and satisfaction substituting at a local Christian school, where she has found a wealth of historical texts and thrilling novels that have enthralled her. They are out there. They just aren't being used in our public schools.

Noah Webster stated, "Every child in America should be acquainted with his own country. He should read books that furnish him with ideas that will be useful to him in life and practice. As soon as he opens his lips, he should rehearse the history of his own country."

How many of our children can do that? Today our children are missing the crucial understanding of what makes America great. Do you want to know what our children are missing? Would you like to know what our schools *used* to teach our children before patriotism became a political taboo? A few years ago, I came across a reprint of an elementary school history book originally published in 1880. American patriots who still clearly remembered their fight for independence were the authors. It is compiled of stories from people who were actually there, making history. Many of the children who originally read from this text were grandchildren of the very men and women who fought for our independence.

One of my favorite stories from the book is "The Capture of Fort Ticonderoga." The story tells of Colonel Ethan Allen and the Green Mountain Boys. The courage and fortitude of Ethan Allen inspired me so much that I named my youngest son Ethan. The story goes as such:

In Vermont, called … the Green Mountain state, the men had formed themselves into a company under their colonel, Ethan Allen, and called themselves the Green Mountain Boys.

On the morning of the very day of the meeting of Congress which made George Washington commander-in-chief, Ethan Allen, with a detachment of these volunteers, set out to surprise Fort Ticonderoga.

Allen in a voice like thunder, so his followers say, demanded the instant surrender of the fort.

The commander, frightened, and only half dressed, threw open his door, saying, 'By whose authority do you'—But Allen broke in upon him with, 'In the name of the Great Jehovah and the Continental Congress do I command you to surrender.' No resistance was attempted; and so a large quantity of cannon and ammunition which the English had stored there, and which just then was so much needed by the troops at Boston, fell into the hands of the Americans, without the loss of a single man.[7]

This is what they were learning in school in the 1880s. One hundred years later, in the 1970s, I was learning about the melting pot. In 2001, my daughter was learning how to use tarot cards in her history class, and my son was learning the importance of accepting alternate lifestyles in his science class. And we wonder why our society has degenerated into a culture of spoiled, selfish, confused adults with no motivation?

America's schools are not producing American citizens. They aren't even producing free thinkers. What they are producing is a mass civilization of disrespectful, uninterested, uninformed followers who haven't the faintest idea of what America is about.

For the last four decades, American heritage has been systematically replaced with socialist propaganda. We can't even count on the fact that we, as their parents, know the truth. How many of you reading this have ever heard of the great American melting pot? How many of you who *have* heard of it have forgotten all about it? Eye-opening, isn't it? What else have we been denied? What else have we forgotten? If the schools aren't going to do their job, then we need to. There are three things we must do to preserve our country. It requires minimal effort but offers immeasurable return.

First, we must educate ourselves. Our freedom documents were inspired by God, constructed by honest, courageous men, and sealed with the blood of patriots. It is an injustice to God and our founders to ignore them. It is imperative that we study our freedom documents. We need to read them and understand them. Further, we need to read about our founders and learn of our heritage. Current technology has made this incredibly simple and enjoyable through a virtual library of Web sites on the Internet. I have listed some sources I recommend throughout this book and in the resource section in the appendix. One book I particularly recommend is *The 5000 Year Leap: A Miracle that Changed the World,* written by Cleon Skousen. There is no way you can read this book and not be changed. *The 5000 Year Leap* is an excellent place to start, and I strongly encourage every American to read it.

The second thing we need to do is to teach what we have learned to our children. We cannot count on someone else to do it. We must take on the responsibility ourselves. It doesn't need to be tedious. There are many children's books that have the power to instill a love for America in the hearts of young and old. I have included many of these in the resource section as well.

Third, we need to call our schools on the carpet. We need to find out what our children are and aren't learning. Look through your children's textbooks. Sit in their classrooms. From one who has spent the last twenty years doing so, I assure you, you will be shocked. Our teachers can only do so much. They are so overtaxed and overburdened with unnecessary regulations, restrictions, and paperwork that is nearly impossible for a teacher to teach anymore. And with all that money we pay for education, most of it never even reaches the teacher or classroom.

Our schools have become little corporations with an overabundance of administrators and teams of lawyers that have become necessary to weed through all the red tape required to educate our children today. We have become top-heavy, and we need to simplify and get back to the basics. We need to be teaching our children about America. We need to be teaching them what it means to *be* American.

The only way the government school system is able to get away with its treachery is because we are not paying attention. It is time we did. It is time we held our schools accountable for what they are teaching our children. After all, it is our American tax dollars that are paying for our children's education. Shouldn't those tax dollars be used to produce American citizens? Shouldn't our money be used to teach American history as it really was?

I have two dear friends who were not born in this country, and yet they are more "American" than most of the people who were. We are citizens by birth, and yet how many of us could pass our own citizenship test? This is our wake-up call. We don't know what we have. It's time we find out just how great America is. And it's time we teach our children. If we are too busy to do this, then America is lost.

From Our Founders

You will think me transported with enthusiasm, but I am not. I am well aware of the toil and blood and treasure that it will cost to maintain this Declaration, and support and defend these States. Yet through all the gloom I can see the rays of ravishing light and glory I can see that the end is worth more than all the means; that posterity will triumph in that day's transaction, even though we [may regret] it, which I trust in God we shall not.
~John Adams

What we obtain too cheap, we esteem too lightly. Heaven knows how to put a proper price upon its goods; and it would be strange indeed, if so celestial an article as Freedom should not be highly rated.
~Thomas Paine

I will not believe our labors are lost. I shall not die without a hope that light and liberty are on a steady advance.
~Thomas Jefferson

If a nation expects to be ignorant—and free—in a state of civilization, it expects what never was and never will be.
~Thomas Jefferson

A general dissolution of the principles and manners will more surely overthrow the liberties of America than the whole force of the common enemy.... While the people are virtuous, they cannot be subdued; but once they lose their virtue, they will be ready to surrender their liberties to the first external or internal invader.... If virtue and knowledge are diffused among the people, they will never be enslaved. This will be their great security.
~Samuel Adams

A morsel of genuine history is a thing so rare as to be always valuable.
~Thomas Jefferson

Other Notable Quotes

Let [the Constitution] be taught in schools, in seminaries, and in colleges, let it be written in primers, in spelling books and in almanacs, let it be preached from the pulpit, proclaimed in legislative halls, and enforced in courts of justice. And, in short, let it become the political religion of the nation.
~Abraham Lincoln

Liberty lies in the hearts of men and women; when it dies there, no constitution, no law, no court can save it.
~Learned Hand

Suggested Books & Resources:
School House Rock DVD
A More Perfect Union DVD (can be ordered through the National Center for Constitutional Studies at www.nccs.net or by calling 800-388-4512)
The 5000 Year Leap: A Miracle that Changed the World by W. Cleon Skousen
A Patriot's History of the United States by Larry Schweikart and Michael Allen
The Making of America by W. Cleon Skousen
American History Stories You Never Learned in School by Mara L. Pratt, MD
American Minute by William J. Federer

WHITE WIGS AND FAT CATS

Whatever may be the judgment pronounced on the competency of the architects of the Constitution, or whatever may be the destiny of the edifice prepared by them, I feel it a duty to express my profound and solemn conviction ... that there never was an assembly of men, charged with a great and arduous trust, who were more pure in their motives, or more exclusively or anxiously devoted to the object committed to them.
-James Madison

A few years ago, while in the midst of reading the Federalist Papers, I taught a class to a group of high school students on the United States Constitution. As I began the class, I asked the students what they knew about the Constitution. One of the boys in the class raised his hand and said, "It's just an old document written by a bunch of fat cats in white wigs."

My heart sank. How could such an amazing document written by those remarkable men be dismissed with such callous disrespect? As the discussion continued, other students shared their feelings. One young woman said the Constitution was written by men for men and gave no rights to women. Another said the Constitution was old and out of date and should be rewritten to fit our current times.

As I sat there and listened to the students share their opinions, I ached inside that the youth of our nation were so horribly deceived. I determined right then and there that I would take the opportunity available to me to teach and enlighten the people of this nation about our heritage, our history, and our Founding Fathers. I knew I couldn't change the world in one day, but on that day, I had the power to influence twenty-two students in a small classroom in Dayton, Ohio, and I was going to make the most of the opportunity.

When the forty-minute class ended, twenty-two of America's future leaders left the classroom wiser, eager to learn more, and asking me to come back and teach again. It was an incredibly enlightening experience for both the students and me. I left the school that day feeling like I had done something great. I may not have saved the world, but I had planted seeds in young hearts and I knew the power and potential of those seeds to grow. And grow they did … for just a few weeks after I taught the class, I received an e-mail from Katie, one of the students from the class.

Katie stated in her letter that she went home from class that day committed to read the Constitution. She said she had not only read the Constitution but she also read every one of the books I had suggested to the class that day and wondered if I had any more suggestions, which I gladly gave her. As she closed her letter to me, Katie said, "I had no idea how amazing our Founding Fathers were. They aren't the people they teach us about in school. You should teach everyone what you taught us. It would change the world."

Changing the world may be an exaggeration from an excited teenager, but who knows, if there were more teenagers out there excited about our Founding Fathers and our nation's history, maybe it *would* change the world. In any case, I decided Katie was right—I *should* teach everyone I can what I taught those students that day. American schools do not teach about the great men of our past, and they should. If they did, the people of this nation would know that our Founding Fathers were not "fat cats in white wigs" but great, incredibly knowledgeable, and humble men who revered God, adored women, and cherished freedom. I have the greatest respect for them and I owe them a debt of gratitude I don't feel I could ever repay. But maybe by sharing their stories, by giving them back their sacred honor, I can in some small way repay the debt and show them how grateful I am for their sacrifices.

There were fifty-six men who signed the Declaration of Independence. They have been labeled as exclusionists, but the truth is they were the most inclusive group of men the world had ever seen. They believed with their very souls that freedom was an inalienable right given by God to *everyone*, not just a few. Equality was not distinguished by color or gender in the Declaration of Independence, and life was not determined by age or weeks of gestation. The world had never seen such a group of men before. Each one of them signed his own death sentence as their wives and families stood by their commitment and honored their courage. These men pledged their lives, their fortunes, and their sacred honor to the revolution and the fight for freedom. Some of them lost their lives. Many of them lost their fortunes. But it wasn't until my generation that they lost their sacred honor.

I wonder if our Founders and their wives knew this would happen. What a tragedy it would have been for them to see the future and know that the incredible sacrifices they were making would be forgotten, even ridiculed, by the very future generations they fought to protect. They gave everything so *we* could live free, and what do we have to show for it? How do we honor them?

Today our Founding Fathers are ridiculed, mocked, and maligned. Their biographies have been falsified, their histories rewritten, their contributions belittled. It is an absolute travesty that utterly breaks my heart, and it all began with one small statement made by a group of women.

The whole entire premise that our Founding Fathers were exclusionists comes from one small sentence from one short letter written by Abigail Adams to her husband John in the spring of 1776. This short correspondence between husband and wife has become the very basis for NOW's platform and the root of their "man-hating" agenda. NOW states on their Web site: "The exclusion of women from the United States Constitution was not accidental. Equality has been deliberately denied. For more than two centuries since this country was founded, men have refused constitutional recognition of women's legal and civil rights."[1]

Women were *not* excluded from the Constitution. That is an outright lie. Is it true that the word "woman" is not mentioned anywhere in the Constitution? Yes, it is true. But there is also no mention of the word "man" in the United States Constitution either. The Constitution is gender-neutral. It is also race-neutral. There is no mention of color anywhere in the United States Constitution. These men were not exclusionists. They bent over backwards to stand against British law, customs, and tradition to include *every* citizen of this nation, regardless of color, gender, income, or creed. And that *was* revolutionary. But that is not what some women want you to know. They want you to believe that our Founding Fathers were exclusionists because it makes women look weak and gives them power to "save" you from your plight and they back up their claims with the following statement.

In 1776, Founding Father John Adams denied his wife Abigail's demand that the constitution of the new nation "put it out of the power of the vicious and lawless to use [women] with cruelty and indignity and impunity," as English law allowed. His response? "Depend upon it," he wrote, "We know better than to repeal our masculine systems."[2]

The more I read these quotes from John and Abigail, the more suspicious I became. There was obviously more to their letters than this brief excerpt, and I wanted to know more. So I began searching in earnest, trying to find the complete text of the letters. Finally, I did. And just as I suspected, there was so much more to this correspondence than the minuscule part that feminists quote from—so much more.

I would like to share a portion of their letters for you. The letters were written in March and April 1776 in the heat of the Revolutionary movement. Abigail was in absolute support of this movement. She was completely aware of the British oppression and stood behind her husband at great sacrifice to herself and her family.

Abigail was also keenly aware of the injustices of British law and tradition on women. Abigail saw this freedom movement as an opportunity to benefit women. With this in mind, Abigail wrote to her husband.

> I long to hear that you have declared an independency. And, by the way, in the new code of laws which I suppose it will be necessary for you to make, I desire you would remember the ladies and be more generous and favorable to them than your ancestors.
>
> Do not put such unlimited power into the hands of the husbands. Remember, all men would be tyrants if they could. If particular care and attention is not paid to the ladies, we are determined to foment a rebellion, and will not hold ourselves bound by any laws in which we have no voice or representation.
>
> That your sex are naturally tyrannical is a truth so thoroughly established as to admit of no dispute; but such of you as wish to be happy willingly give up the

> harsh tide of master for the more tender and endearing one of friend.
>
> Why, then, not put it out of the power of the vicious and the lawless to use us with cruelty and indignity with impunity?
>
> Men of sense in all ages abhor those customs which treat us only as the (servants) of your sex; regard us then as being placed by Providence under your protection, and in imitation of the Supreme Being make use of that power only for our happiness.[3]

When you read the complete text of these letters, as well as other correspondences between John and Abigail, you get a sense of their relationship. Both John and Abigail were greatly concerned for the fate of America. They were both devoted to the cause of freedom and were willing to sacrifice everything to ensure it. They were also both courageous patriots and completely devoted to one another.

Abigail had a respect for her husband and John, in turn, had a great admiration and respect for his wife. John also had a sense of humor that, from reading their letters, I believe was probably both a great comfort to Abigail and an aggravation at the same time. This, as well as the fact that John did not seem to be a letter-writer, helps a person better understand John's answer to his wife's plea. He addressed his wife's concerns in the final part of his letter to her.

> As to your extraordinary Code of Laws, I cannot but laugh. We have been told that our Struggle has loosened the bands of Government everywhere. That Children and Apprentices were disobedient—that schools and Colleges were grown turbulent—that Indians slighted their Guardians and Negroes grew insolent to their Masters.
>
> But your Letter was the first Intimation that another Tribe more numerous and powerful than all the rest were grown discontented.—This is rather too coarse a Compliment but you are so saucy, I wont blot it out.

> Depend upon it, We know better than to repeal our Masculine systems. Altho they are in full Force, you know they are little more than Theory. We dare not exert our Power in its full Latitude. We are obliged to go fair, and softly, and in Practice you know We are the subjects. We have only the Name of Masters, and rather than give up this, which would compleatly subject Us to the Despotism of the Peticoat, I hope General Washington, and all our brave Heroes would fight. I am sure every good Politician would plot, as long as he would against Despotism, Empire, Monarchy, Aristocracy, Oligarchy, or Ochlocracy—A fine Story indeed. I begin to think the Ministry as deep as they are wicked. After stirring up Tories, Landjobbers, Trimmers, Bigots, Canadians, Indians, Negroes, Hanoverians, Hessians, Russians, Irish Roman Catholicks, Scotch Renegadoes, at last they have stimulated the [women] to demand new Priviledges and threaten to rebell.[4]

When I finished reading John's letter to his wife, I didn't feel oppressed. I felt like giving a big YEE HAW! John Adams recognized the power of women and basically declared the rebellion a done deal now that the women were taking a stand and joining the fight. As if to say, "Look out, King George, the women of America have just engaged!"

The letters shared between John and Abigail were touching, sincere, and completely inspiring. Of all the letters written, all the journals recorded, all the documents penned by these men and women of the Revolution, feminists could only find one tiny snippet of one correspondence—that had to be taken out of context—to make a bold statement that our founders were male chauvinist oppressors. NOW's entire "women's rights" platform begins with this lie.

NOW's claim that the "exclusion of women from the U.S. Constitution was not accidental" is preposterous. Not only was it not on purpose, it *didn't* happen! I defy you to find one place in the Constitution where it states only a man may vote, or that only a man may run for Senate, Congress, or even president of the United States. It isn't there. It doesn't exist.

The Constitution doesn't deny anyone the right to vote. It isn't even implied. The Constitution didn't *declare* women couldn't vote or hold property. It was British tradition that *assumed* it. Our Founding Fathers realized it was a bad system, and Abigail figured if they were going to make new laws and a set up new government, this would be the perfect time to get rid of those archaic and barbaric British customs once and for all.

The Constitution doesn't segregate races either. It specifically mentions age, place of birth, and residence, but there is no reference to gender or race. Look for yourself. I assure you, you will not find one reference that supports NOW's claim—and you won't find it in the Bill of Rights either.

Our Founding Fathers weren't oppressors of women. On the contrary, they had the greatest respect and admiration for them. If blame needs to be placed for women's suffrage being denied, it should be directed to the individual states, not our Founding Fathers. The Fourteenth and Nineteenth amendments exist because British customs and tradition were bigoted, not because our Founders were. We were not intentionally denied anything—our Founders saw to it when they formed the government for "We the People" and not "We the White Male Land-owners." Their goal was freedom and equality for all, not a few, and they hoped that someday we would achieve it.

Unfortunately, that truth is not told, and the feminists' statement has been accepted by society as truth and recognized as fact. This is in large part because the majority of citizens in this country have never even *looked* at the Constitution, let alone read it. If we don't know what it says, if we don't know the history of our people, then we can be easily deceived into believing women *were* purposefully left out of the Constitution and that our Founding Fathers *were* self-serving exclusionists who just wanted to protect their investments and keep women in their place.

The success of this feminist strategy is evidenced in a documentary on George Washington that aired on the History Channel. Don't be fooled by the name. Not everything aired on the History Channel is historically accurate. The documentary on George Washington is a good example. The so-called "documentary" portrayed George Washington, our most revered and respected Founding Father, as an insecure child who was oppressed by his mother, coveted his neighbor's wife, and accidentally assassinated a French official, causing the French and Indian War—and that was all within the first ten minutes.

The documentary went on to say that Washington was an opportunistic gold-digger who went after rich young women in town like a werewolf and only married Martha on the rebound because of her money.

According to the "documentary," Washington lobbied for the position of commander of the Continental Army by wearing his uniform to every session of congress. The "documentary" also stated that had Washington applied for such a high position today, he wouldn't even be considered because he had no real war record (except, of course, for single-handedly causing the French and Indian War). This is what is being portrayed on the History Channel, for crying out loud!

When David McCullough's book *1776* was released, *Newsweek* ran a spread on George Washington and made the following statement about our first president: "He enjoyed parties and particularly the company of attractive women … [Washington was] prone to self-doubt and flashes of self-pity. Washington was insecure, hated New Englanders, obsessed over the smallest details of decoration of Mt. Vernon, and was hungry for fame."[5]

I can't even tell you just how preposterous this is. I'd like to tell you who the real George Washington was. Not the one you hear about in school, in the media or on the History Channel, but the one who actually lived more than two hundred years ago. I will tell you about the George Washington who loved his wife, adored his children, and cherished liberty—the humble man who would lead a nation to freedom. The History Channel documentary did get a few things right: George Washington did marry Martha, he did fight in the French and Indian War, he did lead the Continental Army, and his name was George Washington. That's pretty much where reality and fantasy part ways, however.

George Washington was not only the commander-in-chief of the Continental Army, he was also a surveyor, a planter, a soldier, and a statesman. He served as the chairman of the Constitutional Convention and was an active Episcopalian. Despite what you hear from feminists, media, and educators today, George Washington was considered the most popular man in the colonies. In speaking of General Washington, Henry "Light Horse Harry" Lee made the now-famous statement, "First in war, first in peace, first in the hearts of his countrymen." Does this sound like a man who was obsessed with power and was bigoted toward women and blacks? Do you really think the colonists would so highly respect a gold-digging werewolf? I guarantee you, after reading about the women of George Washington's time, they wouldn't have stood for such nonsense. And they certainly wouldn't have revered a man who would treat women with such wanton disrespect.

Surely the story was accurate when it claimed George Washington's mother was verbally abusive and oppressive to George right? Wrong! When

George left home to begin what would be a lifetime of civil service, his mother Mary told her son, "Remember that God is our only sure trust. To Him, I commend you my son, neglect not the duty of secret prayer." Does this sound like the words of an abusive mother? I guess, in today's world, putting God first in your life *is* considered pretty oppressive.

What about the claim that the young George Washington was on the prowl—after anything in a dress with money; or his so-called "affair with his neighbor's wife"? When George Washington was fifteen, he wrote in his own handwriting, *110 Rules of Civility and Decent Behavior in Company and Conversation*. Among them were:

> 108) When you speak of God, or His attributes, let it be seriously and with reverence. Honor and obey your natural parents although they be poor.
> 109) Let your recreations be manful not sinful.
> 110) Labour to keep alive in your breast that little spark of celestial fire called conscience.

Call me crazy, but this doesn't sound like the words of a gold-digging werewolf on the prowl. If you studied the real history of George Washington, you would be absolutely appalled at what educators are calling history today. One of the best books available on the subject is *The Real George Washington* by Jay A. Parry. If you want to know who George Washington really was, I recommend that book, but here are just a few things you should know about the person who was known throughout the colonies as America's most indispensible man.

George Washington was the son of Augustine Washington and his second wife Mary. He was a descendant of King John of England and a descendent of nine of the twenty-five Surety Barons of the Magna Carta. George Washington grew up in and around Fredericksburg, Virginia. Our family lived in Fredericksburg for four years, and I absolutely loved it. The history there is just astounding. When you visit George Washington's birthplace and boyhood home, it gives you chills. I found it more inspiring than even Mt. Vernon. I don't know how to explain it. There's just such a humbling atmosphere there. And the small shop they have at George Washington's boyhood home in Fredericksburg is full of books about the *real* George Washington.

Just a few decades ago, these stories could be found in our school textbooks. Now you have to search for them. For instance, the account of

George Washington at the Battle of Monongahela was included in student textbooks in America until 1934. The story is absolutely inspiring.

During the French and Indian War (you know, the one George Washington caused), he fought alongside British general Edward Braddock. On July 9, 1755, the British were on the way to Fort Duquesne, when the French surprised them in an ambush attack.

The British, who were not used to fighting except in an open field, were being massacred. Washington spent the entire battle riding back and forth across the battlefield delivering General Braddock's orders. As the battle raged, every other officer on horseback, except Washington, was shot down. Even General Braddock was killed, causing his troops to flee in confusion.

A few days after the battle, on July 18, 1755, Washington wrote to his brother, John:

"But by the all powerful dispensions of providence, I have been protected beyond all human probability or expectation; for I had four bullets through my coat, and two horses shot under me, yet escaped unhurt, although death was leveling my companions on every side of me!"[6]

Fifteen years later, Washington was traveling with a friend through the very woods where the battle had taken place. They met an old Indian chief who spoke with Washington through an interpreter.

> I am a chief and ruler over my tribes. My influence extends to the waters of the great lakes and to the far blue mountains.
> I have traveled a long and weary path that I might see the young warrior of the great battle. It was on the day when the white man's blood mixed with the streams of our forests that I first beheld this chief [Washington].
> I called to young men and said, mark yon tall and daring warrior? He is not of the red-coat tribe—he hath an Indian's wisdom, and his warriors fight as we do—himself alone exposed.
> Quick, let your aim be certain, and he dies. Our rifles were leveled, rifles which, but for you, knew not how to miss—'twas all in vain, a power mightier than we, shielded you.

> Seeing you were under the special guardianship of the Great Spirit, we immediately ceased to fire at you. I am old and soon shall be gathered to the great council fire of my fathers in the land of shades, but ere I go, there is something bids me speak in the voice of prophecy:
>
> Listen! The Great Spirit protects that man (pointing at Washington), and guides his destinies—he will become the chief of nations, and a people yet unborn will hail him as the founder of a mighty empire. I am come to pay homage to the man who is the particular favorite of Heaven, and who can never die in battle.[7]

The Indian warrior later said, "Washington was never born to be killed by a bullet! I had seventeen fair fires at him with my rifle, and after all could not bring him to the ground!"[8]

George Washington was a man of great character. During the Revolution, he was riding by a group of soldiers who did not know who he was. They were in the process of trying to lift a very large, heavy beam. As General Washington neared, he noticed a young corporal standing by yelling commands at the men. "Now you have it," he shouted. "All ready. Pull!"

As Washington looked on, he quietly asked the corporal why he didn't help the men. The man angrily replied, "Sir, do you realize that I am the corporal?!"

Washington politely raised his hat and said, "I did not realize it. Beg pardon, Mr. Corporal."

Then General Washington dismounted from his horse, and went toward the men and helped them, giving all his strength until the beam was raised. Before leaving, General Washington turned to the corporal, while wiping the perspiration from his face and said, "If ever you need assistance like this again, call upon Washington, your commander-in-chief, and I will come."[9]

The confused corporal turned white when he realized who he had been talking to. And that, my fellow Americans, is who George Washington was. That is why he was well loved and respected. He not only had character, he had principle, integrity, and backbone; all characteristics that are seriously lacking in our elected leaders today.

Another character trait Washington had that is seriously lacking today is a genuine respect and trust in God. He petitioned Him often. One such occasion was so powerful it inspired an artist, Arnold Friberg, to make a painting of it. We know it as *The Prayer at Valley Forge,* and a copy of it is proudly displayed atop the fireplace mantel in our home. The story behind the dramatically stirring painting is even more extraordinary.

In the freezing winter of 1777, General George Washington suffered from a severe lack of supplies for his troops camped at Valley Forge. Soldiers died at the rate of twelve per day. While the British army slept in tents and ate warm meals, Washington's troops were starving, and many even lacked the simple necessities such as blankets, shirts, and shoes. General Washington recorded their desperate state in his own words.

> No history now extant can furnish and instance of an army's suffering such uncommon hardships as ours had done, and bearing them with the same patience and fortitude. To see men without clothes to cover their nakedness, without blankets to line on, without shoes (for the want of which their marches might be traced by the blood from their feet)…and submitting without a murmur, is a proof of patience and obedience which in my opinion can scarce be paralleled.[10]

It was reported from a committee to congress that the feet and legs of many of these brave men froze until they were black and had to be amputated. Bloody footprints in the snow and the sight of his men starving and exposed led General Washington to woods of Valley Forge where he dropped to his knees to seek divine guidance.

It was then that Isaac Potts, a local Quaker, past by the scene of General Washington—Commander-in-chief of all the Continental Armies, on his knees praying to God for his beloved country. Isaac Potts was so touched by the scene and the prayer he heard that night, he deeply reconsidered his idea that a soldier and Christian could not co-exist in one person. When he returned home to his wife that night he declared, "…if George Washington be not a man of God, I am mistaken, and still more shall I be disappointed if God does not through him perform some great thing for this country."[12]

The most telling thing about President Washington's character is found in his resignations. While most of us today focus on what a president does while in office, the most remarkable thing about George Washington is that he left office. The world had never seen anything like that before. Just think about other great military commanders and revolutionary leaders before *and* after Washington such as Caesar, Santa Anna, Napoleon, Lenin, and Hitler. They all seized the power they won in war and they didn't give up that power until they either died or were defeated by someone else. None of them willingly walked away from their power, but George Washington did—twice. First, at the end of the Revolutionary War when he resigned his military commission and returned to Mount Vernon to once again be a farmer, and the second time at the end of his second term of office when he refused, despite all the pleadings of the people, to run for a third term.

George Washington could have been king if he wanted. He could have taken power of all the colonies after the war. That was the custom: You kept the power and the lands you won in war. But George Washington didn't want to be president, let alone king. He served as president because the people loved him and asked him to. He had fought for liberty because he *believed* in it, and was dedicated to preserving it.

At the end of the war, the American painter Benjamin West was commissioned by King George III to do a painting. While in his service, King George III asked the painter what Washington was going to do now that he had won independence. Benjamin replied, "They say he will return to his farm."

"If he does that," said the king, "he will be the greatest man in the world."

George Washington was a remarkable man. He was a man of conviction, compassion, and valor, and he was surrounded by men like him. It was a *time* of patriots—a time of heroes. There are so many examples of courage, service, and faith. From homes to churches to farms and storefronts, America was filled with the lives and stories of great men. Patriots were found everywhere—even behind the pulpits of America's churches, as witnessed in 1775 when Pastor John Peter Muhlenberg preached a message on Ecclesiastics 3:1: "For everything there is a season, and a time for every matter under the Heaven." He closed his message by saying, "In the language of the Holy Writ, there is a time for all things. There is a time to preach and time to fight." He then threw off his robes to reveal the uniform of an officer in the Revolutionary Army. That afternoon at the head of three hundred men, he marched off to join General Washington's troops.[13]

Chaplain James Caldwell may not be a name you remember, but I bet you'll recognize his words. In June of 1780, General Wilhelm of the British army crossed to New Jersey from Staten Island with five thousand troops. The Colonial Army drove them back, but not before the British shot and killed Reverend Caldwell's wife, the mother of their nine children.

Two weeks later, as the British troops once again made the advance, led this time by General Clinton, they again met with resistance from the Colonial Army. American general Nathaniel Greene's regiment were courageously firing from behind the church fence when they suddenly ran out of the paper wadding used to hold the gunpowder in place in their muskets.

Chaplain James Caldwell, remembering his wife, quickly ran past the British fire, entered the Presbyterian Church, and collected all the copies he could carry of Isaac Watts's *Psalms, Hymns, and Spiritual Songs*. He carried them back through enemy fire and distributed them to the American troops exclaiming, "Now put Watts into 'em boys! Give 'em Watts!"[14] The Americans held their ground, and by the next day, the British withdrew.

Robert Morris, who is known as the financier of the Revolution, gave thousands of dollars of his own money to feed and clothe Washington's handful of half-naked, half-starving militia. George Washington always knew he could come to Robert Morris for support. On one occasion, General Washington sent word to Robert asking his friend for funds to support a vital campaign he was planning. Robert had spent his fortune paying for the revolution and did not have enough to meet the General's needs so he went to a Quaker friend and asked him for a loan to cover the requested costs.

The Quaker asked Robert what security he could offer for the loan. "My note and my honor," said Mr. Morris. The Quaker replied: "Robert, thou shalt have it."[15]

The money was sent to General Washington and because of Robert's sacrifice, General Washington crossed the Delaware and changed the entire direction of the war.

Time after time, Robert Morris gave of his own resources and raised money on his own credit to keep Washington and his men supplied with their needs. One record remarked: "If it were not [proven] by official records, posterity would hardly be made to believe that the campaign … which … closed the Revolutionary War, was sustained wholly on the credit of an individual merchant."[16]

When the war ended, this self-made millionaire spent three years in debtor's prison after he lost everything—all for the sake of liberty.

Thomas Nelson, Jr. was another man of valor. When the Revolutionary War started, most of the farming in the colonies came to an abrupt halt when all the men left to fight the war. Without the men to farm the land, many families were left destitute. General Nelson used his own money and resources to support the families of many of his poorest soldiers. More than a hundred families were spared from starvation and destitution because of Thomas Nelson's sacrifice and benevolence. In the battle of Yorktown, General Cornwallis had taken the Nelson home as a headquarters. Knowing it was General Nelson's home, the army refused to fire upon it. When Thomas Nelson found his home was not being fired upon, he asked his men why. They said it was out of respect for him. Thomas Nelson then took the cannon himself and fired upon his own home. That home was the collateral he used to raise $2 million for the Revolutionary cause. When the war was over and the loans came due, Congress refused to honor them, and Thomas Nelson lost his property and died without a cent to his name.

Thomas Jefferson lost his wife and baby. Samuel Adams lived in near poverty his whole life. John Hart was hounded and hunted as a criminal while his wife lay dying. Richard Stockton was thrown in prison, his lands were destroyed, and he ended up literally begging for food and money to keep his family alive. John Martin died a broken man when his neighbors, friends, and some of his own family disowned him after he signed the Declaration of Independence. His last words to his family and friends before he died in 1777 were, "Tell them that they will live to see the hour when they shall acknowledge it [the signing] to have been the most glorious service that I have ever rendered to my country."

Our Founding Fathers were not just a bunch of men in white wigs. They were the best and brightest the world had to offer. They were not fat cats out to secure their financial estates. Most of them lost everything, and they all knew they *had* everything to lose but they stood by their principles in spite of all the threats and oppositions launched against them. They were everything we look for in elected leaders today—men of principle and integrity who respected God, cherished their families, and put their country *above* their own self-interests. They believed in a cause *greater* themselves and they were willing to sacrifice everything for that cause. For them, it truly *was* liberty or death. Many of our Founding Fathers lost everything. Each of them *gave* everything. And yet, we honor them for nothing.

John Adams spoke to us in our day as if he knew this would happen. "Posterity," he said, "you will never know how much it cost the present generation to preserve your freedom. I hope you will make good use of it. If you do not, I shall repent in heaven that ever I took half the pains to preserve it." We cannot let the dedicated sacrifices of these great men and their families be for naught. We cannot allow these honorable men to continue to be maligned, ridiculed, and disrespected. We must read the stories of their lives, we must teach our children about them; for if we do not, their memories and their sacrifices will be lost forever.

Those men who signed the Declaration of Independence, those who fought in the war for independence, and those who were part of the Constitutional Convention were all men of valor not just in their day, but in ours as well. They weren't perfect men, but they were men who were able to *overcome their imperfections* in order to accomplish great things. They were some of the greatest men who ever lived. We need more like them.

It is my earnest prayer that someday we as a people will come to understand and revere the lives of these remarkable men. I pray that we will acknowledge that their commitment to freedom was the most glorious service they ever could have rendered to their country—and to the world.

From Our Founders

Before God, I believe the hour has come. My judgment approves this measure, and my whole heart is in it. All that I have, and all that I am, and all that I hope in this life, I am now ready here to stake upon it. And I leave off as I began, that live or die, survive or perish, I am for the Declaration. It is my living sentiment, and by the blessing of God it shall be my dying sentiment. Independence now, and Independence forever!

~John Adams

The time is now near at hand which must probably determine whether Americans are to be free men or slaves; whether they are to have any property they can call their own; whether their houses and farms are to be pillaged and destroyed, and themselves consigned to a state of wretchedness from which no human efforts will deliver them. The fate of unborn millions will now depend on God, on the courage and conduct of this army. Our cruel and unrelenting enemy leaves us only the choice of brave resistance, or the most abject submission. We have, therefore, to resolve to conquer or die.

~George Washington

Principally, and first of all, I resign my soul to the Almighty Being who gave it, and my body I commit to the dust, relying on the merits of Jesus Christ for the pardon of my sins.

~Samuel Adams

Freedom is not a gift bestowed upon us by other men, but a right that belongs to us by the laws of God and nature.

~Benjamin Franklin

A ... virtuous citizen will regard his own country as a wife, to whom he is bound to be exclusively faithful and affectionate; and he will watch ... every propensity of his heart to wander towards a foreign country, which he will regard as a mistress that may pervert his fidelity.

~Alexander Hamilton

To the corruptions of Christianity I am, indeed, opposed; but not to the genuine precepts of Jesus himself. I am a Christian in the only sense in which he wished any one to be; sincerely attached to his doctrines in preference to all others ...

~Thomas Jefferson

The patriot who feels himself in the service of God, who acknowledges Him in all his ways, has the promise of Almighty direction, and will find His Word in his greatest darkness, a lantern to his feet and a lamp unto his paths. He will therefore seek to establish for his country in the eyes of the world, such a character as shall make her not unworthy of the name of a Christian nation ...

~Francis Scott Key

The cause of America is in a great measure the cause of all mankind. Where, some say, who is the king of America? I'll tell you, friend, He reigns above.

~Thomas Paine

The brief exposition of the Constitution of the United States, will unfold to young persons the principles of republican government; and it is the sincere desire of the writer that our citizens should early understand that the genuine source of correct republican principles is the Bible, particularly the New Testament or the Christian religion.

~Noah Webster

Suggested Books & Resources:

Lives of the Signers (reprint of 1848 text) by Wallbuilder Press 1995)
America's God and Country by William J. Federer
The Real George Washington by Parry, Allison, Skousen
The Real Thomas Jefferson by Andrew M. Allison
The Real Ben Franklin by Andrew M. Allison
Prelude to Glory (nine-volume set) by Ron Carter
Unlikely Heroes by Ron Carter
John Adams (HBO Miniseries) Disk 1, Episodes 1 and 2 DVD

GOD IS TOO CONTROVERSIAL

*Hurricane Rita, this is like the ninth hurricane out this season.
Maybe this isn't the time to take God out of the Pledge of Allegiance.*
-Jay Leno

I think by now we have all become blatantly aware of the status of God in our society: He just doesn't fit in anymore. He is definitely *not* politically correct. In 2004, soon after Homemakers for America was formed, I received some advice from an agent with a PR firm. He suggested I would get a lot more support and do a lot better building our membership if I took God out. "God is too controversial," he told me. "What if you changed your *God, Freedom, and Family* motto to *Family, Freedom, and Faith?*" I was stunned. Taking God out of our motto wasn't even something I could consider. It wasn't that I wouldn't change it; it was that I couldn't.

Our Founding Fathers wrote over and over that God not only protected them in the battle for independence but also guided them in constructing the Constitution. How could I possibly start an organization to preserve our nation's heritage and legacy if I didn't include the very being who made it all possible?

I thanked the professional PR rep for his kind advice and promptly dismissed it. This wasn't the last time I was given such advice. I have been encouraged numerous times by various professionals that I should remove God. I met one woman who was so thrilled with our organization that she offered to do all our Northwest Coast PR for us at no charge. She said she just wanted us to make some changes to the Web site before moving forward. She made several suggestions on wording, photos, and placement that were all very good ideas, and we gladly made the changes. Once the suggested changes were made, we began discussing the PR campaign.

"There is just one more change that needs to be made before we launch the campaign," she said.

"What's that?" I asked.

"It's that *God* thing," she answered. "It's just too restrictive and offensive. If you change it to *faith,* it will have the same effect without the negative impact."

I wasn't sure how to respond. "Well," I began, "I am sure that this is a wise strategy from your perspective, but from mine, it is not even possible. It isn't that I *won't* remove God from our motto, it's that I *can't*. It just isn't right. Our money doesn't say 'In faith we trust.' The Pledge of Allegiance doesn't state 'one nation under faith'; we don't swear 'so help me faith'; and Thomas Jefferson didn't say 'adore faith.' He said 'adore God,' and that will remain the HFA motto."

Obviously frustrated, the woman paused and then encouraged me to pray about my decision. Yes, you read that right. The woman suggested that I pray to God and ask Him whether or not He should be taken off our Web site. Oh, the irony of it all.

Just why is it, do you think, that God has become so controversial? If a person wants to do something that breaks the rules, the easiest thing to do—so you can continue doing that thing—is to *change* the rules. But when you have something like the Ten Commandments staring you in the face, and God all over our money and government buildings, it makes it kind of hard to justify immoral actions. So the answer is, of course, simply get rid of God and His laws. There is only one problem with that—all our nation's laws are *based* on *God's law*. All of the principles of liberty our nation was founded on, and which our Founding Fathers wrote so much about, were based on God's law. So it only stands to reason that if you want to change the moral code of rules and ethics in America, you have to get rid of God. But what you *cannot* do is claim He was never here and has nothing to do with it. God was the reason for America, and He has *everything* to do with it. Our Founding Fathers knew this, and they testified of it again and again.

From the time Columbus discovered America, it was about God. The Pilgrims landed on Plymouth Rock because of their belief in Him. America won its independence from England because of Him, and the Constitution was written with divine guidance by Him. This is not just my own beliefs, it isn't just my truth, it is *the* truth—it is what was, and the history of our nation proves it. So why is it, then, that prayer has been removed from schools and public squares? Why are the Ten Commandments being banned from government buildings when they have adorned them for two hundred years? Why are our public schools forbidding the Declaration of Independence to be taught in schools because it mentions God? And why is the ACLU trying to take God out of our Pledge of Allegiance and off of our money? It is all because the children of America have been taught in school for the last three decades that the public display of God and religion is unconstitutional by using the little phrase "separation of church and state"? You've heard it in the courts, in the media, and in public squares, but those words cannot be found anywhere in the Constitution of the United States, because they are not there. There is no such rule of law. In fact just the opposite is true.

The Constitution doesn't protect us *from* worshipping God; it protects our right *to* worship Him—according to the dictates of our own conscience. So where does the statement come from? Ironically, the phrase comes from a letter written by Thomas Jefferson to the Danbury Baptist Association in order to *protect* the right to worship God. The Association wrote the letter to Thomas Jefferson soon after he was sworn in as president of the United States.

The purpose of the letter was to ask President Jefferson for his assistance, hoping that he would persuade the state of Connecticut—as well as the other states in the Union—to make laws respecting religious freedom and not laws that would restrict, reward, or punish one religion over another—which is what was happening at that time. Religious bigotry is something the world has been facing since the beginning of time and our Founding Fathers knew the great tragedy of setting up a national religion and they knew the federal government should have no part in regulating it in any way. The Baptist Association that wrote this letter understood very well these same things. They also understood the sovereignty of states' rights.

At that time, the Baptists felt there was a lack of religious liberty in the state of Connecticut and that the Congregationalist Church was using the state government to pass laws that favored their church and its members above all other denominations. There was a religious hierarchy established through the Congregationalist Church with direct ties to the government, making it very difficult for members of other denominations to receive justice. So when Thomas Jefferson was elected, knowing he was a man who firmly believed in the free exercise of religion, they decided to petition him for help. They wrote in their letter while they knew he was not a national legislator and that the national government had no power to destroy the laws of the states, they hoped that he would "prevail through all these states and all the world, till hierarchy and tyranny be destroyed from the earth." They further wrote that despite the freedom outlined in the Constitution, state governments considered religion as the first object of legislation making what rights and privileges the people of the state enjoyed more like favors granted by the state then inalienable rights to which they were guaranteed.

Thousands of years of history proved the great danger in governments regulating religion in order to dictate the consciences of man, and Thomas Jefferson was well versed in history. So, in an effort to change the climate in Connecticut, the Danbury Baptist Association wrote the following to the president of the United States:

> Our sentiments are uniformly on the side of religious liberty—that religion is at all times and places a matter between God and individuals—that no man ought to suffer in name, person, or effects on account of his religious opinions—that the legitimate power of civil government extends no further than to punish the man who works ill to his neighbors.[1]

Thomas Jefferson, standing firmly on the individual rights of every American to worship how, where, and what they may (as long as it does not infringe on the rights of others) wrote the following response to the Association:

> Believing with you that religion is a matter which lies solely between man and his God, that he owes account to none other for his faith or his worship, that the legislative powers of government reach actions only, and not opinions, I contemplate with sovereign reverence that act of the whole American people which declared that their legislature should "make no law respecting an establishment of religion, or prohibiting the free exercise thereof," thus building a wall of separation between church and State.[2]

The "separation of church and state" that Thomas Jefferson was referring to was the "wall" that allows American citizens the right to worship God as they see fit. Thomas Jefferson was not stating that God had to be removed from our money and the Ten Commandments be purged from every public building. He was simply stating that the Congress would not establish a national religion or make any laws that would regulate religion—thus protecting *religion from* the government, not the other way around. Congress would not put one church above another. They would not make a statement declaring one church the only church. They would not, as was done for centuries in Europe, dictate the beliefs of one's conscience, and Jefferson hoped that the same sentiment would prevail in every state in the Union.

Thomas Jefferson—himself a devout believer in God—would be absolutely mortified to know how his words have been used and sentiment manipulated to eliminate the very being that he recognized as self-evident. In fact, to our Founding Fathers and their families, God was so self-evident that I doubt it ever occurred to them to even consider the need to address a godless nation. Thomas Jefferson's statement is often used as a means to do the very thing the Founding Fathers worked so hard to avoid—regulate religion. Today, that is exactly what is being done.

Our government dictates to us how and where we can pray. They dictate where we can read our Scriptures, where we can talk about religion, and when we can wear a cross as a religious symbol. I assure you, this is not what our Founders had in mind. John Adams confirms this with the following statement. "It is the duty of all men in society, publicly, and at wrote seasons, to worship the supreme being, the great creator and preserver of the universe. And no subject shall be hurt, molested, or restrained, in his person, liberty, or estate, for worshipping GOD in the manner most agreeable to the dictates of his own conscience; or for his religious profession or sentiments; provided he doth not disturb the public peace, or obstruct others in their religious worship."[3]

I was raised by a mother who went to great lengths to teach me of the importance of recognizing God's hand in everything. She taught me about American history, our Founders, and most importantly—God's providential hand in establishing this nation. I know these things because my mother taught them to me. But what if she hadn't? What if my mother hadn't taken the time to share her love of God and country with me? Would I have found it on my own? I don't know. I'm just glad she took the time. I repay her every day when I share that same passion with my *own* children. And now, I have the opportunity to share it with you.

Several years ago, I had a friend who told me she didn't believe in God. "If there's a God," she said, "why does he allow so much pain in the world?" I hear that argument all the time, but when my friend said it, I just couldn't find a way to answer her. Her statement was filled with grief and devastation over the recent loss of her three-year-old daughter, who died very unexpectedly from a brain tumor. You can't do anything in circumstances like that except hold their hand and tell them how sorry you are. This woman had a real reason to grieve. What I couldn't seem to explain to her is that I *know* there is a God and that knowledge is what makes all the pain in the world bearable.

What people today have forgotten is that God not only created us, He gave us agency—the freedom to choose. This agency is commonly referred to as free will. God hopes we will choose Him, but He doesn't demand it. He hopes we will choose to obey those Ten Commandments that adorn the United States Capitol, but He doesn't force us to do so. A murderer has just as much free will as a preacher. The difference is the consequences. Agency and rights are *not* the same thing. Agency is the law of God that man is free to choose his actions (though he does *not* get to choose the consequences of those actions). A right is a legally protected privilege—which the government can, when desired by the people and on the local level, regulate.

The United States is ruled by the people, and that is why the local and state governments are set up the way they are—so the people have the government in their own backyard and don't have to walk to Washington, D.C. to protect their rights or petition for laws. But when the federal government takes on authority it has no right to assume and passes laws that restrict the states, then the people lose their power to rule their government and the government begins to rule over them. And that is exactly what has happened to cities and states throughout America.

It doesn't matter whether or not a city wants to display a nativity scene on the front lawn of their City Hall at Christmas—the federal government says they can't. It didn't matter that the people of Alabama wanted to keep a monument displaying the Ten Commandments in the Alabama Supreme Court building—the government said it had to be removed. When cities and states lose their right—their legally protected privilege—to make and keep laws, the people of this nation lose their voice, and tyranny and oppression rule from Washington. And if the people want redress, instead of going to their own City Hall or State House, they have to travel all the way to Washington, D.C., and then hope they get heard. This is exactly what our Founding Fathers were trying to stop. They knew a centralized government was unjust. They knew it would end up enslaving the people. And they knew this because they witnessed it firsthand under King George.

The colonists tried to work with parliament and the king, but they had no recourse. All the laws, taxes, and restrictions put on them came from one man on an island thousands of miles across the ocean. Our Founders formed our government of checks and balances so there would not be one power stronger than another, and they put strict restrictions in the Constitution to keep the federal government from becoming the kind of tyrannical institution they fought against. And yet, that is what we face today—tyranny, only now it is coming from Washington. And that tyrannical, oppressive government is dictating to us where and when we can pray, what we can believe, and when and where the Ten Commandments can be displayed.

The Ten Commandments battle is probably the most absurd of all because they are displayed all over our nation's federal and state buildings. They are the foundation of all our laws. They are the standard by which America prospered and became a free nation. Why is this such a controversy? Who would have a problem with the Ten Commandments being displayed? An adulterer would obviously have a problem with "Thou shalt not commit adultery." A thief would take offense with "Thou shalt not steal." And a murderer would certainly take issue with "Thou shalt not kill." So if it is those who commit the crimes who find offense, why do we care? What we have today is not a world where God has forgotten His children. We live in a world where God's children have forgotten Him.

Ronald Reagan once wrote, "We can't have it both ways. We can't expect God to protect us in a crisis and just leave Him over there on the shelf in our day-to-day living."[4]

Alexander Solzhenitsyn was a Russian author who was imprisoned for eight years by Joseph Stalin. His crime was writing letters and articles in opposition to the new government. He, like many others, was imprisoned for censorship—because his own beliefs did not agree with the government—the same reason thousands of Europeans were sent to concentration camps in World War II. When Alexander was asked about the moral decline in modern culture that would allow such things to take place, he said, "Man has forgotten God; that is why this has happened."

The evils that we live with today are not proof that there is no God. They are proof that we have forsaken him. As soon as the Ten Commandments became controversial, our nation began a downward spiral, which has only accelerated since the "free love" era. If we, as women, mothers, and homemakers, were teaching our children and influencing our homes using the Ten Commandments, we would live in a much different world. If we were taking the time to teach our children of America's godly heritage, we would not live in a nation where God was ostracized. Instead we would live in a nation where God was revered for His hand in creating it. That is the way America used to be.

I would like to assure the media, the Supreme Court, and the American public that I, as a Christian, am not out to baptize the nation (though it certainly couldn't hurt), or take over the United States government. My desire is simply to see that our nation's heritage and legacy are preserved and our government returned to its simplistic greatness. I want the history of our great nation to be taught in every school, home, church, and community throughout America. It is *our* story, after all. It is *our* heritage and *our* legacy. And as heirs to that legacy, we have the right to worship God, and God has a right to be recognized.

To those who say there is no God, I want to assure you *there is*. For those of you who believe He is not a God of love, I say, you just don't know Him. And to put it plainly, I don't know how anyone can go through this world *without* a knowledge of God's infinite wisdom and benevolent love. You ask, "How can I believe in God in a world like this?" I answer, "I couldn't live in a world like this without a belief in God." That is what our Founders knew and what they believed when they established this great nation. That is what we have forgotten. God is at the helm of our nation's history.

Today we are denied this heritage because of that nonexistent "separation of church and state" clause. We are told we can't learn these things in school because it is religion. But the truth and reality is—it is American history!

God has been a part of America since Christopher Columbus discovered it. Columbus himself attested to the hand of providence guiding his path when he wrote, "When I was very young, I went to sea to sail and I continue to do it today … I have found Our Lord very well disposed towards my desire, and I have from him the spirit of intelligence for carrying it out. He has bestowed the marine arts upon me in abundance and that which is necessary to me from astrology, geometry, and drawing spheres and situating upon them the towns, the rivers, mountains, islands, and ports, each its proper place."[6]

Columbus was criticized and mocked for his beliefs and passions, but he never denied the hand of providence in his life. He said, "God made me the messenger of the new heaven and new earth of which he spoke in the Apocalypse of St. John after having spoken of it through the mouth of Isaiah; and he showed me the spot where to find it."[7]

And of his critics, Columbus said, "Let them call me then, by what name they will, for after all, David, that wisest of kings, tended sheep and was later made king of Jerusalem, and I am the servant of Him who raised David to that high estate."[8]

Of course, stories such as these are left untold today because God is too controversial. But facts are facts. History is history. Whether *you* believe in God or not does not change the fact that Christopher Columbus did. Whether you believe Columbus was led by providence or not, the fact remains, *he* did. That is history. But there is so much more—story after story from the discovery of America to the construction of the Constitution attest to God's influence and the power of his protection over America.

During the War for Independence, there were numerous instances that were recorded. Of course, they no longer appear in our history textbooks either, but every once in a while you will find an old text or a history gem that still includes these remarkable stories. One such treasure is a book entitled *America's God and Country,* written by William J. Federer. This book contains priceless quotes, stories, and biographies that have been all but lost. It is still in print and I highly recommend it.

The story of George Washington's army and their divine protection throughout the Revolution is told, in part, in this magnificent book. The true story of this time in our nation's history is awe-inspiring.

For instance, on August 27, 1776, British general Howe had trapped General Washington and his eight thousand troops on Brooklyn Heights, Long Island, ready to advance the next morning and defeat them. In a desperate move, Washington gathered every vessel, from fishing boats to rowboats, and spent all night ferrying his army across the East River. When the morning came, there were still a large number of his troops dangerously exposed to the British. Then a sudden change in the weather brought a thick fog in over the river and the fog remained, protecting Washington's army, until the last man crossed to safety! The British were never again given such a rare chance of winning the war.[9]

Major Ben Tallmadge, Washington's chief of intelligence, wrote about the incident:

> As the dawn of the next day approached, those of us who remained in the trenches became very anxious for our own safety, and when the dawn appeared there were several regiments still on duty. At this time a very dense fog began to rise (out of the ground and off the river), and it seemed to settle in a peculiar manner over both encampments. I recollect this peculiar providential occurrence perfectly well, and so very dense was the atmosphere that I could scarcely discern a man six yards distance ... we tarried until the sun had risen, but the fog remained as dense as ever.[10]

In January 1781, Lord Cornwallis became infuriated when George Washington defeated an entire British detachment at Cowpens, South Carolina. Cornwallis immediately began pursuing Washington's army with fury. He decided to rest his troops on the banks of the Catawba River, where Washington and his troops had crossed just two hours earlier. During the night, however, a storm arose that prohibited them from crossing the river for days.

On February 3, Cornwallis nearly overtook the American troops again at the Yadkin River. Cornwallis watched the American troops getting out of the river on the other side, but before his troops could cross, a sudden flood ran the river over its banks, which prevented the British army from crossing.

On February 13, only a few hours ahead of the British troops, Washington and his army crossed the Dan River into Virginia. When the British arrived, the river had risen too high for the British to safely cross, and they were once again stopped from pursuing Washington's army.

The British commander-in-chief, Henry Clinton, wrote:

> Here the royal army was again stopped by a sudden rise of the waters, which had only just fallen (almost miraculously), to let the enemy over, who could not else have eluded Lord Cornwallis's grasp so close was he upon their rear.[11]

General George Washington sent a letter to his friend Brigadier General Thomas Nelson in August 1778 which stated:

> The hand of providence has been so conspicuous in all this that he must be worse than an infidel that lacks faith, and more wicked that has not gratitude to acknowledge his obligations ...[12]

And later, in November 1781, General Washington wrote to Thomas McKean, president of the Continental Congress, speaking of the battle of Yorktown:

> I take particular pleasure in acknowledging that the interposing Hand of Heaven, in the various instances of our extensive Preparation for this Operation, has been most conspicuous and remarkable.[13]

God's divine intervention was apparent throughout the war for independence but it didn't stop there. The hand of providence continued to guide them and was ever present in the hot, steamy summer of 1787. It has been called the "Miracle in Philadelphia," and it began with General Washington uttering the proclamation, "Let us raise a standard to which the wise and the honest can repair. The event is in the hand of God,"[14]

A group of men from various regions, professions, incomes, and religions came together to join efforts in an undertaking that would change the world; their purpose was to form a government of the people, for the people, and by the people. Freedom was their message, and securing it was their goal. It was the first time in history when men would join together to freely write a new constitution for their own government.

Ideas, concerns, and strategies were traded, but it was difficult to come to any kind of consensus on certain issues, such as representation and slavery. After a few weeks, the convention deteriorated to a battle of wills. Quarrels between the states became the format of each meeting. Arguments ensued, tempers flared, and many historians believe that George Washington's presence and the delegates' immense respect for him was the only reason the convention held on as long as it did.

General Washington's dignity and demeanor held the convention together. He remained thoroughly impartial as he presided at the convention, and only shared his personal beliefs between sessions. He was respected and revered, but even that was not enough to hold the convention together forever. Soon everyone present became greatly concerned that the convention—and the Union—was about to break up.

At this crucial moment in history, a lone voice spoke out from the back of the room. Quietly, Benjamin Franklin, the respected elder statesmen, then eighty-one years of age, stood and addressed the convention.

> In the beginning of the contest with Britain, when we were sensible of danger, we had daily prayers in this room for Divine protection. Our prayers, Sir, were heard, and they were graciously answered. All of us who were engaged in the struggle must have observed frequent instances of a superintending Providence in our favor ... And have we now forgotten this powerful friend? Or do we imagine we no longer need His assistance?
>
> I have lived, Sir, a long time, and the longer I live, the more convincing proofs I see of this truth: that God governs in the affairs of man. And if a sparrow cannot fall to the ground without His notice, is it probable that an empire can rise without His aid?
>
> We have been assured, Sir, in the Sacred Writings that except the Lord build the house, they labor in vain that build it. I firmly believe this. I also believe that, without His concurring aid, we shall succeed in this political building no better than the builders of Babel ... and what is worse, mankind may hereafter, from this unfortunate instance, despair of establishing government by human wisdom and leave it to chance, war, or conquest.
>
> I therefore beg leave to move that, henceforth, prayers imploring the assistance of Heaven and its blessings on our deliberations be held in this assembly every morning before we proceed to business.[15]

The words of this humble man became the turning point of the convention. The delegates reconsidered their priorities and commenced with the task of crafting a new constitution and assuring the freedom and security of this new nation.

At the young age of twenty-two, Benjamin Franklin wrote his own personal epitaph, which he wished to be remembered by. At the time of his death, his words were a last fitting tribute to the humility of this man and his personal conviction that there is a God and a future estate.

The Epitaph of Young Benjamin Franklin

The body of
B. Franklin, Printer
(Like the Cover of an Old Book
Its Contents torn Out
And Stript of its Lettering and Gilding)
Lies Here, Food for Worms.
But the Work shall not be Lost;
For it will (as he Believ'd) Appear once More
In a New and More Elegant Edition
Revised and Corrected
By the Author.

This is what American history is really about. These are the people who lived at the time. *They* were there. *They* recorded these events firsthand. How dare we ignore their words?

As George Washington resigned his commission as general of the Continental Army on December 23, 1783, he issued a powerful and emotional statement: "I consider it an indispensable duty to close this last solemn act of my official life by commending the interests of our dearest country to the protection of Almighty God and those who have the superintendence of them into His holy keeping."[16]

I'm not sure that Mr. Washington would be so pleased with our stewardship today. I founded Homemakers for America on the principles of "God, Freedom, and Family" in hopes of reminding the people of America what it is that makes our country so great. It *is* God. That is reality. We can't change history. We can ignore it. We can avoid it. We can even try to rewrite it but you can't change what is. And controversial or not, as our Founding Fathers declared and history records—God *is* America.

From Our Founders

Those people who will not be governed by God will be ruled by tyrants.
~William Penn

God who gave us life gave us liberty. And can the liberties of a nation be thought secure if we have removed their only firm basis: a conviction in the minds of men that these liberties are the gift of God? That they are not to be violated but with His wrath? Indeed, I tremble for my country when I reflect that God is just; that His justice cannot sleep forever.
~Thomas Jefferson

He is the best friend to American liberty, who is most sincere and active in promoting true and undefiled religion, and who set himself with the greatest firmness to bear down on profanity and immorality of every kind. Whoever is an avowed enemy of God, I scruple not to call him an enemy to his country.
~John Witherspoon

The propitious smiles of Heaven, can never be expected on a nation that disregards the eternal rules of order and right, which Heaven itself has ordained.
~George Washington

It is the duty of mankind on all suitable occasions to acknowledge their dependence on the Divine Being ... [that] Almighty God would mercifully interpose and still the rage of war among the nations ... [and that] He would take this province under his protection, confound the designs and defeat the attempts of its enemies, and unite our hearts and strengthen our hands in every undertaking that may be for the public good, and for our defense and security in this time of danger.
~Benjamin Franklin

I should be pained to believe that [the American people] have forgotten that agency, which was so often manifested during our Revolution, or that they failed to consider the omnipotence of that God who is a lone able to protect them.
~George Washington

It is when people forget God that tyrants forge their chains.
~Patrick Henry

Suggested Books & Resources:
The Light and the Glory by Peter Marshall and David Manuel
Three Secular Reasons Why America Should Be Under God by William J. Federer
Persecution by David Limbaugh

WARMONGERS

We are either a united people, or we are not. If the former, let us, in all matters of general concern act as a nation, which have national objects to promote, and a national character to support. If we are not, let us no longer act a farce by pretending to it.
~George Washington

In the fall of 1989, I stood in front of our small black-and-white television in our Louisiana apartment holding my nine-month-old son Jordan, tears streaming down my face as I witnessed the Berlin Wall crumbling right before my eyes. I was standing right there in our little living room, a firsthand witness as history was made and an entire chapter in my life came to an end. I was a living witness to the end of an era of fear.

If you are younger than thirty-five, this probably means nothing to you. But if you can close your eyes and remember where you were when you witnessed that miraculous event, you know exactly how I felt. I don't remember where I was when Elvis died. I don't remember what I was doing when John Lennon was shot. But I will always remember where I was when the Berlin Wall came down, and I will *never* forget where I was on September 11, 2001.

I grew up in a world where nuclear war was a constant threat and the Soviet Union was the world power everyone feared. There was a forty-year standoff between the United States of America and the Soviet Union. I lived through twenty of those years. I remember learning about the Soviet Union when I was in school. I learned about the Berlin Wall and how it divided families. I saw graphic pictures of people being shot while trying to sneak through the Berlin Wall to freedom—and the ditches that would be filled with the bodies of those who didn't make it. I knew what it *meant* to see that wall come down. But the tears I shed that day were not solely tears of joy at witnessing a miracle and knowing the era of fear was over. I stood there in my living room that day weeping because I knew my children would never fully understand what this meant.

My children would never know what it meant to live under the fear of nuclear war. They would never know what it was like to ache for those on the other side of that wall of death. They would never know the symbol the wall held in our hearts. It was a physical barrier that divided freedom and prosperity on the west from tyranny and poverty on the east. I was overjoyed that my children would not live a life of fear, but I was also deeply saddened because I knew my children would never understand freedom as *I* understood it that day. I cried with the people of Germany as they pulled each piece of stone from that cement barrier and families were once again united as they climbed through the rubble. As the wall fell at the hands of the people, I remembered President Reagan's words, "Mr. Gorbachev, *tear down this wall!*"[1] And what I saw was freedom. The people of East Germany—after forty years of tyranny, fear, and oppression—would finally taste freedom. They would finally know peace. And isn't that what we all want?

You might find it interesting to know that according to the National Organization for Women's Web site, "Peace is a *feminist* issue," as if to insinuate that the rest of us are just a bunch of warmongers. No one of any good character *enjoys* war. No one *wants* it. But the fact is, to keep the peace, sometimes war is *forced* on us. I firmly believe that arguments should be settled peaceably, but peace cannot be one-sided. There will always be bullies. You can't force peace on them. And we will never have peace in this world as long as there are people and countries whose goal is to intimidate and destroy others.

I grew up in a world where nuclear war was a constant threat and the Soviet Union was a world power everyone feared. There were a lot of people who promoted "peace" during that time. But their peace was nothing more than an elusive dream. The Soviet Union wanted world domination and they were well on their way to achieving it. How can you have peace when a whole entire country thrives on occupation and domination and you are on their list of conquests?

I would hazard a guess that every one of us has at some point in our lives come face to face with a bully. What happens when you back down? Does the bully then stop because you are being peaceful? The exact opposite happens: the more we back down, the more the bully pushes.

When I was twelve, our family moved to a new neighborhood and I began junior high school in a building of complete strangers. Adolescence is hard enough without adding that kind of complication, and I had a very difficult time adjusting. We all have, to some degree or another, the desire to be accepted, so we all try to find that place where we can find "peace" by fitting into a group. I spent the first six months of seventh grade trying to find my "peace."

I rode a bus to school each day, and that is where my "peace" was first disrupted. Our bus carried both junior high and high school students to school, so we had a wide range of ages represented on my bus. There was a group of high school students who rode in the back of the bus and spent the whole trip terrorizing as many kids as possible—especially the seventh graders.

I remember my first day of school that year. I got on the bus and found a seat near the middle. I don't know if it was because I was new or because I looked lost, but the kids in the back of the bus immediately decided I was a great target. They began yelling obscenities in my direction as soon as I sat down. Through the whole thirty-five-minute bus ride, the kids in the back took turns running up and slapping me and various other kids on the back of the head, while the others laughed and egged them on. By the time we got to school, I was so glad the bus ride was over I nearly fell off the bus trying to get into the school.

As the days and weeks passed, things got increasingly worse. The kids in the back began throwing things at the kids in the front. They grabbed our books and wrote all over them. They tore homework assignments, threw purses out the window, and even started throwing tampons. I was absolutely appalled at their behavior, but I wasn't sure what to do. And if truth be told, I was scared to death. I didn't think I *could* tell anyone, because then I would be a snitch and that would just make me a bigger target. So, I guess out of self-preservation, I just put up with it and hoped they would eventually find someone else to pick on.

About a month into the school year, a new stop was added to our bus route. The family had just moved in, and they had a daughter who was in seventh grade. By the time we got to her house, all the seats on the bus were taken, and she had to find a seat where someone would let her sit three in a seat. The new girl, whose name I later learned was Lisa, had a full head of bright red hair and a face full of freckles. She instantly became the new target. What I saw that day was sickening. As Lisa walked from seat to seat, up and down the aisle, one person after another shook their heads and said she couldn't sit there. As the bus started to move, the girl lost her balance and fell into a seat. The boy she fell on pushed her into the aisle and yelled something at her. Suddenly, the mob in the back of the bus broke out in thunderous laughter and congratulated the boy on his cruelty, and he was swiftly inducted into the "cool" group.

I was absolutely sickened by what I saw, but I must shamefully admit that until Lisa fell and was abjectly humiliated, I considered turning her away from my seat as well. I guess I had hoped that maybe the gang in the back would focus their attention on this new kid and leave me alone. But after this despicable display, I could no longer stand by and do nothing. A shout came from the front of the bus as the bus driver noticed Lisa was standing. "Take a seat!" he yelled. I pushed the girl beside me over and gestured to Lisa. "You can sit here," I said.

The next few weeks were nearly unbearable. While Lisa and I were becoming fast friends, the kids on the bus were starting to realize that if they joined in with the gang in the back, they would no longer be targets. One by one, the kids on the bus started to join the kids in the back until there were only a very few of us left as the targets—and Lisa and I were at the top of the list.

I had three books defaced, my backpack thrown out the window, and several homework assignments torn to shreds. Lisa was equally harassed. There was one girl in particular who found great pleasure in running to the front of the bus and slapping us on the head. Her name was the only one I could remember because it was so unusual—Delia. Lisa and I put up with this for three months, trying our best to ignore them. Then one day, one of the girls in the back came up behind Lisa as she was leaving the bus and shoved a *used* maxi pad down the back of her pants. We were completely appalled and disgusted, and *that* was absolutely the end of our *tolerance*. We just couldn't believe anyone could be so vile and disgusting. Enough was enough.

For weeks, my mother had been asking me if everything was all right. She sensed something was wrong, but my answer was always, "I'm fine. Everything's fine." That day, however, I had another answer. I spent an hour talking to my mom about all the things that had been going on. When my dad came home, we both talked to him. I didn't know where those kids lived. I didn't even know their names—except for Delia. My parents looked her up in the phone book and found her address. It turned out that she just lived down the street from me. My parents called and made arrangements to meet with her parents.

That night, after dinner, my parents and I went to Delia's house. Her parents were older than mine, and they seemed very nice. They offered us refreshments and welcomed us into their home. After we filled them in on what was going on, Delia's mother looked at me with a puzzled face. "Are you sure my daughter was one of these kids doing these things?" she asked.

"Yes," I answered. "I'm sure."

Her father then spoke. "It is just surprising to us because Delia spent all last year being terrorized by these kids, and I just can't believe she would do this when she knows how much it hurts."

Delia's parents then called to her, and she came down the hall from her bedroom. It was obvious from the look on her face that she had no idea I was there. Delia's mother told her what I said and then asked if it was true. I will never forget Delia's courage when she answered with a twisted and obviously ashamed face, "Yes," she said quietly, "it's true."

I felt uncomfortable as I looked at Delia's anguished face. *Of all the kids on the back of the bus,* I thought, *the one we came to see was the one who was just like me.* I immediately understood what she had done—and why—and my heart instantly softened. Then Delia really impressed me when she said, "It won't happen again," and I *knew* what that would mean.

The next day when I got on the bus, I noticed Delia was sitting toward the front and was already being jeered.

"What's the matter, Delia?" the kids yelled. "Don't you like us anymore?"

"Come on back, Delia," a boy yelled. "You can sit with me. I won't bite."

The jeers and slurs continued interspersed with vulgarity and sexual innuendos. I looked at Delia in anguish. She just looked at me and gave a slight smile.

Over the next few weeks, Delia moved further up to the front of the bus as she continued to be brutalized. The gang in the back paid little attention to us after that. Though Lisa and I always befriended and tried to shield Delia, it became apparent that the whole bus was content to let Delia be the target of the gangsters in the back. Everyone just stood by and watched as Delia was attacked and ridiculed day after day. Then one day, Lisa decided it was time to stop this.

You may be wondering where the heck the bus driver was through all of this, right? Well, he was there. But he never did anything about it. I think he was just as terrified of those kids in the back of the bus as everyone else was. So Lisa decided to take matters into her own hands. If the bus driver didn't have the guts to deal with the situation, she would.

After getting off the bus at school that day, Lisa walked straight to the principal's office and told him what was going on. I wasn't there to view the events that unfolded that day firsthand, but I was told that the bus driver was called into the principal's office and informed that if he couldn't get control of the bus, they would hire someone who could. The principal then told the bus driver that he had complete authority to expel anyone, not only from the bus but from school, because the bus was considered school grounds. And the principal assured the bus driver that he would uphold his ruling if he felt someone needed to be expelled. The principal said that if the bus driver needed assistance on the bus, he would be happy to have school security ride with him.

I guess that's all the incentive the bus driver needed. That afternoon when I got on the bus and we were all loaded and ready to go, the bus driver stood up. His voice was strong and confident. "Attention on the bus!" he began. "I have been informed that I have authority to expel anyone on this bus who does not obey the rules of conduct for this educational institution."

The bus driver then pulled some papers from his seat and asked a couple of kids in the front to distribute them. He then continued, "Just in case you don't know what the rules of conduct are, I have listed them for you on the paper you are being given. Each of you is to have this list signed by your parents and returned to me before you get on the bus tomorrow. And for those of you in the back of the bus, your activities will discontinue immediately or you will be assigned seats in the front of the bus. And if that doesn't shape you up, I'll bring in the school security officers to sit with you. And if there are any *further* incidents from any of you in the back," he continued, "I will have you arrested and you will not ride this bus again!"

There was complete silence. Then the bus driver looked at Lisa and me, gave a quick smile, and went to his seat. A sudden sound broke the silence as I noticed that Lisa had stood up and began clapping. Soon the whole front end of the bus was clapping and whistling. I turned to Delia and saw the relief on her face. The kids in the back just sat there stunned as we all returned to our seats and the bus pulled out of the school parking lot.

There were a couple of incidents that came up throughout the year, but the bus driver handled them just as he said he would. And when it came down to expulsions, true to his word, the principal honored the ruling. A couple of kids were expelled but no one ever had to be arrested. I'm sure that was only because the kids in the back knew it was an option, so they didn't push it. And for the rest of the year, we had peace on the bus—not peace because of *tolerance*—peace because of *strength*.

Several years ago, I watched a movie that left a lasting impression on me. The movie, *Red Dawn,* stars a young Patrick Swayze, who plays a teenager caught in the midst of World War III. The film was released in 1984, when our country was still gripped in the era of the cold war. The film depicts a non-nuclear version of World War III, where the Russians and Cubans unite together to attack America. A group of teenagers caught in the crossfire end up becoming freedom fighters, led by Patrick Swayze. They called themselves the Wolverines.

One of the Wolverines is the son of the town's mayor. The mayor, in an effort to "keep the peace," freely turns the city over to the enemy and even helps them do so. There is one scene in the movie where the joint Russian/Cuban army rounds up all those men they feel might be a threat. The Cuban officer then lines the men up for execution. As the executioners ready their weapons, one of the American men starts singing "God Bless America." The mayor is standing by the Cuban and Russian officers as they signal their men to fire. The men open up their weapons and cut the defenseless American prisoners down and the singing suddenly stops. The mayor grimaces and turns his head as blood spatters all over the rocks, and then walks away talking with the Russian and Cuban officers.

I noticed a clear, distinct difference between the man who stood to sing "God Bless America" and the mayor who turned away. It was the same thing I noticed on the bus when I was twelve years old. Some of the kids on the bus found "peace" by being silent. Others found it by joining the enemy. Sometimes "peace" is simply another word for cowardice. Peace and pacifism are *not* the same thing. Kowtowing to a bully does not promote peace. It just encourages the bully. But when you defeat the bully, like we did on the school bus, you promote peace because there is no longer a bully to threaten the peace.

Near the end of *Red Dawn,* there is a heart-wrenching scene where the Wolverine who is the mayor's son confesses to his friends that he is carrying a bug. He went into town and his own father turned him in, so he could promote "peace." The Cubans tortured the boy and made him swallow a homing device. I was only seventeen when I saw the film, and I just couldn't understand how a father could do that to his own son—and all in the name of peace? Even as a teenager, I could clearly see the mayor of the town was more interested in self-preservation than peace for his town.

Peace is not an absence of war. It is a state of being. It is the ability to be at peace despite the storm raging around you. Many of those who promote peace are the very ones who disrupt it. In the 1960s, promoters of "peace" destroyed property, initiated riots, and attacked United States soldiers on college campuses throughout America. Just how did this promote peace? It didn't, of course. But the demonstrators weren't promoting *peace*. They were promoting an agenda—just as they do today.

In March of 2003, the National Organization for Women wrote an open letter to President Bush stating, "Violence often simply begets violence. Women's groups have long favored non-violent, diplomatic means to resolve conflict, including international conflict."[2]

I'm not sure who NOW is including in their list of "women's groups" but they obviously haven't heard of the Daughters of Liberty.

In 1774, when King George rescinded the oppressive Stamp Act, the colonists were overjoyed, believing that England was finally going to treat the Americans fairly. To show their gratitude, the Sons of Liberty in New York City built a large, lead statue in honor of the king's honorable gesture and placed it in the city square. Their good relations with King George were short-lived, however, when he replaced the Stamp Act with even more oppressive taxes, restrictions, and regulations.

The following spring, when the British stationed troops at Staten Island, the Sons of Liberty started a citywide riot. The statue of King George was pulled down and stomped on, as angry men and women yelled, "Liberty! Liberty!" The statue was then melted down to make bullets for the Colonial Army. It was the *Daughters* of Liberty who turned the statue into ammunition. They organized themselves into groups and held a competition to see who could make the most bullets. Ruth Marvin came in with the highest number at 11,592 bullets which, together with the thousands of others cast, were used to fill the guns of the American soldiers to fight the oppressive King George.[3]

Yes, the women of America have always favored peace, but not at the price of freedom. And that is the price we are being expected to pay today. Our very freedom is at stake. The safety of our children and our children's children is being threatened. But that doesn't concern feminists and their many cohorts. When you read further in NOW's letter to President Bush, you realize what does concern them:

> We are also concerned about the very high costs of a war against Iraq. There is no longer a federal budget surplus to fund this war, as tax cuts coupled with continuing economic weakness have pushed tax revenues down, resulting in budget deficits for the foreseeable future. We fear that, as has happened during previous wars, funds will be diverted from education, health, welfare and other vitally needed social programs whose budgets were already downsized. Women will bear the greatest burden of any decrease in domestic spending in order to finance war.[4]

Unbelievable! The feminists are complaining about the war because it is costing so much money. They are up in arms because they fear their myriad of programs may suffer from a lack of funding because of the money being spent to protect our nation from terrorists. Okay, so let me just point out, for those of you who are not familiar with the Constitution: the "domestic spending" the feminists are referring to is completely unconstitutional. Education, healthcare, welfare, and the myriad of other social programs Congress is funding today are not authorized in the Constitution—national security, however, is. And did you read that part about the taxes? The feminists are complaining because the government let us keep more of *our* money. Are they crazy?

I have to wonder if feminists are really opposed to war or are they just afraid we will find out how much of our money they are taking for all their special interest programs to, as they claim, "help women"? According to feminists, tax cuts are bad, government spending is good, the Constitution is obsolete, terrorists are revolutionaries, and we all just need to get along. This is a perfect example of the *negative* influence of women.

When the Berlin Wall came down, a great many Americans sighed in relief, thinking we had finally achieved world peace. And many of the anti-war groups felt we no longer needed the military. What do you think would have happened if the bus driver from my junior high school suddenly caved? Do you think peace would have continued on the bus? You know it wouldn't. Those kids would have gone right back to their old behavior once the authority showed weakness. James Madison knew this. He wrote, "How could a readiness for war in time of peace be safely prohibited, unless we could prohibit, in like manner, the preparations and establishments of every hostile nation?"[16]

America was about to learn this lesson the hard way.

In 1992, the anti-military club found a crusader for their cause, and for eight years, President Bill Clinton gutted the military down to a skeleton force while the anti-war crowd cheered him on for promoting peace. But it didn't promote peace, because on September 11, 2001, our nation was viciously attacked and thousands of Americans were killed. And it wasn't Bill Clinton the nation called on to promote peace. It was the United States Air Force.

As the air force flew their jets over the city of New York, millions of Americans felt safe and protected. Then as we watched our navy, army, and marines, we stood in awe as the joint forces of the United States military were instantly mobilized and stood at the ready. They didn't just appear over the horizon out of nowhere. The men and women of the military have always been there preparing, training, constantly at the ready to protect the United States of America. And they would gladly lay down their lives to keep America free.

I think it is important that we understand the mindset of those who *say* they want peace because they are the ones, who by their very actions (or lack thereof), thrust us into danger. Don't be fooled by the cry for peace. The terrorists and conquerors of the world are watching, just like the kids in the back of the bus were. They are constantly looking for weakness of any kind. Unfortunately, they have recently found it in the statements and actions of our own president. I have been told it is very unpopular, and even dangerous, to speak out against President Obama's actions and policies, but I think it is much more dangerous for us to believe we are safe. We are not. An absence of terrorist attacks does not mean there are no terrorists; it only means that our defenses are strong. But with each sign of weakness, the terrorists of the world become more and more emboldened. We cannot afford *not* to protect ourselves. We cannot afford to let our guard down—our very freedom depends on our strength.

We are not at war with countries; we are at war with the terrorists who live in those countries. Some are the *rulers* of those countries like Cuba, North Korea, Iran, and Venezuela. Some are drug cartels on our southern border. Some are religious extremists who murder and terrorize in the name of their god. Some are militant cartels in Africa. Some are young hoodlums with guns parading as pirates on the high seas. They are *all* watching—looking to see how America reacts under pressure—pushing our buttons to see if we will push back. And they see what I see.

I see a president who does not understand that terrorists will not give up nuclear weapons just because we ask them to. These terrorists are our enemies not because *we chose them* but because *they chose us*. They don't stop being our enemies just because *we* decide we want to be friends. They don't *want* to be friends with us. They want to kill us!

I know it is hard for us to believe that anyone would have such pure evil intentions, but they do. Just look at history. Who would have believed in such a thing as kamikaze pilots or suicide bombers? Who would believe that a person could strap a bomb to a little baby in a stroller and then push that baby into a building to blow it up? Who could fathom such things? And yet, they are happening around the world every day. It doesn't matter if we are nice to *them;* they have no intentions of being nice to *us*.

They have no intentions of giving up their nuclear weapons or the desire to have them, because they seek ultimate power. They have no intention of living peaceably, because they do not know how. They weren't raised that way. They don't know freedom; they only understand tyranny and oppression. I know this is hard for us to understand. It just doesn't compute. But that is what they know. It is what they were taught.

If you were taught from the time you could walk that daisies were poisonous and your little brother died a horrible death because he touched them, you would grow up hating daisies and avoiding them like the plague. Then if years later, someone came along and told you they weren't poisonous at all, you would not believe them, because if you did, it would completely uproot everything you knew to be true. Everyone you knew, loved, and trusted from the time you were born—your parents, your family, your pastor, your teachers—all told you daisies were poisonous and your brother died from them. They have been talking about poisonous daisies every day, several times a day, your whole life. They are *still* talking about poisonous daisies. So you can't believe it isn't true, because if you do, your family becomes wrong and your brother's death is left unexplained. You would feel confused, betrayed, and scared.

Everything you have known and believed would become a lie, and all the people you have known and trusted would be wrong—fighting for a wasted, unjust cause. You can't accept that fate. So, despite all the evidence that daisies are not poisonous, you decide to believe those you trust most and spend the rest of your life believing—and even teaching your own children—that daisies are poisonous. That is why Muslim children grow up believing Israel is a vile enemy that needs to be crushed and America is an abomination that needs to be brought to its knees. They learn this from the time they are born. They hear it every day from everyone they know and trust. To go against it is to deny their family and everything they know, love, and have come to accept as truth. To say Israel is not the enemy is to deny who they are. To suggest peace with the world is an attack on their culture, history, and families. They believe these things just as strongly as we believe the earth is round. You can't reason with that. For them, daisies are poisonous, regardless of what the truth is.

You cannot rationalize with terrorists, because they are *not* rational. You cannot explain to someone who would fly a plane into a New York City high-rise for the purpose of killing thousands of people that using nuclear weapons to kill people is a bad idea. To them, it's just more efficient. Nuclear weaponry is a threat terrorists intend to use to crush this nation and all others that get in their way. *And we really are the only nation standing in their way.* Once they take the United States, the rest of the world will just crumble. *We* are the last line of defense. We cannot afford to be weak at a time like this.

This is not the time to cut our military budget to fund pet projects. This is not the time to pull out of Iraq and Afghanistan. This is not the time to close Guantanamo Bay. And this is not the time to tell the terrorists of the world that the United States is dismantling their nuclear weapons as an example of world peace. The terrorists will not *follow* our example, but they *will* take advantage of the opportunity, and the consequences will be devastating.

I am tired of the terrorists of the world being treated like freedom fighters and heralded as great leaders while the men and women of our military are treated like criminals by the media and members of our own Congress. The men and women of the United States military are not fighting for conquest. They are not fighting for power or riches. They don't even seek honor. They leave their families and their homes to put their lives on the line for complete strangers they will never see, to fight for a cause they believe in—freedom. And they do it for all of us—even those who ridicule them for it. As my husband always says, "They ridicule us, mock us, call us criminals, and protest everything we do, and I will fight to my last breath, and give my life if necessary, to protect their right to do so." Is it any wonder I am a patriot?

My husband and I recently attended a military function where a group of young airmen put together a video presentation honoring all the military service members who have given their lives in defense of our nation since September 11, 2001. The following poem, written by Charles M. Province, was read as part of the presentation. It was a wonderful expression of appreciation for all those who have died in defense of the freedoms we so often take for granted.

IT IS THE SOLDIER

It is the Soldier, not the minister
Who has given us freedom of religion.
It is the Soldier, not the reporter
Who has given us freedom of the press.
It is the Soldier, not the poet
Who has given us freedom of speech.
It is the Soldier, not the campus organizer
Who has given us freedom to protest.
It is the Soldier, not the lawyer
Who has given us the right to a fair trial.
It is the Soldier, not the politician
Who has given us the right to vote.
It is the Soldier who salutes the flag,
Who serves beneath the flag,
And whose coffin is draped by the flag,
Who allows the protester to burn the flag.[17]

©Copyright 1970, 2005 by Charles M. Province

Some call them warmongers. I call them heroes. And the amazing thing is that despite the low pay, adverse conditions, long family separations, and poor living conditions, these men and women continue to volunteer and proudly serve their country—not because they're warmongers, but because they love America and they believe freedom and liberty are worth the cost. As long as there is freedom, there will always be those who fight against it. As long as there is peace, there will always be those determined to disturb it. As long as there is an America, there will always be those who are hell-bent on destroying it.

The end of the cold war was not the end of all war. We stopped one bully, but there are many more. But the end of the cold war did prove one very important thing: "peace through strength" *does* work!

I was wrong about one thing, though: Because of 9/11, my children now understand freedom. They understand the importance of the United States military, and they know the value of "peace through strength." And in the spring of 2003, as I watched the Iraqi people pull down the statue of Saddam Hussein on national television, I once again had tears in my eyes. And as I looked into the eyes of my children gathered around me, I knew they understood too. "This is freedom, kids," I said as we watched together. "This is freedom—and it is worth fighting for."

From Our Founders

For a people who are free, and who mean to remain so, a well-organized and armed militia is their best security.

~Thomas Jefferson

A generous parent would have said, "if there must be trouble, let it be in my day, that my child may have peace."

~Thomas Paine

Whatever enables us to go to war, secures our peace.

~Thomas Jefferson

The tree of liberty must be refreshed from time to time with the blood of patriots and tyrants. It is its natural manure.

~Thomas Jefferson

Every post is honorable in which a man can serve his country.

~George Washington

My anxious recollections, my sympathetic feeling, and my best wishes are irresistibly excited whensoever, in any country, I see an oppressed nation unfurl the banners of freedom.

~George Washington

Every man who loves peace, every man who loves his country, every man who loves liberty ought to have it ever before his eyes that he may cherish in his heart a due attachment to the Union of America and be able to set a due value on the means of preserving it.

~James Madison

It is in vain, Sir, to extenuate the matter. Gentlemen may cry, Peace, Peace!—but there is no peace. The war is actually begun! The next gale that sweeps from the North will bring to our ears the clash of resounding arms! Our brethren are already in the field! Why stand we here idle? What is it that Gentlemen wish? What would they have? Is life so dear, or peace so sweet, as to be purchased at the price of chains and slavery? Forbid it, Almighty God! I know not what course others may take; but as for me, give me liberty or give me death!

~Patrick Henry

We fight not to enslave, but to set a country free, and to make room upon the earth for honest men to live in.

~Thomas Paine

Other Notable Quotes

When you see a rattlesnake poised to strike, you do not wait until he has struck before you crush him.

~President Franklin D. Roosevelt

Patriotism is easy to understand in America. It means looking out for yourself by looking out for your country.

~Calvin Coolidge

Suggested Books & Resources:
American Mourning Catherine Moy and Melanie Morgan
Countdown to Terror by Curt Weldon
They Just Don't Get It by Colonel David Hunt
Shane Comes Home by Rinker Buck
Lone Survivor by Marcus Luttrell

IS THERE TRUTH OUT THERE?

In a time of universal deceit, telling the truth is a revolutionary act.
~ George Orwell

On Wednesday, April 15, 2009, I stood before an audience of eight thousand proud Americans at Courthouse Square in Dayton, Ohio. It was a cold day, much colder than usual for that time of year, but still the people came, not because they were racists, not because they were coerced by Fox News, but because they were fed up with their oppressive government overburdening them with taxes and spending us into oblivion. It was the Dayton, Ohio Tea Party event, and as I walked up to the podium to deliver my speech, I looked out into the faces of all those glorious freedom-loving Americans. I just stood in awe as I thought to myself, *they're here, they really came.*

Just a couple of months earlier, I was approached by a young student from the University of Dayton who told me her boyfriend was organizing a TEA (Taxed Enough Already) Party in Dayton. She asked if I would speak. A few days later, I met her boyfriend, the young UD law student in person. His name was Rob Scott, and he told me that he and his friend Perry, a fellow law student, had decided they would host a Tea Party in Dayton. As I sat and listened to the pure red, white, and blue passion pour from this young man's soul, I couldn't help but marvel at his commitment and dedication to his country. For one so young to be so filled with American spirit *and* respect for the Constitution was inspiring. It gave me hope for our future, and at that time, I was seriously wondering if there was any hope left for the present, let alone the future. But sitting there that day, I saw a part of America that reminded me what we are fighting for and why it is important that we don't give up. And Rob and Perry never did.

In a few short weeks, these law students put together an event that I, as an event planner, marveled at. What was even more astonishing was that Rob, on a college student's meager means, used his own money to pay for the event, and by pulling resources, trading services, and receiving things in kind, he pulled off what any professional would consider impossible. But there I stood on that stage that day in front of thousands of Ohioans from the economically struggling city of Dayton. As I looked out at the masses, I remembered the famous line from *Field of Dreams:* "If you build it, they will come."

It turned out that the Dayton Tea Party, with eight thousand in attendance, was the largest Tea Party in Ohio and one of the largest in the nation. There were no national figures, no big names, no bands—none of the usual things to bring a crowd like that. And yet there they were, and they weren't alone. Thousands more Americans assembled in state houses, community parks, anywhere they could gather and they all came for the same purpose—to tell Washington enough is enough and that "We the People" aren't going to take it anymore.

The message was the same all over the nation, in every town and city where American families of every race, religion, and income joined to have their voice heard. You would think a movement like that would have been on every front page of every newspaper in the country and dominated all the network media airwaves. But that did not happen. In fact, the next day when President Obama was asked what he thought about the Tea Parties, he said he didn't know anything about them. But I assure you he knew, and so did the media, which is exactly why they chose not to cover it. And that is a perfect representation of the American media today.

The lack of media coverage didn't surprise me. I have come to expect it. What did surprise me, however, was their blatant attacks on people like Rob, who sacrificed so much to host a Tea Party, and all the normal, everyday American families who attended them. And it absolutely floored me when it was suggested by our own government that the people who went to the Tea Parties were right-wing extremists and potential terrorists. The media portrayed the Tea Parties as racist, right-wing lynch parties sponsored by the Republican Party and Fox News. It was utterly absurd. And the more I watched the news reports, or lack thereof, of the hundreds of Tea Parties around the nation, the more I found myself wondering, *Is there any truth left in American media? Is there any truth out there?*

Just take a quick look at American media today. From Tea Parties to the economy and the war on terror to presidential campaigns, there isn't much of anything you can call news today. Whatever happened to accurate reporting of the facts and the belief that the people have a right to know? Know what? The media no longer report events; they manipulate them. They're no longer reporting facts; they're promoting an agenda. We are in the midst of the greatest exhibition of propaganda the world has ever seen. And I urge you: *do not believe everything you hear or read.*

Here are just a few examples of what I call "manipulation media."

Bad Economy

In the eight years that President Bush was in the White House, the media was saturated with stories about how bad our economy was. The two general standards the media use to determine the nation's economic status are the unemployment rate and the national debt. Simply going by the media's reports of our nation's economy over the last seventeen years, you are led to believe the economy was booming in the Clinton years, miserable in the Bush years, and now things are looking up. You get the impression from the media that President Obama was left with a horrible economy, and now that he is in office, we are finally starting to recover from the Bush years. That is what the media is reporting. But if we used the media's own standards to judge the economy over those same seventeen years, we get a much different picture.

The chart below, provided by Gateway pundit and based on the Misery Index[1] (the standard the government, media, and economists use to determine U.S. unemployment rate) shows the unemployment rate in the Clinton years, the Bush years, and today. I know many of you may question my resources or the numbers I use, because the media has done such a good job convincing you things are a certain way. (You may not want to believe what I am about to tell you, but I assure you, these aren't my numbers. Please, look them up for yourself.) The Misery Index is available online and lists the unemployment rates each month of every year from 1948 to the present. In fact, I encourage you to look it up. It is very enlightening. And I am a strong advocate of self-education. The more we learn, the less our government can oppress us and the less the media can deceive us. That said, let's take a look at the numbers in the following chart:

Women: America's Last Best Hope

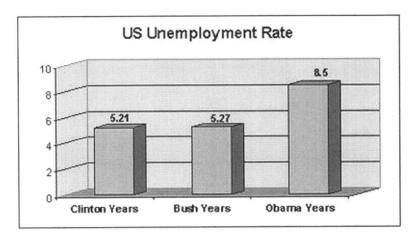

The numbers along the left side of the chart represent the percentage of unemployment. The towers show the unemployment rates for the last three presidents. I find it very interesting how different the picture looks when we compare actual numbers to media reports. If the media were really *reporting* the news, they would show us these numbers, but they don't; they just claim this thing or that thing, and we sit on our couches, watching the evening news, taking it all in as if it is fact. The only problem is, they leave the facts out.

The media praised President Clinton for all the jobs created during his terms in office and hammered President Bush for all the job losses during his. They continually mentioned the record low unemployment rates during the Clinton years. They attacked President Bush for the "skyrocketing" unemployment during his. Yet, when we look at the actual numbers as shown in the chart, we see that the average unemployment rates during the Clinton and Bush years were virtually the same. The only obvious difference in interest rates between the two administrations was how the media reported it.

That brings us to President Obama's term. Now, before you buy into the media's claim that the unemployment rate is so high because President Obama inherited Bush's recession, let me remind you that the unemployment rate was well below 6 percent when President Bush left office. We somehow forget that President Bush inherited a recession when he took office and that despite the monumental challenges he faced throughout his terms in office—9/11, stock market scandals, Hurricane Katrina, and the war on terror—the unemployment rate never went over 6.5 percent until the fall of 2008, when it reached 6.7 percent in November and climbed to 7.2

percent in December. Until that time, the unemployment rate remained a steady 4.5 to 6 percent for five solid years.

The first question we should ask ourselves, then, is why did the increase happen after being steady for so long? Well, two major events happened in the fall of 2008. One, in October the United States Congress passed a $700 billion bailout package known as the TARP, and two, Barack Obama was elected as president of the United States.

Now, before you close the book in disgust, concluding that I am one of those racists out to get President Obama, let me explain why not just one but *both* of these events are important. And since this is a book of common sense and not statistics, I will use the examples of some of my friends to illustrate my point.

In 2006, a friend of mine opened a franchise restaurant in Huber Heights, Ohio. He entered into an agreement with the franchise company, borrowed the necessary money, and received training from the corporate office. The timeline to open the business included finding a location for the restaurant, constructing the interior, hiring workers, and stocking the product—in this case, food. This all could have easily been done in thirty to sixty days, and he would have been open and ready for business. However, there is one glitch to opening any business—government intervention.

My friend had to go to the government for permits allowing him to create *his* store, pay fees allowing him to build *his* store, and sign paperwork committing to pay taxes on what he earned at *his* store. Now my friend, Seth, had been a manager with Wal-Mart before he decided to leap into this endeavor. He put all his savings and experience, time, and energy on the line to fulfill a dream of opening his own business. According to the franchise, Seth would be open for business in less than three months—plenty of time to start paying back his loans and begin generating a return on his sizeable investment. Enter the government.

Within just a few weeks of the process, Seth realized the county government was not going to make this process easy. The county burdened him with paperwork, fees, and inspections that seemed never-ending, but he met each requirement and continued in the process until the county code enforcement officer informed Seth that he was required to have a fire wall—twice the depth and three times the cost of a normal wall. Seth explained to the government official that he was a sandwich shop and that there were not any ovens in the restaurant. The county didn't care. The code required that restaurants have fire walls, and they would not give Seth an operating license unless he had a fire wall.

The battle dragged on for weeks while Seth tried to work within the system and use the county's own regulations to prove he didn't have to have a fire wall. But, as time passed, he realized all he was doing was making the county mad and worried that they wouldn't grant his permits, even if he did have the fire wall. So he gave in and paid the additional expense to have a fire wall built that he didn't need, in hopes of moving closer to opening his store. But it wasn't that easy. Seth found himself facing even more paperwork, inspections, and government red tape, until his costs were so high he worried if he would ever recoup them once the store was open. Of course at this point, he was starting to wonder if the store would ever open. But it finally did. Three months turned into four and then five, and finally seven months later, Seth had his grand opening. He struggled from day one because of the long delay in opening, but he worked hard. He was there every day, putting in long hours. He felt that if he just worked hard enough, he would make a return on his investment, and he still believed in his dream.

Three months after opening, however, Ohio passed an increase in the minimum wage, and Seth had to cut two employees and work longer hours himself to cover the higher costs forced on him, just so he could stay in the black. Seth continued to struggle for another year, until he realized that between the franchise fees and the local and federal tax burdens, he barely made enough to survive. With a baby on the way, Seth decided to go back to Wal-Mart so he could provide for his family. He kept the store open another year until his franchise commitment was fulfilled and then closed the store, leaving the city with less revenue and five employees without a job.

I approached Seth just before he closed his store and told him about a business opportunity another friend of mine was starting, to see if he was interested, since he had experience in running a business. Seth looked at me and said, "That whole thing just scares me. I think I'm just going to stay at Wal-Mart, where I know I'll get a steady paycheck and income for my family."

Now I've heard a lot of legislators on the floor of Congress over the years give heartbreaking stories about single-parent families who are struggling on minimum wage, and single mothers and young families who have lost their jobs, but not one of them mention the reason these families are struggling: the government has put so many burdens and regulations on businesses like Seth's that they can't stay open. And this is just one of thousands of examples.

Small business is the lifeblood of this nation. It isn't the corporations that keep America's economy afloat. It is American families, and it isn't just the government that doesn't seem to get that—it is the media too. One CNN reporter proved that when she covered the Chicago Tea Party and condescendingly threw her microphone in the face of a father holding his young child. I'm sure you've seen or heard the correspondence, but just in case, here is the transcript. You can view it yourself online.

> SUSAN ROESGEN (CNN Reporter): *(Reading some of the signs held by protesters)* Uh, let's see ... 'Drop the taxes,' 'Drop socialism.' OK. Let's see. *(Moves to man holding his young child)* You're here with your two-year-old and you're already in debt. Why are you here today, sir?
>
> MAN: Because I hear a president say that he believed in what Lincoln stood for. Lincoln's primary thing was he believed that people had the right to liberty, and had the right—
>
> ROESGEN: Sir, what does this have to do with taxes? What does this have to do with your taxes? Do you realize that you're eligible for a $400 credit?
>
> MAN: Let me finish my point. Lincoln, Lincoln believed that people had the right to share in the fruits of their own labor and that government should not take it. And we have clearly gotten to that point.
>
> ROESGEN: Wait, wait ... Did you know that the state of Lincoln gets $50 billion out of the stimulus? That's $50 billion for this state, sir. (looking back at camera)
>
> ROESGEN: OK, well, Kyra, we'll move on over here. I think you get the general tenor of this. Uh, it's anti-government, anti-CNN, since this is highly promoted by the right-wing conservative network, FOX. And since I can't really hear much more, and I think this is not really family viewing. Toss it back to you, Kyra.

<u>KYRA PHILLIPS</u>: I know Susan Roesgen is having a hard time hearing me, but wow. That is the prime example of what we're following across the country there. Susan pointed out everything plain and clear of what she's dealing with.

Does this sound like a reporter reporting the news or a woman debating her position? That man was there, like thousands of Americans all across the nation who gathered at Tea Parties, to protest the government's taxing and spending us into the poorhouse, and her comeback was "Did you know that the state of Lincoln gets $50 billion out of the stimulus?" That's the whole point. Where does she think the stimulus money comes from? It comes from the pocket of that man standing there concerned about how much longer and how much harder he is going to have to work to put food on the table when the government takes even more of his pay to cover that $50 billion. The government is taking billions of dollars from the hardworking families of this country and passing it around like clowns throwing candy at a parade. What sense does it make for the federal government to take money from the citizens of this country just to give it to more government to spend on things we have no say in? Why do the media think we would happy about this? And why aren't they reporting the truth?

Apparently I wasn't the only one irritated with the lack of accurate coverage (or any coverage at all) of the Tea Parties. After a huge public outcry on the way this woman reported the Tea Parties, CNN responded by simply stating the woman was doing her job and called it like she saw it. And I guess that about sums up the current state of our media.

My friend Seth learned what all businessmen quickly learn if they intend their business to prosper. One, you can't spend more than you make, and two, the more government intrudes in your business, the more money you will lose. It is those two factors that determine the country's unemployment rate. The president doesn't create jobs, people do. Businessmen know this. But they also know that the government can cause the loss of jobs. The more government restricts, taxes, and regulates business, the more those businesses lose. They have to make up the difference somewhere—either in higher costs, less overhead, or both. Either way, American families lose.

So in November, when American businessmen and -women saw that President Obama—a man who campaigned on spreading the wealth and more government intervention—won the election, they decided it was a time to save and not a time to invest. And suddenly, the unemployment rate jumped to over 9 percent and is still climbing. President Bush was able to keep the unemployment down, not because he created jobs but because he created an atmosphere where business could prosper by reducing taxes and regulations. Families had more of their own money to spend and more freedom to invest in new businesses. Imagine how low the unemployment would have dropped during the Bush years if he hadn't spent so much money, which brings me to my next example of media manipulation.

National Debt

In the eight years that President Bush resided in the White House, the media never wasted a minute talking about the mounting national debt, but they didn't seem to think that same debt was such an issue in the eight years that President Clinton was in the White House. The media talked about the national debt as if it just suddenly appeared when President Bush was elected. They consistently referred to the Clinton years as an economic boom full of surplus and accused President Bush of "wasting" the surplus—because he gave it back to the taxpayers.

During the Bush years, you couldn't get away from the onslaught of slinging insults and accusations on all the money President Bush was spending. The national debt became such a huge part of the news that children in elementary schools were saving pennies to do their part to help pay down the debt. They would have been better off buying Skittles and gumballs, but the media ate it up.

Day after day, we faced one story after another about how high the national debt was and how long it would take to pay it off. Then suddenly on January 19, 2009, that all changed. The national debt was no longer a story at all, let alone a major one. With the way the media dropped their reporting of the national debt, you would think it disappeared overnight. But it didn't. It's still there. So what happened on January 19, 2009? Barack Obama was sworn in as president of the United States. I'm just stating facts here. Isn't everything I just said true? And if so, then you've got to ask yourself, if the national debt was such a huge issue from 2000 to 2008, why isn't it an issue anymore? If the national debt was a major news story then, why isn't it now? If the media were *reporting* news, it still would be.

The national debt *was* a huge issue during the Bush years, just as it was during the Clinton years—and *every* year since our founding that our nation has carried a debt. George W. Bush *was* spending like there was no tomorrow and the media *should* have been reporting it. But if the media felt it newsworthy then, why aren't we hearing anything about it now, when our national debt jumped almost $4 trillion since President Obama took office? When anyone brings up the issue, the media seem to totally blow it off. "Oh, that little thing? Well, President Obama had to do that because he inherited Bush's debt and he needs to fix it." Is anyone really buying that?

For the sake of argument, let's look at the numbers. When President Bush took office, the national debt was $5.727 trillion—an absurd amount of money. But thanks to President Bush's "compassionate conservatism" with his No Child Left Behind, Medicare expansion, and his myriad of other unconstitutional pet projects to "show compassion to the needy," he increased the national debt by more than 70 percent. By the time President Bush left office, thanks in large part to the midnight passage of the $700 billion TARP fund, our national debt had risen to $9.849 trillion. Of course the media should have been reporting that—as well as naming the names of every member of Congress who voted for it, after all, it is Congress that allocates spending the money, not the president.[2]

If Congress had stood up for the people instead of bowing to the president, we wouldn't be in such miserable debt. This was definitely a newsworthy story. Unfortunately that is where the story ends—at least in the media. For just three months after the TARP was passed, with one strike of his pen, President Obama signed the $780 billion Stimulus Bill, soaring our national debt to $11 trillion, and he isn't done yet.

The Tea Parties were organized because the people of this country are angry. We are tired of all the spending, and we are fed up with our elected leaders telling us it's for our own good and the media trying to convince us we should be happy about it. If the media hammered on President Bush for a $9 trillion national debt, they should be sounding a battle cry for the $11 trillion (and rising) debt President Obama is carrying. So why aren't they? And why are they spending so much time trying to convince us it is all President Bush's fault and the debt isn't a big deal anymore. Why are they treating the issue like an outfit that was so last season? If they really are *reporting the news,* then why aren't they reporting this? One must wonder if there is some agenda driving them, and it all seems to be wrapped around which party is in the White House. The media claims they are *reporting news* when in actuality they are doing nothing more than propagating personal opinion and manipulating facts and interviews to back up that opinion, and that brings us to my next example of media manipulation.

The Iraq War

I began this chapter stating that I have come to expect media manipulation, and the war in Iraq is why. I had a unique vantage point of the Iraq War and the media's coverage of it while my husband was stationed at the Pentagon. Now I want you to understand that everything I have learned and all the things that I share in this book are all things that I have learned in a relatively short amount of time. So maybe that will explain why I had no idea what the Fox News Channel was or that it even existed until a few months after the war in Iraq began.

My husband was the air force public affairs liaison with Combat Camera. His job was to obtain footage, clear it for release, and then send it out to the media as requested. In March of 2003, when the Iraq war began, my opinion of the media plummeted to depths even I didn't think possible.

During the first few months of the war, my husband lived at the Pentagon—literally. I rarely saw him. He worked around the clock, releasing video and still photos to the media. As the major conflict ended and the job of rebuilding began, the stories and images being aired through the media became very disturbing to me. Everything out of the media drew a picture of a country and a people that didn't want us there. The media gave the appearance that we were invaders—unwanted oppressors. One day I shared my concerns with my husband.

"Our troops are being targeted daily," I told him. "Why do these people hate us? Why are we there if the Iraqi people don't want us? Why don't we just leave?"

"Don't believe everything you see, Kimberly," he told me. "What you see in the media isn't what's really going on."

"What do you mean?" I asked.

"I look through hundreds of photos and video segments every day. Ninety-five percent of what I see is positive, and most of the Iraqi people want us there." My husband then told me how whole villages in Iraq were adopting U.S. military units. Soldiers were being invited into Iraqi homes for dinner every week. U.S. military doctors were treating Iraqi men, women, and children for various ailments. Convoys were handing out candy to Iraqi children. And he had viewed several photos of Iraqi citizens holding signs that said "Thank you, America" and waving American flags. Of course my husband saw the photos of the car bombs and snipers as well, but in the mainstream media, that's *all* you saw.

Day after day, I saw reports of Iraqi citizens who hated America. I never saw one report of the things my husband was seeing, even though the information was being sent to them daily. I looked at my husband in frustration. "If they're only going to report the negative," I said, "then don't give them anything but the good stuff."

"A week ago, that's all I released because that's all there was to release," he said. "They still didn't run it. They just re-ran the old negative stuff over and over again."

I couldn't believe it. I was so angry. Why wasn't the media telling the truth? Around that time, the home school co-op I was involved with started promoting a news subscription to *World* magazine for our current-events studies. The leader of the group said she had been receiving the magazine for years and loved it. "And," she added, "it comes with a free book." *Free* sounded good to me, so I signed up, and about a week later, my free book arrived in the mail. I didn't know who the author was, but the patriotic cover and the title, *Let Freedom Ring,* caught my attention immediately. I sat down and started reading right then.

Three chapters into the book, I wanted to know who this guy was. I liked everything he had to say. It was like he was echoing my thoughts, feelings, and passions. So I turned to the cover and read about the author—a guy named Sean Hannity. The bio mentioned he was a radio talk show host and the co-host of *Hannity and Colmes* on the Fox News Channel. When my husband came home from work that night, I asked him if he knew what the Fox News Channel was. He looked at me like I was some kind of alien. "Yeah," he answered. "It's a cable news channel. We watch it at the Pentagon."

"Why don't we get it?" I asked him.

"We only have the fifty-channel package with our satellite company. You need the one hundred-channel package to get Fox News."

The next day, I called our satellite provider and ordered the one hundred channels. We have had Fox News in our home ever since. Despite what the other media outlets claim, I don't watch Fox News because I am brainwashed or too stupid to think for myself; I watch it because I finally found a news network that reports truth and facts. They have great programming and commentators who really make you think. My absolute favorite is Glenn Beck's show. I watch every weekday while making dinner, and the more I watch his show, the more I realize how much I don't know. And I want to know. I want to know about what our elected leaders are doing. I want to know how they're spending our money; I want to know about the history of our country and our government. I just want to know. And I want to know why the only place I get this information is on Fox News or the Internet.

The great tragedy is that most Americans still get their news from the big three networks. That's where I got my news until a few years ago. It was like a family tradition. I grew up watching NBC's *Today* show every morning while getting ready for school. I still remember Willard Scott giving his morning weather report as Mom kissed us good-bye and scooted us out the door. I come from a whole family of *Today* show viewers but not one of us watches NBC anymore. We all watch Fox News.

I can't even stomach the big three networks anymore. And CNN is even worse. I'd rather have no clue what the weather is like and be blind to the day's events than to sit through even two minutes of that garbage they call news. Every once in a while, I'll turn on one of the big three networks just to see if anything has changed and compare them with what Fox is reporting. I am always stunned at the difference, and then my heart sinks, knowing how many people are getting *their* version of the news. But what if there were other options? What if Fox News was available on local channels?

Well, that got me thinking. Fox network has its own channel, just like NBC, CBS, and ABC. What if Fox News had a morning show and an evening news program on the Fox network affiliates like the other networks do? Well, I know what the outcome would be: it would only be a matter of time before everyone was watching Fox and dumping the other stations. But I thought it was worth looking into. So I wrote up a petition and started circulating it throughout the Dayton area. The petition simply said that those who signed would like to have the option of a Fox News morning show and evening news program on the local Fox affiliate. I collected more than three hundred names in two weeks. When one of my friends asked me what I was going to do with the petition, I said I was going to send it to Fox News. And I did.

I spent two days bouncing around the network phone system from one person to another until I finally found someone I could send the petitions to. He was one of the network executives in charge of affiliate relations. I told him what I had done and asked if I could e-mail him the petitions with a letter I had written. He said I could, so I sent it to him that day. It was October 2004.

A week after I sent the letter, I received a call from the network/affiliate liaison at Fox News. He told me my letter received a great amount of attention and was viewed by Roger Ailes, the founder and president of Fox News. Mr. Ailes asked his executive staff to look into the idea and see if it was feasible. The Fox executive told me Mr. Ailes was very interested in the proposal but came to the conclusion from speaking with his staff that it is not feasible under the present conditions.

"What does that mean?" I asked.

"It means," said the Fox executive, "that we could only do it if we had the support of the Fox Network in Los Angeles and several of our local affiliates."

"What about the petition?" I asked him.

"You'd have to collect a lot of signatures," he said. "And they can't all be from Dayton."

"How's five thousand signatures a state?" I asked.

There was a long pause. "Yeah," the Fox executive said, "that'd probably do it." Then he added, "And you're just tenacious enough to get it done."

Yes, I am. So we posted the Fox News petition on our Web site and collected a couple thousand signatures. I sent them to the network in Los Angeles and was completely ignored. I guess we need more signatures, so if you want to sign the petition, you can do so through our Web site. And if you'd like, we'll give you the phone number of the executive who keeps ignoring our petitions—just in case you'd like to give him a call.

The manipulation media is just aghast over this whole talk radio phenomenon, and Fox News has been a thorn in their side since it hit number one. They really don't get it. The media really thinks the problem is Fox News. They keep asking themselves in exasperation, "Why do people keep listening to this stuff?" And I'm sure they believe if Fox News would just go away, life could get back to the "good old days" when the media could lie to the people in peace and they didn't have to worry about a thing like competition—which is no doubt why the manipulation media supports things like the Fairness Doctrine. They don't want fair; they want a monopoly. Fox News, talk radio, and the Internet put *fair* into the media, and now the manipulation media wants to take it away. They will do anything they can to keep the truth from the people so they can exploit whatever agenda or promote and protect whatever candidate or elected official they happen to be promoting at the time. But I just want the truth. Is that really so hard to do—tell the truth, give the facts?

I don't need the media telling me what to think; I just want them to give me the information and the facts. I am smart enough to make up my own mind and form my own opinion, but I think that is the problem. I think that is exactly what they are afraid of. If we had the facts, we would know the truth, and that would cause us to think, act, and *vote* differently. I don't think that's a chance the media are willing to take, and I think their coverage of the Tea Parties proves it. The Dayton Tea Party is the perfect example. The coverage of the event was lame at best, and what coverage we did get mainly came from an opinion columnist, Martin Gottlieb, who stated in the Dayton Daily News he "was doing his job and called it like he saw it."

Mr. Gottlieb's article, which ran in the op-ed section of the newspaper, called the event an anti-Obama rally and stated that the crowd was 99 percent white. He was very careful to pick his quotes and the signs he referenced, so as to back up his claim, and made every effort to diminish the size of the crowd and impact of the event. What he left out was the fact that most of the signs targeted *both* political parties and that the speeches were directed to government—especially Congress—and clearly stated that *both* parties were to blame. And he totally ignored my speech, because the entire thing was about calling *both* parties on the carpet and *voting them both out* in the next election. But that didn't get reported. Instead, we got Mr. Gottlieb's summary of the event. You could almost see him looking down his nose sneering as you read his "take" of the crowd.

> Any president who proceeds as boldly as Obama has will generate some sort of backlash. But any Obama people looking over this event would likely be pleased. There was nothing there that might resonate with the American mainstream. There was just a lot of ideologically-mongering. The word ideological is perhaps misleading, because we're certainly not talking about a lot of academics here. The crowd seemed—guessing here, of course—mainly blue collar. But we're talking about people with very fairly special takes on things.[3]

It isn't really Mr. Gottlieb's article that bothered me. After all, it was an opinion column, which is just that—someone's opinion, and that opinion will of course be based on the perspective, experiences, and personal beliefs of the person giving it, so I feel his opinion was quite understandable. And I am sure he would find mine the same. So my issue is not Mr. Gottlieb's biased opinion; my issue is that the *Dayton Daily News* sent no one, except an opinion columnist, to cover the event, which left Mr. Gottlieb's opinion to stand as a representation of the "news."

If the intent of the *Dayton Daily News* is truly to inform the residents of the community on the news and events of the day by reporting the news, then the newspaper failed miserably. A true and honest news report—with the purpose of informing the public—would have included the names and backgrounds of the speakers, quotes from those in attendance, photos of the enormous crowd, the statement from the Dayton Police Department estimating the crowd attendance at 8,000, and a complete printing of each of the speeches given. *That* would be reporting the news. But that is not what the media do these days. They don't report, they interpret.

What does it say about the newspapers and TV stations around this country when a major event of historic proportions takes place in their own towns and there is more information about it on Facebook and YouTube than the local newspaper or TV newscast? The local media sure didn't have any trouble saturating us with coverage every time Barack Obama came into town to campaign. It was like they were his personal promotional team. If they had given the same coverage to the Tea Party, I would call it news. But given the facts, I would have to call it the blatant manipulation of public thought in an effort to promote and protect an agenda.

I am going to assume from the lack of "news" reported on the Dayton Tea Party and the major impact it had on our community that the *Dayton Daily News* has made the decision not to be a newspaper but an opinion paper that makes up, ignores, and/or completely distorts the news. If this is the path they have chosen, then they are in good company. There are several other newspapers around the nation seeing a major drop in circulation and suffering financially as well, for making the same choice to disenfranchise the everyday Americans who drive this great nation and our economy. They are the everyday Americans, the potential customers of these media outlets, that are desperate for "news" and discovering it is harder and harder to find.

People all across America are dropping their newspaper subscriptions, deciding the sports section and store ads just aren't worth it anymore. It is never a good idea to insult and belittle your current or potential customers. It just isn't good business, and in today's economic climate, I would think the media would be much more concerned with that than with promoting a political agenda.

I frequently get calls from the *Dayton Daily News* asking me to renew my subscription—which I canceled some time ago. Each time they call, I give the same answer, "I will not buy your paper as long as you continue to print propaganda in the name of news and employ gossip columnists under the guise of reporters. When that changes, call me." I wonder how many other calls like that newspapers around the country receive each day. Daddy Warbucks must be funding these newspapers for them to be so obstinate and unchanging, in a climate of economic turbulence, that they would completely ignore and even insult their current or potential readership. How many subscriptions can they lose before they get the message and decide that making money is important? Perhaps that is why Senator Benjamin Cardin introduced a bill in Congress to allow newspapers to become non-profit, so they are eligible for non-profit tax breaks—and I'm sure a lot of government grants as well. The senator calls it the Newspaper Revitalization Act and hopes it will save the failing industry, which he blames on the economy.

Reuters reported, "A Cardin spokesman said the bill had yet to attract any co-sponsors, but had sparked plenty of interest within the media." Well, I'll bet it has.

Senator Cardin stated, "We are losing our newspaper industry. The economy has caused an immediate problem, but the business model for newspapers, based on circulation and advertising revenue, is broken, and that is a real tragedy for communities across the nation and for our democracy."

No, Senator, the real tragedy is that the government once again feels the need to intervene in our lives, rescue a business the American people don't want, and then make us pay for it. He even admits that the reason the industry is failing is because circulation and advertising revenue are "broken." They aren't broken. They are working just fine. Consumers guide the market, not the government, and the consumers are tired of the media bias. They are going to talk radio, Fox News, and the Internet—not out of convenience but because these are the only places they can find real news. And when circulation drops, advertisers stop advertising because they realize they're wasting their money advertising in a paper nobody reads or on a news network nobody watches. Rush Limbaugh isn't having a problem making money. Fox News doesn't seem to have a problem getting advertising.

Isn't that just like the government to come to the aid of another bad product? Our government is the poster child of lost causes no one wants to fund. If you can't get the people to fund it willingly, well, they'll make us pay for it with our taxes—which of course they will have to keep raising to fund all their lost causes nobody else wants. And that's what it's going to have to come to: either the media starts giving the consumers what they want or they get government bailouts and we pay for them anyway—kind of like the way we pay for National Public Radio now. And what's next? Do we bail out CNN and Air America too? Can you even imagine your tax dollars going to keep those people on air? No wonder the media is so opposed to the Tea Parties—they are for *stopping* all these bailouts, and the media is counting on them to stay afloat.

The media offended a lot of people with their biased reporting and the blatant lack of reporting of the Tea Parties, but I am even more emboldened and impassioned than ever by their choice to ignore and minimize the event. The media only go out of their way to minimize and marginalize something when they fear it. They were there. They know the impact of this event, and I assure you, no matter how hard they try, they cannot squash this movement. They can minimize it all they want. They can ignore it, interpret it, alter and manipulate it, but it still won't change what is. The people of America are angry, and we are rising up against an oppressive, tyrannical government, and the media that support them, to say enough is enough!

All I expect is the truth. I just want the news. If I found it in the *Dayton Daily News*, I would subscribe to it. If I found it on CNN, I would watch it. But it isn't there. All we want are the facts. Just give us the information. We are intelligent enough to form our own opinions and perfectly capable of doing so. Just report. Give us the information and we'll decide what we think about it. Which is why the motto for Fox News resonates with so many Americans—*We report, you decide*. Wow, imagine that. If the rest of the media would embrace that motto, there would be a lot fewer newspapers failing and CNN wouldn't be scrambling for viewers.

Note to media: how about if instead of trying to shut down Fox News, talk radio, and the Internet, you start looking at them as a model of success because they are the only ones in media succeeding right now.

The Tea Parties are not done. There *will* be more. And more and more people will attend. We are *making* history, and if the media doesn't start covering it, they will *be* history. Is there truth out there? Yeah, you just have to look harder to find it.

From Our Founders

When truth has fair play, it will always prevail over falsehood.
~Benjamin Franklin

Advertisements contain the only truths to be relied on in a newspaper.
~Thomas Jefferson

There is but one straight course, and that is to seek truth and pursue it steadily.
~George Washington

The man who reads nothing at all is better educated than the man who reads nothing but newspapers.
~ Thomas Jefferson

Nothing can now be believed which is seen in a newspaper. Truth itself becomes suspicious by being put into that polluted vehicle.
~Thomas Jefferson

Suggested Books & Resources:
BIAS: A CBS Insider Exposes How the Media Distort the News by Bernard Goldberg
Slander by Ann Coulter
Arrogance by Bernard Goldberg

FORT KNOX

The principle of spending money to be paid by posterity, under the name of funding, is but swindling futurity on a large scale.
~Thomas Jefferson

The Internet has created a unique voice for the people of America. Three or four times a week, I will receive an e-mail that has passed from computer to computer, bouncing all over the fruited plain, until it arrives in my inbox. One such e-mail arrived a few months ago, and I decided it was worth keeping. This is what it said:

We need more money? Remind me what the Boston Tea Party was all about?

Accounts Receivable Tax
Building Permit Tax
Capital Gains Tax
CDL License Tax
Federal Unemployment Tax (FUTA)
Food License Tax
Fuel Permit Tax
Hunting License Tax
Liquor Tax
Marriage License Tax
Property Tax
Real Estate Tax
Social Security Tax
Road Usage Taxes (Truckers)
Recreational Vehicle Tax

Court Fines (indirect taxes)
Corporate Income Tax
Dog License Tax
Federal Income Tax
Cigarette Tax
Fishing License Tax
Gasoline Tax
Inheritance Tax
Local Income Tax
Luxury Taxes
Medicare Tax
Septic Permit Tax
Service Charge Taxes
Sales Taxes
Road Toll Booth Taxes

School Tax
Unemployment Tax
Toll Bridge Taxes
Telephone Usage Charge Tax
Traffic Fines (indirect taxation)
Vehicle License Registration Tax
Workers Compensation Tax
Telephone and Local Tax
Telephone Federal Universal Service Fee Tax
Telephone Recurring and Non-recurring Charges Tax

Well Permit Tax
Local Surcharge Taxes
Trailer Registration Tax
Toll Tunnel Taxes
Utility Taxes
Vehicle Tax
Watercraft Registration Tax
Telephone Federal Excise Tax
Telephone Minimum Usage Surcharge Tax
GST on everything including your funeral

COMMENTS:
Not one of these taxes existed 100 years ago and our nation was prosperous, had absolutely no national debt, had one of the largest middle classes in the world, and Mom stayed home to raise the kids.

Amen! The above list is just the beginning of the oppression launched against the citizens of this country. There are an awful lot of Americans who, like me, are fed up with the mounting tax burden placed on American citizens—as evidenced by all the Tea Parties. I am not opposed to taxes. I know they are necessary. It is our duty as American citizens to pay taxes for roads, national defense, public buildings, etc. But that is not what our taxes are being used for. In fact, the money the government takes from its people is spent in so many other places that they constantly need to take more of our money so they *can* cover things like roads and national defense. A lack of money is *not* the problem—it is how the money is spent, and if Congress continues to spend money like there's no tomorrow, there won't be any more money to take, because we'll all be broke. As Great Britain's former prime minister Margaret Thatcher so eloquently stated, *"The only problem with socialism is you eventually run out of other people's money."* Congress seems to be on the fast track to find out just how quickly they can get to that point, and every state and local government in the country is right on their heels, filling in any gaps the federal spenders may have left open. And no matter how hard we try to get a leg up, the government always seems to drag us down with their hand deep in our wallets at every turn.

I have a friend who came to me a few years ago angry and in utter frustration. She had just finished filing her taxes and said the forms and the filing system were so confusing that she and her husband had to seek professional help just to figure everything out. Her family lived in a town where they taxed your individual income, and her husband worked in another town that taxed individual income as well. Because they lived and worked in two different places, there was a formula they were supposed to use to get discounts—not exemptions, but discounts on the amount they were required to pay to *both* towns. They were told the money was to support the infrastructure of the communities and the schools in the towns. "I thought that's what my property taxes were for," she protested, "to support the roads, emergency services, and the schools." She was told there was not enough revenue to cover the costs from property taxes alone.

When my friend came to me, she was looking for someone to explain to her why she just got a bill from the school. Then she asked the million-dollar question: "If I am paying income taxes to the federal government, the state government, the county government, and *two* different cities, as well as taxes on my property for the purpose of supporting the schools, then why am I holding a bill in my hand for school fees and a list of supplies I have to buy before my son can go to school? Just what are my tax dollars being used for if I have to buy pencils and Kleenexes for my son's classroom?"

If more people asked questions like this, maybe we would finally get some answers. Instead, we just go along as if this is the way things are and have always been—running off to Wal-Mart to fill the school list like it is some kind of back-to-school tradition. What it is, actually, is tyranny and oppression on a grand scale.

"How can they get away with this?" my friend asked. And the only answer I could give was, *"Because we let them."*

It is our right as American citizens to decide where *our* money will be spent and to not be burdened or oppressed by unnecessary spending. It is *our* right and *our duty* as American citizens to demand *constitutional* spending. Yes, there is such a thing. You can find it in that elusive document called the United States Constitution.

Article One Section 8 clearly outlines what the federal government is authorized to collect taxes for. I urge you to familiarize yourself with this document, because when you do, you will realize that the majority of the programs we are funding with our tax dollars today are *not* on the list. Medicare, Social Security, welfare, food stamps, Head Start, education—

none of these programs is included on the list—and yet, our hard-earned money is being taken from us to pay for them.

All of these programs were instituted under the pretense of good intentions for the "public good," and I am sure the people who started them really did have the best of intentions, but the problem is that "we the people" have no say in the process. We have been completely stripped of our rights. Once our money is taken from us and in the hands of the government, it is gone. And our elected leaders spend it as if it were lottery winnings. They don't look at tax dollars as your daughter's college tuition or your mother's retirement home. It is a living cashbox that continues to replenish itself year after year. And when the coffers get low, our elected leaders find new ways to take from us so they can keep spending.

In 1821, Thomas Jefferson said, "The multiplication of public offices, increase of expense beyond income, growth and entailment of a public debt, are indications soliciting the employment of the pruning knife."[1]

In 1821, we didn't have the Department of Education, the Internal Revenue Service, the Department of the Interior, or the myriad of other departments that currently fill the Beltway. Today there are hundreds of agencies and public offices that didn't exist when Mr. Jefferson made this bold statement. Imagine what he would think today. Why, if the founders had tried to institute such oppression on the people in Thomas Jefferson's day, there would have been a national uprising. The people would not have tolerated such blatant arrogance and disregard of liberty.

Can you imagine the outcome if you lived in the Revolutionary era and government charity was introduced? You use the last dollar you have to your name to buy bags of seeds to plant wheat. You then spend the next four months tilling, planting, and tending the wheat, and another month harvesting, bagging, and storing it. Then you take your bag of wheat to the mill, where you grind it into flour so you can make bread to feed your family.

Then you return home, make the bread dough, knead the dough, and let it rise. Finally you get to the part where the bread goes into the oven. So you gather the wood, start the fire, heat up the bricks, and gently place your bread in the oven to bake. Of course you must keep the oven at just the right temperature, so you continually monitor the heat, adding wood as needed to the fire. In many cases, you go through this process in the heat of the day in midsummer, and of course, you are wearing a corset and full-length skirt and sleeves to your wrist. Wiping the dripping perspiration from your brow, you finally take the hot bread from the oven and set it on the table to cool.

Suddenly, there is a knock at the door. The mayor comes in, cuts your loaf of bread in half, and starts out the door. "What are you doing?" you ask.

"I am taking half of your bread for your neighbor down the street. She was too sick to make bread today, and I told her I would make sure she had bread to feed her family."

"How I am supposed to feed *my* family?" you ask, obviously outraged that this man just barged into your house and stole half of your labors.

The mayor turns to you, agitated. "You're in good health," he says. "Make more bread." Then he takes your family's meal out the door with him.

If things were that obvious today, maybe more Americans *would* be outraged. The problem is, the Sixteenth Amendment made robbing from the people much more sneaky. You never even see a good portion of your pay, so you don't even count it as income anymore. Maybe that's the problem. If you were receiving 100 percent of your income and you had to write a check for taxes, there'd be a national uprising. Our elected leaders knew this, and that is why they amended the Constitution to make income tax legal. It was one of the first steps in the trail of tyranny which we live with today.

I was talking to my friend Gerry, a small-business owner, who owns the UPS store in my town. His answer to the problem was pretty simple and straightforward and filled with determination: "There is only one way to stop this—we have to take their money away!" That is not as absurd as you may think. Remember, Congress has no money. The "revenue" they always talk about comes from taxing the citizens of this nation. They have no money unless it comes from us, and because of that, we *do* have the power to take their money away, and it is as simple as repealing the Sixteenth Amendment. I have no doubt the people who passed the Sixteenth Amendment had the best of intentions. They wanted more power to help the poor and needy—to provide charity to those less fortunate. And who doesn't want that, right?

I am firm believer in charity. My religion has taught me it is the pure love of Christ, and I try to practice it at every opportunity I can. I don't do it for earthly reward. I do it because of the good feeling that comes from serving others. However, if that service is *forced* on me, I find no joy in it. That is the problem with coerced compassion. You, the giver, do not get to decide who you will give to and what you will give. There is no joy in the gift, and you often become resentful of those receiving your gift and even worse, the receiver begins to look on the gift as an entitlement that is owed to them.

Let's go back to our bread story and fast-forward a few years. The woman who was sick has now passed on, and her children and their children are sitting around their dinner table. A neighbor comes to visit them and asks why they are sitting at the table. "We're waiting," they say.

"Waiting for what?" asks the neighbor.

"Our bread. It is dinnertime, and we are waiting for our bread."

"Where does the bread come from?" asks the neighbor.

"We don't know," answers the family. "It just always comes."

"Why don't you make your own bread?" asks the woman.

"Why," says the family, "when the bread is always brought to us?"

Now, let's fast-forward another generation. This time, the family is sitting around the living room when there is a knock on the door. It is the city magistrate bringing their half loaf of bread. "Well, it's about time," complains the mother. "You get later and later every day."

"And all you bring us is this measly half a loaf of bread," says the father. "How are we supposed to live on that?"

"I'm sorry," says the magistrate, "that is all we have set aside for you. It is plenty to live on."

"Well, I want more," says the father, walking to the window. "Look at those people across the street. They have four loaves every day. What do they need with four loaves? It's not fair that they have four loaves and we only have half a loaf. If you want my vote in the next election, Magistrate, you'll make sure my family gets a full loaf of bread."

Fast-forward a few months to the next election and what you find are two candidates trying to win votes.

"I'll make sure every family gets one full loaf of bread."

"One loaf of bread, well how can a family live on that? I'll make sure every family gets *two* loaves of bread!"

And on and on it goes. Do you see the absurdity of it all?

If someone came to my door and told me that my neighbor was sick and wasn't able to feed her family, I would gladly give my *whole* loaf of bread, fresh out of the oven, to her. It would literally be a labor of love. I would find great joy in giving that gift, and it would seem like such a little thing to go through the process again to make another loaf of bread for my own family.

But if the gift is forced on me, then with each step in the process of making another loaf of bread, I would become angrier and angrier, until absolute resentment set in, wondering why they can't make their own bread and worrying how I can continue to provide for my own family when the government keeps coming and taking my bread.

That is the difference. I'm all for helping the poor and needy. I just don't want to be coerced into it. It should be my choice. The redistribution of wealth is not a new thing. The founders witnessed it themselves. While Americans largely believed in hard work and the freedom to succeed to whatever heights your labor takes you, Europe was acting on the theory that the role of government was to take from the "haves" and give to the "have-nots." The popular theory in Europe was that by redistributing the wealth among all the people, all would be equal. It was a miserable failure in Europe, and our Founding Fathers found it the perfect example of what *not* to do.

Thomas Jefferson was strongly opposed to the idea of redistribution. He said, "[A] wise and frugal government ... shall restrain men from injuring one another, shall leave them otherwise free to regulate their own pursuits of industry and improvement, and shall not take from the mouth of labor the bread it has earned. This is the sum of good government."[2]

The book *The 5000 Year Leap* clearly and simply details the principles of liberty this nation was founded on. Principle number seven is Equal *Rights* not Equal *Things*. Simply stated, the role of government is to protect equal rights, not provide equal things.

Where is the equality in the bread story? Neither the woman who had her bread taken nor the woman who received it were treated equally. You see, when we allow the government to make these kinds of decisions, no one wins. If the government was insuring the equal rights of both women, they would have made sure that both women had the freedom to provide for themselves and the freedom to give to others. But that right was stolen when the government took from the one woman to give to the other, and because of this, neither woman received equal rights.

So you may say, at least the woman who was sick received the bread, and that made it more equal, right? Not so. The woman who receives the bread only receives what the government decides to give her. If we were comparing our bread example to government programs today, we would realize just how unequal—and unjust—they are. By today's standards, the government official would come to the home of the woman who made the bread and take half of her loaf. He would then go home, eat the majority of that loaf, and then take the leftover crust to the sick woman so she can feed her family. That is not justice and it is *not* compassion.

So let's go back to our story. The magistrate has just left the woman's home with the bread he took from her. She is standing in her kitchen, looking at her little children sitting around the small, modest table, realizing she has just enough to feed her little family, when a knock comes at the door. She walks to the door and answers it to find the local pastor standing in the doorway.

"Good evening, Pastor," she says. "How can I help you?"

"Well, sister, there is a woman in our parish who is sick and unable to feed her family, and we were hoping you could share some of your bread with her."

"Oh, Pastor," she said, "the magistrate just came and took half of our bread. I only have enough to feed my little family and there is none to spare."

"Yes," says the pastor, "we have been running into that a lot tonight. The magistrate collected the bread to give the very sister I have come to talk to you about, but he only gave her a crust of bread, which is not nearly enough to feed her family."

"But, Pastor, the magistrate took half our loaf of bread for the woman. How is it that she only received a crust?"

"The magistrate and his friends are eating well tonight. He keeps a portion of the bread for taxes, to cover paying his wages as a tax collector, and some more to cover the cost of collecting the bread."

And that is, as clearly and simply as I can put it, our government in a nutshell. There is no compassion. It is nothing more than a job for them, and most of what they collect goes to the self-serving interests of the people we elect to make things "fair." What is fair about stealing from the labors of the people?

What if our story had a different twist to it? What if instead of the magistrate coming and taking the bread, it was one of the townspeople? If some guy from town came in and took your bread, no one would see that as compassionate. All they see is a thief. Stealing is stealing. It doesn't cease to be stealing just because the person from town happens to be the mayor.

When the government can forcibly take our money, and with no accountability whatsoever, spend it however and on whatever they want—and the people have no say in the matter—then that government becomes a monarchy and/or dictatorship, and history repeats itself all over again. This is what our founding families fought against. This is the tyranny and oppression that they sacrificed everything to oppose. Why are we embracing it now? The reason America is so great is not because we provide equal things, it is because our Constitution guarantees equal rights.

Coerced compassion has never worked, and it never will. Germany is the perfect example of that today. The citizens of Germany are required by law to pay a church tax. The tax requires that German residents pay 10 percent of their income to a church. You can choose which church you want the money to go to, but you can't choose whether or not you pay it. The only exception is if you are an atheist. Suddenly, half the German population becomes self-proclaimed atheists. Force is not compassion, it is oppression, and the people will always find a way around it.

The point is, by dividing the people of this nation into haves and have-nots, our government is creating a system where the have-nots start to believe they can never *have,* which leads to hopelessness and despair, and keeps people dependent on government and believing they can never do for themselves.

I recently had an opportunity to teach my children the principle of Equal Rights versus Equal Things. We have developed a system of rewards in our home that has really motivated our children to work hard, work together, and keep their toys picked up. I know, that sounds like a miracle in and of itself. Basically, we use colored popsicle sticks which we call Kudos to reward the children for the work they do, kindness shown, how well they do their jobs, etc. They can then use Kudos they earned for privileges such as electronics time and trips to the park or the library.

We have a strict rule in our house that you can only play computer, video games or have TV time if you can pay for the time with Kudos. Each Kudo is worth 5 minutes of time so this suddenly gave the children an incentive to be more cooperative and do a better job with the chores and assignments. But things really started to change when we initiated the weekly Kudos Auction.

We were having a real problem with the children leaving their toys and personal items throughout the house so I came up with a plan. I found an old wicker basket with a hinged lid in my closet to use as an auction box. I told the children that every time I found something of theirs around the house I was going to put it in the auction box. Once an item went into the auction box it no longer belonged to them and would be up for sale at the auction we would hold each Sunday evening. The children would use their Kudos to buy the things in the auction box.

I was amazed at how well this worked. Suddenly our children started to pay more attention to their personal property and make sure it stayed in their rooms. They worked harder at their jobs so they could earn more Kudos and even started volunteering for jobs. The Kudos developed such a high value that the children started saving them instead of using them for electronics time.

One week my daughter lost her PSP (handheld video game) to the auction box. The children worked overtime that week. The kids were making each other's beds, doing each other's chores, helping with the garden—anything they could do to earn more Kudos in hopes of winning the coveted prize that lay at the bottom of the auction box.

My 5-year-old son, Ethan, became Mr. Service that week. I overheard him talking to his sister, "Amber," he said, "I folded your socks for you, so can you go tell mom so she'll give me Kudos?" It was so cute.

I overheard Amber, who is 11, ask Noah, my 9-year-old son, if he wanted to play Wii with her. "Are you kidding," Noah said, "I'd have to spend twelve Kudos just to play one hour. I can't afford that. I'm saving for the Kudos Auction!"

It was like that all week. I've never seen the children work so hard and be so kind to each other. Amber even cleaned the whole kitchen herself one day. Finally the day of the auction came. I pulled the box into the middle of the floor and told the children to go and get their Kudos.

Noah had the most Kudos at 106. Amber had 92 and little Ethan, as hard as he worked all week, only had 46. I saw the gears turning in Noah's head as he realized that if he just held out and didn't buy anything else in the auction, he would get the PSP. At the same time, I realized Amber was building her strategy trying to figure out how she would convince Noah to spend his Kudos so she could buy her PSP back. Ethan, on the other hand noticed he had much less than his brother and sister and started crying. And right there, at that very moment in time, I had the perfect teaching moment.

I picked up Ethan and held him in my lap trying to comfort him. Then I looked at Amber and Noah and said, "You know you guys, Ethan worked really hard this week don't you think so?"

They both agreed that he had.

"But you know, no matter how hard he works, you guys will always earn more Kudos because you are older and bigger and can do more jobs."

They clearly realized I was right and started feel very bad for their little brother.

"You know, I was thinking that since you guys have so many Kudos maybe you should share some with your little brother who doesn't have very many."

Ethan suddenly stopped crying and began listening intently to the conversation. It was Amber, my 11-year-old who was first to speak. "But Mom, I worked hard for these Kudos."

"I know but so did Ethan and you know, if he was old enough and strong enough, he would earn a lot more Kudos. Don't you think we should consider that?"

"Well, I guess," said Amber.

Noah, being the sweet, compassionate little boy he is, said, "I'll give Ethan some of my Kudos."

"That is so nice of you Noah," I said.

Not to be outdone, Amber then joined in saying she would give some of hers as well.

"That is so nice of you guys." I then reached over and took 10 Kudos from each of them.

"Hey," Noah yelled. "What are you doing? I said some."

"That is some," I said.

"We should get to decide how many Kudos we give to Ethan," Amber said.

"Well," I said, "I just want to make sure it's fair. You both still have so many and Ethan still won't have as many as you. Don't you think you can afford to give him ten when you have so many?"

"I guess," they both said.

"Great," I said, "now let's count your Kudos again. Let's see, Noah you have 96, Amber you have 82 and Ethan, wow, Ethan now you have 66!"

Ethan was elated. He liked this kind of sharing.

"Can we start the auction now," Noah asked.

"Sure." I opened the auction box and then paused a moment. "Then again," I said, "I'm still not sure this is fair."

"What!" Amber protested, "I gave him ten Kudos that's plenty fair."

"Well, I'm not sure Ethan will think it's fair. I mean, you and Noah still have so much more than he does."

"That's because we earned them," Amber said.

"I've saved them all week," said Noah, "I didn't play Wii one time."

"Yeah," said Amber, "and Ethan played lots of times. He used his Kudos on video games. That's why he doesn't have as many."

"Well, that's true," I said, "he did use some of his Kudos to play video games but he is so young and doesn't really understand the consequences of his actions. He didn't really understand that if he used his Kudos to play video games that he wouldn't have them for the auction. I don't think we should hold that against him do you?"

"I'm not giving him anymore of my Kudos," Amber protested.

"Well, if Ethan thinks it's fair then we'll just go ahead with the auction." Then I looked at Ethan. "Ethan, do you think it's far that Noah and Amber have more Kudos than you and can buy more things out the box?"

"No," he said starting to cry again, "they'll get all the good stuff and I won't."

"You're right, Ethan, that *doesn't* seem fair. Amber, Noah, give Ethan ten more Kudos each."

"What!" they both yelled at once.

"You heard me, give Ethan 10 more Kudos."

"I earned these Kudos," Amber yelled, "I cleaned the whole kitchen by myself…"

"And I cleaned the backyard," said Noah.

"And," said Amber barely taking a breath, "and do you know how hard it was to be nice to my brothers all week? Believe me, I earned those Kudos!"

"Whether you earned them or not, I am in charge and my job is to make things fair for everyone. Give Ethan your Kudos or you will be grounded from all electronics for a week."

"What?" Noah and Amber shouted in disbelief.

"Do it," I said.

Amber and Noah ripped the kudos out of their hands in protest and threw them in Ethan's pile. Ethan suddenly became uncomfortable. "It's okay, Mommy, they can keep their Kudos."

"There, see," said Amber, "he doesn't want them and she reached to take her Kudos back."

"No," I said stopping her hand, "we have to be fair. Ethan will keep the Kudos. Now, let's see, Amber you have 72, Noah you have 86, and Ethan, wow, Ethan, you have 86 too! Isn't this much more fair. Now you all have the same."

Noah just seemed happy to still have more than Amber but was obviously unhappy at what had just transpired. Amber however, was livid.

"We don't have the same," said Amber, "now I have less than anybody. This isn't fair it's stupid. I worked hard all week for these Kudos. If I had known you were just going to take them from me I wouldn't have bothered working at all."

"Amber," I said, "I agree. This is *not* fair. You should get to keep what you earn and you should get to choose who you give your Kudos to and what you spend them on."

Amber and Noah looked at me in complete confusion.

"What you have just witnessed here today is a lesson in economics. It is called the redistribution of wealth and it is what our government is doing to the people of this country right now. Remember how you felt and what you learned today."

Now, for those of you who are wondering about little Ethan and how he handled everything, don't worry. Ethan was not traumatized in the least. About half-way through the conversation he became completely disinterested and went in the next room to play with his Lincoln logs. And once we came to the end of our lesson in economics he came back to the table gathered his original Kudos (plus twenty extra that I gave him for being such a good sport) and was happy as could be as he spent all his Kudos buying back his toys from the auction box.

Amber and Noah, and even Ethan left the auction that day much wiser and strongly resolved to stand against the two new words they learned that day—tyranny and oppression. Noah and Amber had their Kudos returned, Ethan was twenty Kudos richer and I told the children they could skip math the next day because of their ability to endure such a brutal economics lesson. I can't wait until we have our lesson on justice.

We do not live in the feudal system in America. No one's destiny is determined by birth. That was Europe's way of doing things, not ours. In Europe, if you were born a peasant, you died a peasant. If you were born a noble, you died a noble. And the only way you could ever be king was if your father was king—unless, of course, you conquered your own kingdom, which sometimes happened. But in America, anyone born here can grow up to be president. There are no limitations to success. If you are born into poverty, there is nothing that requires you to stay there. That is the beauty of America. We have the freedom to be whatever *we* want to be. We have the freedom to succeed as much as *we* want to succeed. Do we really want the government limiting that? Do we really want the government dictating the rules of success and failure? Just because someone has something you don't have, it doesn't mean they are privileged and you are not. It simply means that with hard work and dedication, *you* can have it too.

And when you do, when you have dedicated your time and energy to achieve the success you worked so hard for, do you really want the government taking it away? Do you really want your life's work to be given to someone who doesn't work and has no desire to do so? Why, then, would anyone want to work at all? Isn't that what the Pilgrims learned? Isn't that what my children learned? If they can get it, surely the rest of us can.

Every time I think of this idea of redistribution, I think of the movie *The Pursuit of Happyness*. It is a true story based on the life of a young black man named Chris Gardner from San Francisco. If you haven't seen it, you should. It is an excellent movie that motivates and inspires greatness. Chris Gardner is real. His story is true. How can we watch that movie and witness everything that man went through to lift himself and his son from homelessness, and then think it is okay to take away everything he worked so hard for?

The Pursuit of Happyness is the American dream on the big screen. It is the perfect example of equal *rights,* and Chris Gardner is an American hero for having the courage to pursue that dream. So why do we think it is okay to steal from him now, just because he became one of the most successful businessmen in the country? And what about Farrah Gray? Now there's another inspiring story. Farrah is the author of *Reallionaire: Nine Steps to Becoming Rich from the Inside Out*. His book is the amazing story of his life and the mother who inspired him.

Farrah Gray was a young black boy who grew up in the projects of Chicago with his mother and siblings. Every day, Farrah saw his mother—a single parent with four children—work herself to near exhaustion to provide for their family. They lived in a run-down apartment that rarely had hot running water, and was infested with roaches. Then one day, while he was in school, his teacher asked him what he wanted to be when he grew up, and he told her he wanted to be an entrepreneur. His teacher laughed and told him he couldn't do that because his family was poor. Farrah was very upset by the comment.

When he got home from school that afternoon, he told his grandmother what his teacher had said and asked if it was true that he wasn't smart enough to be an entrepreneur. His grandmother's answer is what changed his life.

"Do not let anyone tell you what you can be," she said. "Do not let anyone tell you that you are not good enough or smart enough. Remember that nobody is better than you. Everybody puts on their pants one leg at a time. I want you to wake up every morning and say, 'Why not me?'"[3]

Farrah did become an entrepreneur, first selling homemade products door to door at the age of seven and then starting his own food company for kids called Farr-Out Foods, which he sold at the age of fifteen for $1.5 million.

Don't Chris Gardner and Farrah Gray have a right to the fruits of their own labors? Don't they have the right to choose what they do with their own wealth that *they* worked so hard for? Of course they do, but the government does not seem to agree, because like the rest of us, Congress controls 100 percent of Chris Gardner's and Farrah Gray's income. The government decides how much of our income we get to keep, and we are required to prove to them—through the IRS—why we should be allowed to keep any of it. We are asking the federal government for permission to keep our own money. If that isn't a reason to repeal the Sixteenth Amendment, I don't know what is.

So, you ask, what then do we do about the poor, the downtrodden and the suffering? Well, I like our Founding Father's formula. W. Cleon Skousen outlines it clearly in *The 5000 Year Leap*. Dr. Skousen spent years studying the works and writings of the Founding Fathers. On the subject of public charity, he wrote the following: "Nearly all of the Founders seem to have acquired deep convictions that assisting those in need had to be done through means which might be called 'calculated' compassion." Dr. Skousen sums up the Founders' sentiments in the following list.[4]

1. Do not help the needy completely. Merely help them to help themselves.
2. Give the poor the satisfaction of earned achievement.
3. Allow the poor to climb the "appreciation ladder"—from tents to cabins, cabins to cottages, cottages to comfortable houses.
4. Where emergency help is provided, do not prolong it to the point where it becomes habitual.
5. Strictly enforce the scale of "fixed responsibility." The first and foremost level of responsibility is with the individual himself; the second level is the family; then the church; next the community; finally the county, and, in a disaster or emergency, the state. Under no circumstances is the federal government to become involved in public welfare. The Founders felt it would corrupt the government and also the poor. No Constitutional authority exists for the federal government to participate in charity or welfare.

Dr. Skousen is absolutely right; the Founding Fathers wrote the Constitution with strict restrictions on what the government could and could not do, and charity was not on the list. James Madison, the author of the Constitution, stated, "[T]he government of the United States is a definite government, confined to specified objects. It is not like the state governments, whose powers are more general. Charity is no part of the legislative duty of the government."[5]

Alexis de Tocqueville, a French historian who toured America in the early 1800s, cautioned, "The American Republic will endure until the day Congress discovers that it can bribe the public with the public's money." Well, it sure didn't take Congress long to figure that out and use it to its fullest. And there are plenty of organizations lining up with their hands out to take advantage. Feminists are always there bright and early—and persistently.

The National Organization for Women has spent years lobbying in Washington for special-interest programs that *you* are paying for—programs that keep people enslaved to the government for their very support. There is an old saying: "Give a man a fish and you have fed him for today. Teach a man to fish and you have fed him for a lifetime." Our government has become a virtual fish factory. Uncle Sam has been handing out fish for decades, and now the people have forgotten how to cast their nets.

The people of America used to be self-sufficient and self-reliant. That is how America was built. But government benevolence has turned millions of Americans into glorified beggars. Whatever happened to John F. Kennedy's famous words, "Ask not what your country can do for you; ask what you can do for your country"[6]?

That is the motto we should be living by. Unfortunately, our government has slowly crept into the charity profession, and now millions of Americans rely on the government for their very livelihood. Of course, if you suggest taking that livelihood away, you would be considered heartless and uncaring. But who is the better friend? Who is more genuine in their giving? Is it the one who gives the fish and has all the power over another's life and death? Or is it the one who teaches the other *how* to fish and gives them power over themselves?

Thomas Jefferson was adamantly opposed to big government and coerced compassion. He stated, "If we can prevent the government from wasting the labors of the people, under the pretense of taking care of them, they must become happy."[7] He further stated, "The most sacred of the duties of a government [is] to do equal and impartial justice to all citizens."[8] How can we be impartial if we are taking from one to give to another? The answer is simple—we can't.

For years, these principles were taught in our nation's schools, churches, and communities, but over the years, little by little, they have been stripped from us by people who cared more about power than freedom. Coerced compassion is just another tool used to tear the fabric of our liberty.

Years ago, there was a story that used to appear in our school textbooks. My mother remembers reading the story in elementary school, so sometime between then and when I was in school, it disappeared from our books. I often wonder, if stories like this were still taught in schools, would we be where we are today? I don't think we would. Our children wouldn't tolerate it.

The story, entitled "Not Yours to Give," was told by Colonel David Crockett while he was serving as a United States congressman.

During Mr. Crockett's term in office, a bill was introduced in Congress that would have appropriated money to benefit the widow of a distinguished naval officer. Several members of Congress rose to give riveting, compassionate, and compelling speeches on behalf of the bill and the gracious woman who would benefit from it. Then the time for the vote came, and just as the speaker was about to open the issue for a vote, Davey Crockett arose and said …

> Mr. Speaker—I have as much respect for the memory of the deceased, and as much sympathy for the suffering of the living, if there be, as any man in this House, but we must not permit our respect for the dead or our sympathy for part of the living to lead us into an act of injustice to the balance of the living. I will not go into an argument to prove that Congress has not the power to appropriate this money as an act of charity. Every member on this floor knows it.
>
> We have the right as individuals, to give away as much of our own money as we please in charity; but as members of Congress we have no right to appropriate a dollar of the public money. Some eloquent appeals have been made to us upon the ground that it is a debt due the deceased. Mr. Speaker, the deceased lived long after the close of the war;

he was in office to the day of his death, and I never heard that the government was in arrears to him.

Every man in this House knows it is not a debt. We cannot without the grossest corruption, appropriate this money as the payment of a debt. We have not the semblance of authority to appropriate it as charity. Mr. Speaker, I have said we have the right to give as much money of our own as we please. I am the poorest man on this floor. I cannot vote for this bill, but I will give one week's pay to the object, and if every member of Congress will do the same, it will amount to more than the bill asks.[9]

Colonel Crockett then took his seat. No one replied. The bill was put to a vote and, instead of passing unanimously, it was defeated. Later, one of Colonel Crockett's friends asked why he had opposed the appropriation of funds to the widow. Colonel Crockett explained that several years earlier, he was standing on the steps of the Capitol with some members of Congress, when they noticed that Georgetown was engulfed in fire. Colonel Crockett and his associates immediately took a carriage to Georgetown, but it was too late to help. Several houses were burned and many families were left homeless and had nothing but the clothes on their backs. The weather was very cold, and when Colonel Crockett saw so many children suffering, he felt that something ought to be done for them. The next morning, a bill was introduced appropriating $20,000 for their relief. Colonel Crockett stated, "We put aside all other business and rushed it through as soon as it could be done."[10]

The next summer, Mr. Crockett was campaigning in the Tennessee countryside when he came upon a man by the name of Horatio Bunce. Horatio told Mr. Crockett he was wasting his time campaigning at his house, because he had no intentions of voting for him. Colonel Crockett was shocked and asked Horatio why he felt so strongly. Horatio answered, "You gave a vote last winter, which shows that either you have not capacity to understand the Constitution or that you are wanting in the honesty and firmness to be guided by it. In either case, you are not the man to represent me. But I beg your pardon for expressing it that way."[11] He then assured Mr. Crockett that he believed he was an honest man but said that "your understanding of the Constitution is very different from mine."[12]

Horatio then referenced the $20,000 bill that was passed for the

Georgetown fire victims. Mr. Crockett was taken aback and said to the man, "Well, my friend, I may as well own up. You have got me there. But certainly nobody will complain that a great and rich country like ours should give the insignificant sum of $20,000 to relieve its suffering women and children, particularly with a full and overflowing treasury, and I am sure, if you had been there, you would have done just the same as I did."[13]

Horatio looked at the congressman. "It is not the amount, Colonel, that I complain of," he said, "it is the principle. In the first place, the government ought to have in the Treasury no more than enough for its legitimate purposes. But that has nothing to do with the question. The power of collecting and disbursing money at pleasure is the most dangerous power that can be entrusted to man ... while you are contributing to relieve one, you are drawing it from thousands who are even worse off than he."[14] Colonel Crockett listened intently as Horatio continued.

"If you had the right to give anything," he said, "the amount was simply a matter of discretion with you, and you had as much right to give $20 million as $20,000. If you have the right to give at all, and as the Constitution neither defines charity nor stipulates the amount, you are at liberty to give to any and everything which you may believe, or profess to believe, is a charity and to any amount you may think proper. You will very easily perceive what a wide door this would open for fraud and corruption and favoritism, on the one hand, and for robbing the people on the other. No, Colonel," Horatio said, "Congress has no right to give charity. Individual members may give as much of their own money as they please, but they have no right to touch a dollar of the public money for that purpose." [15]

Horatio then went on to explain that there were, at that time, 240 members of Congress. If they had shown their sympathy for the sufferers by each contributing one week's pay, it would have amounted to more than $13,000. Then Horatio said, "There are plenty of wealthy men around Washington who could have given $20,000 without depriving themselves of even a luxury of life. The congressmen chose to keep their own money, which, if reports be true, some of them spend not very creditably; and the people about Washington, no doubt, applauded you for relieving them from necessity of giving what was not yours to give. The people have delegated to Congress, by the Constitution, the power to do certain things. To do these, it is authorized to collect and pay moneys, and for nothing else. Everything beyond this is usurpation, and a violation of the Constitution.

"So you see, Colonel," Mr. Horatio Bunce continued, "you have violated the Constitution in what I consider a vital point. It is a precedent fraught with danger to the country, for when Congress once begins to stretch its power beyond the limits of the Constitution, there is no limit to it, and no security for the people. I have no doubt you acted honestly, but that does not make it any better … and you see that I cannot vote for you."[16]

Colonel Crockett said he felt "streaked" and responded to the man in hopes of winning his confidence. "Well, my friend," Colonel Crockett began, "you hit the nail upon the head when you said I had not sense enough to understand the Constitution. I intended to be guided by it, and thought I had studied it fully. I have heard many speeches in Congress about the powers of Congress, but what you have said here at your plow has got more hard, sound sense in it than all the fine speeches I ever heard. If I had ever taken the view of it that you have, I would have put my head into the fire before I would have given that vote; and if you will forgive me and vote for me again, if I ever vote for another unconstitutional law I wish I may be shot."[17]

Horatio chuckled and replied, "Yes, Colonel, you have sworn to that once before, but I will trust you again upon one condition. You are convinced that your vote was wrong. Your acknowledgment of it will do more good than beating you for it. If, as you go around the district, you will tell people about this vote, and that you are satisfied it was wrong, I will not only vote for you, but will do what I can to keep down opposition, and perhaps, I may exert some little influence in that way."[18]

Horatio Bunce kept his word, and Colonel Crockett served another term in Congress, where he would be given the opportunity to keep his word. So this was the story Colonel Crockett related to his friend, explaining why he couldn't vote for the bill. After he finished his story, he looked at his friend and said, "Now, sir, do you know why I made that speech yesterday?" His friend did not answer. "There is one thing which I will call your attention," said Colonel Crockett. "You remember that I proposed to give a week's pay. There are in that House many very wealthy men—men who think nothing of spending a week's pay, or a dozen of them, for a dinner or a wine party when they have something to accomplish by it.

"Some of those same men made beautiful speeches upon the great debt of gratitude which the country owed the deceased—a debt which could not be paid by money—and the insignificance and worthlessness of money, particularly so insignificant a sum as $20,000 when weighed against the honor of the nation. Yet, not one of them responded to my proposition.

"Money with them is nothing but trash when it is to come out of the people. But it is the one great thing for which most of them are striving, and many of them sacrifice honor, integrity, and justice to obtain it."[19]

Now do you understand why this story is no longer found in our textbooks? With such a testimony, how could we possibly justify the myriad of grants, earmarks, and special-interest programs that our government funds? The federal government can only allocate money when it benefits the whole. It has *no* power to spend on individuals or isolated groups—*none*. It is absolutely *against* the Constitution of the United States.

There is no magical treasure chest in Washington, D.C., and there are no money trees on the Capitol lawn. It comes from the people. It is *our* money. If Congress thinks all these programs are such a good idea, then they should be the ones to open their wallets and pay for them.

My husband and I have eight children to put through college, a family to support, and a retirement to plan for. It is *our* hard-earned money that is being taken and *our* hard-earned money that is being spent, and we have no say in where it goes. Recently, it was suggested by a friend that I apply for government grants to fund some of the programs of Homemakers for America. I have thought a great deal about this and I just can't get the words of Horatio Bunce out of my mind, "Congress has no right to give charity. Individual members may give as much of their own money as they please, but they have no right to touch a dollar of the public money for that purpose."[20]

I don't want Homemakers for America to ever receive "coerced funds" from the United States government. We will rely on the gifts and support of those who *choose* to support us, not those who support us by default. I will not allow your child's tuition, your parents' retirement home, or your personal savings to be spent against your will on Homemakers for America. I will not rob the people, no matter how great the cause. It is time to stop "coerced compassion" in every form and heed Thomas Jefferson's words: "The same prudence which in private life would forbid our paying our own money for unexplained projects, forbids it in the dispensation of the public moneys."

If Homemakers for America is to survive—and thrive—it will do so because *you*, the people, chose it! And I hope you will.

From Our Founders

To take from one, because it is thought his own industry and that of his fathers has acquired too much, in order to spare to others, who, or whose fathers, have not exercised equal industry and skill, is to violate arbitrarily the first principle of association, the guarantee to everyone the free exercise of his industry and the fruits acquired by it.
~Thomas Jefferson

Industry pays Debts, Despair increases them.
~Ben Franklin

A wise and frugal government, which shall restrain men from injuring one another, shall leave them otherwise free to regulate their own pursuits of industry and improvement.
~Thomas Jefferson

We must not let our rulers load us with perpetual debt. We must make our selection between economy and liberty or profusion and servitude.
~Thomas Jefferson

A departure from principle becomes a precedent for a second; that second for a third; and so on, till the bulk of society is reduced to mere automations of misery, to have no sensibilities left but for sinning and suffering ... And the fore horse of this frightful team is public debt. Taxation follows that, and in its train wretchedness and oppression.
~Thomas Jefferson

I think we have more machinery of government than is necessary, too many parasites living on the labor of the industrious.
~Thomas Jefferson

It is incumbent on every generation to pay its own debts as it goes. A principle which if acted on would save one-half the wars of the world.
~Thomas Jefferson

History records that the money changers have used every form of abuse, intrigue, deceit, and violent means possible to maintain their control over governments by controlling the money and its issuance.
~James Madison

Equal rights for all, special privileges for none.
~Thomas Jefferson

The democracy will cease to exist when you take away from those who are willing to work and give to those who would not.
~Thomas Jefferson

I, however, place the economy among the first and most important republican virtues, and public debt as the greatest of the dangers to be feared.
~Thomas Jefferson

Other Notable Quotes

Property is the fruit of labor-property is desirable—it is a positive good in the world. That some should be rich, shows that others may become rich, and hence is just encouragement to industry and enterprise. Let not who is houseless pull down the house of another; but let him labor diligently and build one for himself, thus by example assuring that his own shall be safe from violence ...
~Abraham Lincoln

Collecting more taxes than is absolutely necessary is legalized robbery.
~Calvin Coolidge

Suggested Books & Resources:
The Fair Tax Book by Neal Boortz
IRS vs. the People: Time for Real Tax Reform by Jack Kemp and Ken Blackwell
The Interesting History of Income Tax by William J. Federer
New Deal or Raw Deal by Burton W. Folsom
The Tragedy of American Compassion by Marvin Olasky
The Forgotten Man: A History of the Great Depression by Amity Shlaes

Web sites
Citizens Against Government Waste *www.cagw.org*
Citizens for a Responsible Government *www.responsiblegov.net*
Americans for Tax Reform *www.atr.org*
Citizens for Tax Reform *www.repealthetax.com*

STIMULATING FACTS

A government big enough to give you everything you want is big enough to take away everything you have.
~Thomas Jefferson

Imagine for a moment looking through a window in your neighborhood and seeing a family sitting around a warm, glowing fireplace, reading stories and laughing together. Suddenly you notice a spark burst through the fireplace screen, landing on the carpet behind the couch the family is sitting on. They don't realize what has happened, so you shout from the yard outside, trying to warn them, but they can't hear you. You notice a small black spot appear in the carpet as smoke streams upward. You shout louder and move closer to the window, hoping to warn the family as a small flame bursts open on the floor and spreads onto the fabric along the bottom of the couch.

In desperation, you leap to the window and pound on the glass, shouting a warning to the family. *Finally,* they turn around and look at you, and then, with annoyed faces—irritated by the invasion of privacy—they come over to the window and *close the blinds!* You are standing on the outside, frustrated, hopeless, and distraught over the impending doom that you know awaits the family, realizing there is nothing you can do to stop it.

You now have a good picture of how I, and probably many others, feel right now. Our freedom is under direct attack. America is being torn down piece by piece, and no one seems to care or even realize it. Those of us who do care shout warnings to the masses, trying to help them understand, but the louder we shout, the more we are ignored. They are too busy with their lives to worry about a few "alarmists." We must be overreacting, right? I wonder if that's what people thought when they were warned about Hitler and Stalin.

I have spent a lot of time studying world history. I have read of the rise and fall of nations; of vicious men, inhumane violence, and heinous crimes against humanity. I know of the horrible wars and injustices of the past, and I don't want to see them repeated. And though we witness terrible violence, oppression, and inhumanity around the world today, I have always believed America was a haven from such oppression because we know what it means to be free and we would *never* give that up. But in reviewing what I have learned from history, I find that, to my great horror, the same conditions and circumstances that led to the progressive downfall of nations past have taken strong root in our own beloved America.

I see what is happening. I know the path we are on, so I sound the warning cry, hoping everyone else will open their eyes and see what I see. But I am dismissed as an alarmist and considered a fanatic. I know I can't be alone. I know there have to be more Americans who are seeing what I see and feeling what I feel. And I know they must be wondering, like me, when the rest of the nation will wake up and see our impending doom, and when they do, if it will be too late.

There are a lot of people—particularly in the media and the government—who are saying that "alarmists" like me are only angry because we lost an election. But those of us who see what's going on know that is oversimplifying a very real and dangerous threat to our liberty that we know began long before November 2008. It is a threat we have faced even before we were a nation and one that we have been fighting against ever since. It is the threat of separation and subservience.

In the years that led up to our nation's fight for independence, we struggled with both of these. We were subservient to a monarchal government that dictated what freedoms we could and couldn't have and continuously oppressed us with unjust laws, taxes, and regulations.

There were two categories of people living in America at that time: those who were loyal to the monarchy, known as loyalists, and those who were deeply rooted in the idea of freedom. Both groups believed in obeying the law and recognized themselves as subjects of the king, but what that meant to each group was quite different.

England, at this time, was still living the feudal system. Everyone had status by birth. That status determined who you could marry, the work you would do, where you would live, and how you addressed others. Once the *Mayflower* landed on Plymouth Rock, feudalism became a thing of the past. The spirit of America caught on right away. Suddenly, those who were considered a lesser status, such as peasants, who were destined for a life of peasantry, were in a new world where they could own land and property, keep what they earned, and prosper according to their own labors.

There were no kings and courts in America. There were no titles and statuses. However, as more and more people came to America and cities were established, the king decided to take a more active role in governing the colonies. Those who once governed themselves suddenly found nobles and lords, appointed by the king, sailing to America to govern them. And these new governors didn't come alone. They came with armies, businessmen, and magistrates. There soon became two very different groups of people in America: those who made their livelihood *because* of the king and those who made their livelihood *in spite* of him. Neither group had much respect for the other.

For more than a hundred years, American colonists tilled the land, built homes, opened businesses, and created communities. And then, with each passing year, they saw more and more encroachments from the monarchy. Large mansions, churches, and whole city blocks were built to house the king's governors and their courts. The British lords, who were used to being addressed a certain way because of their noble status became infuriated when the colonists didn't appropriately recognize that status. The nobles looked at the colonists as a ragtag band of uncultured peasants. The colonists saw the nobles as lazy snobs. The nobles looked down their noses at the colonists, and the colonists rolled their eyes at the nobles.

Despite their differences, however, they made an effort to get along, because they saw themselves as fellow countrymen. But as the king became more and more oppressive, the local monarchists became unbearable. The nobles were living in luxury, and the colonists were paying for it in ridiculous, unfair, and unjust taxes. The monarchists, of course, felt this was completely acceptable because that was the way it was done in England. In America, however, the people had forged the land by the sweat of their brow and felt the monarchists were coming in to take from their labors—and they had *no* say in the matter.

To make things worse, the king operated on the philosophy "what's mine is mine and what's yours is mine." If the king's soldiers needed a place to stay, the colonists were expected to put them up in their houses. If they needed a horse, the colonists were expected to give them one. If they were hungry, the colonists were expected to feed them. This obviously did not sit well with the colonists and as they protested, things just went from bad to worse.

The number of British troops increased in colonial cities. They walked the streets day and night and at times harassed the colonists. They looked at the colonists as subjects and often treated them with disdain. I am, of course, speaking in generalities, but it was enough of a problem that the colonists started meeting in small groups at local pubs and churches to debate solutions to their predicament, for as the Roman historian Tacitus said, "A desire to resist oppression is implanted in the nature of man." The colonists were definitely being oppressed, and it was, therefore, only natural that they would resist the oppression.

During this time, a very popular pamphlet was published, called simply, *Common Sense*. It was written by Thomas Paine and inspired the colonists to seek for a better way of government. Then, in the spring of 1775, a man of humble stature named Patrick Henry stood in St. John's Church in Richmond, Virginia, and delivered a speech to the House of Burgesses that would inspire generations of Americans for more than two centuries. A little over a year later, the Declaration of Independence was signed, and the vision of a better way soon became a reality.

But it wasn't long before well-meaning people (who thought they knew better than our Founding Fathers) slowly began adding land, programs, services, and charity into the federal government. And it wasn't long after that that power began to corrupt, just as our Founding Fathers feared. By the beginning of the twentieth century, the government started on a path of rapid growth with the establishment of compulsory education, the Sixteenth and Seventeenth Amendments, land acquisitions, and increase of government departments and bureaucracies that would have Thomas Jefferson spinning in his grave. In almost the blink of an eye, we had dismantled all the great things in the Constitution that protected us against oppression and tyranny, and now the federal government has almost complete control of every aspect of our lives.

The Department of Education gives complete control of our children's education to the government. The Department of Agriculture gives control of our farms and agricultural resources to the government. The Department of Labor gives government control of private business. I could go on and on. In 1801, when Thomas Jefferson became the third president of the United States, there were four cabinet positions. Sixty years later, when President Lincoln was elected, there were seven. Today there are twenty-two, and each of those cabinet positions forms a department filled with layers upon layers of bureaucracy. And as if that wasn't enough, in 2001 President Bush established yet another agency that would add to the already inflated executive branch of the government—Homeland Security.

In an effort to "keep us safe" from terrorists, Congress passed the Patriot Act and established Homeland Security, giving the federal government even more expansive power. The Patriot Act was a direct blow to our individual rights, and Homeland Security was a completely unnecessary expansion of government that gave extensive, commanding powers to the president of the United States—power that was *never* intended for *one* person.

I remember watching the State of the Union address as President Bush announced the forming of this new agency. I thought, "Can he do that? Can he just start a whole new government bureaucracy and appoint a new cabinet position without even asking us?" Apparently, in a "crisis" you can do a lot of things for the "safety and security" of the people.

Homeland Security—the very name gives me the willies. In 1933, after the building where the German parliament met was set on fire, Hitler used the "crisis" to pass the Enabling Act through parliament in an effort to "protect the people" and *secure the homeland*. It was this very act that allowed Hitler to seize complete control of the government and proclaim himself Fuhrer. Do we really want the president of the United States to have this kind of power?

I know national security is a major concern for all of us—and it should be. But just what is an organization with a name like "Homeland Security" securing us from? I am one of those crazy few people in America who actually read the Patriot Act in its entirety—both of them. And while there are a lot of things that I feel are very important, and needed, there are a lot of other things that should never have been included, and as usual, those voting on the bill didn't consider the unintended consequences, and probably didn't even read it. It is pretty scary what the government now has the power to do under the pretense of "protecting us." When I finished reading the Patriot Act, I thought, "Thank goodness we have a man of moral character in the White House," but I knew that would not always be the case. "What would happen," I thought, "if monarchists got a hold of that kind of power?" It didn't take long for me to get my answer.

In the spring of 2009, the office of Homeland Security issued a report stating that those who fit the terrorist profile could include anyone with anti-government feelings or those who prefer local/state government over the federal government controlling everything.

The report entitled "Rightwing Extremism: Current Economic

and Political Environment Fueling Resurgence in Radicalization and Recruitment" contains the following definition:

> Rightwing extremism in the United States can be broadly divided into those groups, movements, and adherents that are primarily hate-oriented (based on hatred of particular religious, racial or ethnic groups), and those that are mainly antigovernment, rejecting federal authority in favor of state or local authority, or rejecting government authority entirely. It may include groups and individuals that are dedicated to a single issue, such as opposition to abortion or immigration.

This is what happens when we trade our liberty for security. And once again, our Founding Fathers, in their infinite wisdom, realized this. Benjamin Franklin warned, "Those who would give up essential liberty to purchase a little temporary safety, deserve neither liberty nor safety." And in the end that is exactly what we will get—we will be neither free nor safe.

In August 2008, while campaigning for president, then Senator Barack Obama stated, "We cannot continue to rely only on our military in order to achieve the national security objectives that we've set. We've got to have a civilian national security force that's just as powerful, just as strong, just as well-funded." If your jaw dropped to the floor like mine did when he made this statement, then you know your history. For those were the words Hitler used when explaining the purpose of the Gestapo. And now, because of the Patriot Act and Homeland Security, the president of the United States has the power to form this well-funded civilian national security force. The word *force* alone sends chills up my spine.

What do you suppose will be the mission and purpose of this *force?* Who will they be protecting, and who will the government consider a threat—homeschoolers, Christians, gun owners, fair-tax supporters, those who oppose abortion, those who speak out against illegal immigration, those who don't want government-run healthcare? Just who will be considered an "enemy of the state"?

This is the result of well-meaning people with good intentions who don't understand the importance of the Constitution or the purpose of a Republic. In his book, *The Mainspring of Human Progress,* Henry Grady Weaver writes:

> Most of the major ills of the world have been caused by well-meaning people who ignored the principle of individual freedom, except as applied to themselves, and who were obsessed with fanatical zeal to improve the lot of mankind-in-the-mass through some pet formula of their own …. the harm done by ordinary criminals, murderers, gangsters, and thieves is negligible in comparison with the agony inflicted up human beings by the professional "Do-Gooders," who attempt to set themselves up as gods on earth and who would ruthlessly force their views on all others—with the abiding assurance that the end justifies the means.[1]

It is the "do-gooder" mentality that gets us into most of our problems. I know we all want to be safe, and I know it is hard to see pain and suffering, but sometimes the method we use to "fix" the problem is worse than the problem itself. My son learned this the hard way while at the beach several years ago.

Jordan was only four or five years old at the time. Our family was picnicking at a beach in San Diego, and a small seagull came near our blanket. Jordan thought he looked very hungry and decided he would give this poor little bird a piece of bread. Suddenly, as if from nowhere, hundreds of birds descended on the beach, surrounding our picnic blanket. Some of the birds became aggressive as they tried to get a piece of bread, chip, cracker, or anything else they could reach. One of the birds even nipped Jordan's finger and grabbed his sandwich right out of his hand.

My husband came to the rescue and chased the birds off to invade someone else's lunch. Jordan was crying and obviously *not* understanding why the birds were so "mean." It was a great teaching moment.

I explained to Jordan that the birds had come to rely on people for their food. "People have fed them for so long," I said, "that many of the birds don't know how to get their own food anymore. They will fight for their food because they think they will starve if we don't give it to them."

Jordan looked up at me with his big blue eyes. "Maybe people can teach the birds how to get their own food again," he said. "Maybe we can teach them how to catch fish."

"That's a great idea," I said, "but the birds might think it is easier to just get their food from us because fishing is a lot of work."

"What if we stopped feeding them?" Jordan asked.

"Then," I said, "they would *have* to learn how to fish."

Jordan learned a valuable lesson through his own experience. Experience is our greatest teacher. We learn through our own experiences and from the experiences of others. Studying history is an excellent way to learn from others' experiences. But, like our children who sometimes seem destined to repeat *our* mistakes, we often have to experience things ourselves before we can completely grasp the lesson. Maybe we will have to *experience* tyranny and oppression for us to truly understand and cherish freedom. Maybe we are *incapable* of learning from our founders' experiences. I sure wish we would all come to our senses and realize that our Founding Fathers knew what they were talking about.

Our Republic wasn't just some whim of an idea our Founding Fathers threw together to try out new things. It was the result of studying thousands of years of other people's experiences and learning from them. So before we decide to scrap the whole thing for the sake of change, let us remember that change, in and of itself, isn't necessarily a *good* thing. We need to be careful when we cry out for change, because we never know what we may get.

In the 1920s, Germany was in the midst of a major depression. It wasn't just a financial depression; the people of the country were depressed. The country suffered great economic loss and deep humiliation due to the war. The Treaty of Versailles forced the German government to admit blame for the war and required reparations in money and property be paid to the Allied countries. This angered many Germans who, refusing to accept the humiliation of defeat, believed they had been betrayed by their own countrymen. It was a very difficult time for the people of Germany. They were tired, angry, frustrated, and looking for a change. Their change came in the form of a man named Adolf Hitler.

In Russia around the same time (1917), a revolution was brewing. The people were tired of the tyranny they had suffered for years under a monarchal dictatorship. They were oppressed, restricted, and persecuted by the government. They were tired, angry, frustrated, and desperately seeking change. Vladimir Lenin offered it to them.

In both of these cases, the men who launched their prospective revolutions used the "have-not" philosophy to win loyalty among the working class or the so-called "blue collar" workers—the tradesmen, the factory workers, the linemen. They were the families who worked hard every day just to provide for their homes and families. Some of these families became resentful that they had to work so hard for so little, when others seemed to have so much. The change promised by Hitler and

Lenin seemed the answer to all their ills, but the change they got was not something they could have even imagined.

Hitler and Lenin gave hope to people. They talked of equality, fairness, spreading the wealth, and taking care of the common man. It was what everyone needed to hear. It was the hope of a brighter future, where everyone would be cared for, everyone would have a job, no one would go hungry, and there would be no more suffering—but it was all a masterful plan of deception. Lenin and Hitler created an atmosphere of subtle deceit that crept up on the people, little by little, until it was too late to stop it. And it wasn't long before the people realized Hitler and Lenin (and later Stalin) weren't about "fairness" at all; they were obsessed with power. They didn't want equality for all; they wanted to be above everyone else. They wanted to be the new "haves." They would strip the old "haves" of all their power and dignity and teach them a lesson. It wasn't a revolution; it was a conquest. It was simply a changing of the guard from one oppressive, tyrannical government to an even worse one. There was nothing patriotic or loyal about it. It was sinister, self-serving, and maniacal. And Hitler and Lenin succeeded by intoxicating thousands of men and women with greed and lust while seducing and corrupting the children. But it *was* change, right?

It is very important that we know our past. If we don't, we *will* repeat it. Can we really afford to repeat the mistakes of the German and Russian people? Can we really afford that kind of change? The things Lenin and Hitler introduced weren't new ideas; they were old, bad ones. Wealth redistribution was not a new concept; we had already tried it in America long before Lenin's revolution and realized Communism for what it was—a miserable failure. We witnessed firsthand the oppressiveness of the feudal system in Europe; we saw the dangers of monarchies and big governments. We knew how easily power corrupts, and our Founding Fathers, in all their infinite wisdom, shunned all of these forms of government when forming this new nation. They were the ones who offered change—change the world had never before seen—based on the successes and failures of thousands of years of government. What our Founding Fathers introduced *was* the new original idea—freedom for all! There was no more revolutionary idea than that.

Freedom was something everyone wanted. It has been fought for by people and countries for centuries. The Jews fought for freedom from the Romans. William Wallace led a band of Scots to fight for freedom from England. Joan of Arc fought for it, Martin Luther fought for it, Gandhi fought for it, Harriet Tubman fought for it. The Pilgrims fled England to have it. The American Revolution, the Alamo, even the Civil War were all fought for freedom. Freedom is in our very souls. And once that freedom is lost, it is almost impossible to get it back. So before we decide to go to the government to solve our problems, let us look back in history and consider the cost of that choice. What are we giving up to have national healthcare? What are we trading to "save" the economy? What price do we pay for looking to the government to "fix" things? The answer can be found in our own history, and it certainly seems to be repeating itself.

The cycle of freedom is quite interesting when we put it on paper—even more so when we put it on a graph and see how the cycle repeats itself. The spirit of freedom is in all of us. When our freedom is limited, restricted, or even taken away, we humble ourselves, suddenly remember there is a God, and ask Him for help. Then, realizing we are inherently free, we find courage within ourselves and fight for our freedom. Liberty is the result. That is what our Founding Fathers left to us—liberty that they fought for. They already paid the price and freedom became *our* inheritance.

Because of that freedom, we prospered. We became the wealthiest nation on earth. The greatest inventions and discoveries of the world, from the cash register to the airplane (and beyond) came from right here in the United States, because we were free to create, build, produce, and design. We are free to conceive ideas and theories and test them. We are were free to try and free to fail—which is the very thing that led to most of our successes.

We became a nation of great abundance, and within a short time, that abundance became our focus and we became complacent about preserving the Republic. As time passed, we forgot what the republic even was, what it meant, and what it stood for. Then while we were busy doing other things, little by little, the government encroached on our lives in an effort to "help" us, until we became dependent on the government for many of our needs and wants. And now, we are once again on the verge of bondage—slaves to our own government.

In 1770, just six years before America proclaimed independence, a Scottish professor of history by the name of Alexander Tytler made the following conclusion from his years of researching world history and civilizations.

> A democracy cannot exist as a permanent form of government. It can only exist until the voters discover

that they can vote themselves largesse from the public treasury. From that moment on, the majority always votes for the candidates promising the most benefits the public treasury with the result that a democracy always collapses over lousy fiscal policy, always followed by a dictatorship. The average of the world's great civilizations before they decline has been 200 years. These nations have progressed in this sequence: From bondage to spiritual faith; from faith to great courage; from courage to liberty; from liberty to abundance; from abundance to selfishness; from selfishness to complacency; from complacency to apathy; from apathy to dependency; from dependency back again to bondage.[2]

Using the following diagram of this cycle of democracy as Tytler refers to it, where do you feel America is right now?

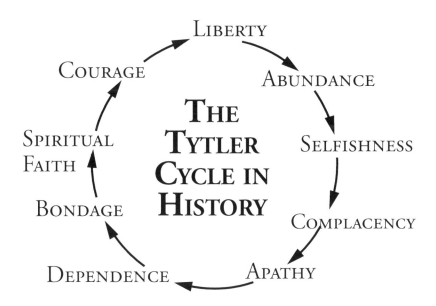

After years of complacency and apathy that led to continuous encroachments on our freedom, we find ourselves in the very same situation our founding families faced over two hundred years ago—despite all their efforts to prevent it. And now, after all these years, there are once again two different groups of people in this country—those who make their livelihood *because* of the government and those who make their livelihood *in spite* of it. It has become so out of control that our own Congress has taken the place of King George as the oppressor, and greedy men and women hang around Capitol Hill like courtiers at the king's palace, amassing wealth *because* of the government. These people don't want smaller government—it would cut into their profits and inhibit their lifestyle.

We see the fruits of our labors being taken away by the bushel load as Congress has adopted King George's philosophy, "What's *mine* is mine and what's *yours* is mine"! If Congress wants to fund a pet project, we're expected to cover the cost of it. If Congress wants to bail out a bank, we're expected to pay for it. If Senator Reid wants a train from Disneyland to Vegas, we are expected to give it to him. If Congresswoman Pelosi wants a jet to ease her travel from D.C. to California, she takes it—and *we* get the bill. It is no wonder they're loyal to the government—*they're living off of it.*

Then there are the people who are loyal to the government out of perceived necessity, because they have come to depend on government for their very survival through "benevolent" programs like Medicare, welfare, and food stamps. They don't want smaller government—they want an increase in benefits. And so, we have these two groups in our country once again—the loyalists who support *government* because they depend on it, and the patriots who support the *Republic* because they depend on themselves. Despite our differences, we try to get along because we are fellow countrymen, but as the loyalists ask for more and more money, it is becoming increasingly difficult to suppress tensions, because the loyalists are living off the labors of the patriots.

Today's loyalists are loyal to the government for one of two reasons—either out of necessity or out of sheer greed. Those who are loyal out of necessity feel they *need* the government. Those who are loyal out of greed *use* the government. I refer to these loyalists as monarchists because they use the government to amass wealth and status—much like the British nobles did.

Monarchists support big government just like the British nobles supported the king, because they want to be in the king's court, where they have special rules and enjoy high status. Today's monarchists feel they are above rule and regulation. What applies to us simply does not apply to them. Congress is always passing laws and regulations that they exclude themselves from. And government officials often act as if they are above the law, with two sets of rules—one for the nobles, and one for the lowly peasants.

For a monarchist, the government is their power base and they will use any means necessary, and at their disposal, to keep and increase their power. So they use things like "crises" to add to their power. Simple incidents, like a fire in Georgetown (referenced in a previous chapter), where well-meaning people have a real desire to help those who have suffered loss, becomes a regulated program that needs a mammoth bureaucracy to run it. Do you really think Congress just handed over $20,000 to those families in Georgetown who lost their homes? Of course not. After all, it is public money and Congress needs to be accountable to the public, right? So how do they account for that $20,000 of compassion?

Well, first you have to set up a committee to oversee the process. The committee—probably made of members of Congress and local do-gooders—will then meet to draft a plan on how to disperse the funds. Who will get the money? How much will they get? Will it be based on loss, income, family size? All these things will need to be determined, so there will, of course, need to be forms printed up to collect the information. And there will need to be an office set up where the families who were affected by the fire can come and fill out the paperwork. Then the committee realizes someone will have to collect the forms and review them to see how much each family will receive in government funds.

After weeks of meetings, the committee decides all this paperwork, and meetings with the families to review each case, are going to take way more time than they have, because they have luncheons to get to and more projects to appropriate funds for. There are so many worthy causes, so many people in need, so many pressing things that need their attention. So they decide to hire a staff to run the program.

The staff will, of course, need oversight and Congress doesn't have time to deal with that, so they decide to hire an oversight manager. But the oversight manager can't act without approval from Congress, and Congress can't authorize the manager without congressional oversight (is your head spinning yet?), so the president establishes the Georgetown Fire Relief Association for Families or GFRAF—because every government program must have an acronym to be official.

Of course, the president can't just establish a new program without Congress approving it, so a bill is written, which is passed back and forth through Congress while senators and representatives add little things here and there (all for the good people in their states and districts, of course) until the bill finally hits the floors of Congress and it is passed unanimously in both the House and the Senate.

The office of the Georgetown Fire Relief Association for Families finally opens their doors to accept applications nine months after the Georgetown fire was extinguished. The $20,000 that was designated for the welfare of the fire victims is put into the bank account of the newly organized GFRAF, and the program is placed with a congressional committee for oversight.

Six months later, members of the House Health and Human Services Committee meet with the GFRAF oversight manager for an accounting of the program. The oversight manager reports the start-up costs at $5,000 to purchase supplies and equipment and lease office space for one year. Printing costs totaled $1,000 and salaries for the combined staff are $50,000 annually. Added to this are all the "additions" members of Congress made to the bill establishing the GRFAF, which totaled $300,000, and you have a grand total of $376,000 for a $20,000 benevolent program to help the poor fire victims of Georgetown, Virginia.

After reviewing the accounting, members of the committee ask the oversight manager to report on the progress and success of the program. "Well," says the oversight manager, "we opened our doors and began receiving applications nine months after the Georgetown fire. What we found was, out of the forty-two families affected by the fire, all but two families had already rebuilt their homes and recouped their losses with aid and support from their local churches and community. The two families who did not rebuild their houses moved in with extended family and relocated to other parts of the state."

"So," asks one of the committee members, "how many families filled out applications for assistance?"

"None, sir."

"Not one?" repeats the committee member.

"No, sir, not one."

"So, what you're saying is, we still have $20,000 to spend."

"Well, um, yes sir," stutters the oversight committee chairman, "I guess that is what I'm saying."

So for the next few hours, the oversight committee chairman and members of the Health and Human Services Committee discuss how they can use the program to help all the other needy families in Georgetown. They decide the program should drop the word "fire" so that GFRAF—which becomes GRAF—can distribute funds to families of Georgetown who have been affected by *any* disaster—including job loss or debilitating illness. The committee determines that with their new expanded benevolent intentions, $20,000 isn't enough, so one of the Congressmen on the committee introduces a bill in Congress for an additional $20,000 to be added to the program. The bill passes through the House and Senate committees, as $150,000 in more *additions* are added by various members of Congress (to support the needy people in their states and districts), and a month later, the bill is passed unanimously in the House and Senate.

As the years pass, Congress decides that they shouldn't restrict their benevolence to Georgetown when there are so many people suffering all over the country, so they drop the "G" in GRAF and add an "A" for *American,* renaming the program the American Relief Association for Families or ARAF. After a few years, Congress starts receiving letters from constituents complaining that the ARAF discriminates against people with no families and families of alternate lifestyles. Members of Congress, not wanting to be accused of being bigots or homophobes, race to the media to assure the public they are very concerned about the failings of the system and are scrutinizing the program policies as they speak. The congressional aides and lawyers then spend weeks rewriting the policies and procedures of the program to include every form of "family" they can think of, and release a three-hundred-page manual introducing the "new and improved" program. So ARAF becomes ARA—American Relief Association—which, several years later and after considerable reflection on behalf of members of Congress becomes WRA or World Relief Association because there are so many needy around the world—and think of all the *good* we can do.

The original $20,000 program has become so inclusive and so large over the years that the staff has had to be increased each year to cover the workload. And with more staff, you need managers to manage the staff and managers to manage managers, and in just a few years, the initial staff of five has grown to more than five thousand. The seven-hundred-square-foot office they started in is now a series of forty-thousand-square-foot office buildings that make up the WRA complex. And the annual budget is now in the billions. But think of all the people they're helping, right? Yes, let's take a moment and talk about all the people the government is helping.

Twenty years ago, I was one of those people being "helped" by the government when our family met with unforeseen circumstances. I was one of those people who had to sit in long lines, waiting to be escorted into a dismal office, where a government employee—who didn't want to be there—interrogated me for thirty minutes on our income, home life, and employment, just so our children could receive medical care.

I was one of those people who spent hours in the government health unit every six months waiting for my children to have their iron tested to see if they still qualified for W.I.C. I was one of those women who had a baby in a government-funded state hospital, where I stood in long lines, forced to have tests I didn't want, and treated like a burden. I spent six hours in the hospital's OB clinic *just going through the registration process*.

I was sent to one line to fill out paperwork, another line for my blood work, another line for my vitals, another line where I was asked a series of questions about my health, medical history, sexual activity, and home life, and then finally, I was sent to the last line—where I got an appointment to go through the whole mess all over again. It was assembly-line medicine on a grand chaotic scale. It was the most callous and impersonal medical care I have ever experienced, and I vowed I would do whatever it took to get out of that miserable system. If it meant going back to school, working more hours, getting a better job, whatever we needed to do to be able to pay for better healthcare, my husband and I were committed to doing it. And we did.

The thought of a lifetime of that kind of medical care was unacceptable. My family was more important to me than that. I was more important than that. So imagine my shock when people in our country started talking about wanting national healthcare. The first thing that came to my mind was "People actually *want* to be treated this way?" Then I realized that the people supporting it have probably never experienced government healthcare, because if they had, they surely wouldn't be promoting it.

Maybe you think my experience is extreme. Maybe it's just a rare exception. Well, ask yourself this: when have you ever been in any government office where you have been treated with kindness or respect? When have you ever gone to get your driver's license or renew your registration and *not* stood in a ridiculously long line? When have you ever gone to the Social Security office and *not* spent all day? When have you ever been in a government office and actually had someone who works there smile and wish you a good day? Now I must ask you, why do you think a government-run healthcare system would be any different?

I know we are looking for that "change" again, but we need smart change that will actually make things better, not quick change that will treat everybody equally miserably. I think when most people think national healthcare, what they are envisioning is top-notch healthcare for free. Let me remind you, you get what you pay for.

The reason healthcare is so good in America is because it is personal. You get to choose your doctors—sometimes from a list, but you still get to choose them. You get to discuss your health issues and treatment options with your doctor, and you and your doctor decide how you will proceed with treatment. If you don't like what your doctor tells you, you can get a second opinion—and as many more as you'd like until you feel comfortable with your healthcare plan. I know our healthcare system isn't perfect, but it is still the best in the world. People come from countries all over the world to receive the top-notch healthcare America has. Still, there are definitely things we can do to make it more efficient and much more affordable. The most immediate and effective way is through tort reform.

Tort is the system we use in America for compensating people for wrongs or harm done to them by someone else. It's what we use to determine whether or not we file a lawsuit against someone—and it is the reason why doctors have to pay outrageously high premiums for malpractice insurance, which has directly contributed to the rising cost of healthcare. There are lawyers whose whole entire profession exists on preying on the misery of others. They call themselves personal injury and malpractice attorneys, but they are commonly referred to as "ambulance chasers," because that is exactly what they are—only they don't have to chase anyone anymore. They just run commercials and people come to them.

My daughter (at ten years old) came into my room one day and asked a very odd question: "Mom, did you ever take Paxil when you were pregnant with any of us?"

"What?" I asked, completely bewildered and seriously wondering how she even knew what Paxil was. "No," I said, "I didn't. Why?"

"That's too bad," she said. "The guy on the TV says there's a lot of money in it for you if you did."

Great. Thank you, Bender and Bender for providing me with another great teaching moment for my children.

There are many people who have been trying to get tort reform passed for several years. Tort reform would make changes to civil justice that would reduce litigation or damages. The lawyers, of course, hate this idea, because they make an enormous amount of money with these lucrative lawsuits. In fact, they are the only ones who do in many of these lawsuits.

You see, they get paid from the damages awarded to their client—or *clients* as is so often the case. They go on a prowl for clients, like a tiger stalking its prey. Anytime the FDA releases anything negative—no matter how ridiculously small—on any drug, food item, or anything for that matter, law firms race to the TV airwaves to let you know "You could have a claim!" Then people sitting on their couches see the commercial and visions of free money dance in their heads. "Hmm," they wonder to themselves, "didn't my wife take Paxil when she was pregnant?" So they call the toll-free phone number and the lawyer asks a bunch of questions to determine if they have a good enough story to help them win the claim. And they can't have enough good stories—the more clients the better; it just makes their case stronger and increases their chances of scoring big when they collect on the damages—which is why they like *class action* lawsuits so much.

The reason so many people go to these lawyers is because it doesn't cost them anything. The lawyers tell the clients how much they care about their situation, how wronged they were, and convince them they deserve a financial reward for their suffering. "Don't worry," they tell them, "you don't have to pay any money up front. Just sign this little paper here and authorize us to collect our fee of 20 to 40 percent of the damages if we win the case. If we don't win your case, you don't owe us anything."

Of course, it is in the best interest of the lawyers to win the cases so they can collect that hefty 40 percent fee. They will say or do anything to win the case—and win big. Remember, their fee is percentage-based. The greater the damages rewarded, the bigger their score. And one law firm hit the jackpot in 2000 when they won their class action lawsuit against tobacco companies on behalf of Howard Engle and several other smokers. The jury in the case awarded damages of $145 million. Even at only 20 percent, that's a take-home pay of over $20 million for the lawyers—for just one case! And while the lawyers *always* win big in these cases, many times the clients, on whose behalf the cases are filed, do not. This is especially true in the case of class action lawsuits where lawyers can receive hundreds of thousands of dollars and each claimant gets a check in the mail for twenty-five dollars.

The whole thing is a major racket, but instead of pushing for tort reform to curtail this out-of-control abuse of our courts, which is creating total mayhem in our healthcare system, we'd rather blame the doctors. We blame them for charging so much money for their services and accuse them of being a bunch of rich gold diggers who care more about how much money they make than caring for their patients. I cannot even tell you how absurd this is.

When are we going to start holding the gold-digging, self-serving, wealth-amassing lawyers accountable for their contribution to the rising cost of our healthcare? They are the true parasites feeding on the system. The doctors are just trying to survive the consequences of their lawsuits, doing whatever they can to keep practicing amid ever-increasing rises in their malpractice insurance. How much higher can malpractice insurance premiums go before doctors have to close their doors altogether? Add to that all the oppressive government regulations, restrictions, and intrusions—

and the fact that their own patients are accusing them of not caring and making too much money—and I can't understand why anyone even *wants* to be a doctor anymore.

In 2009, I attended a town hall meeting on healthcare where several members of the medical profession, including two doctors and a hospital administrator, answered questions about the realities of government-run healthcare. Several of those in attendance asked questions of the panel members on specific issues relating to H.R. 3200, as well as the healthcare industry in general. Many of them asked the panel for suggestions on how we could fix the problems in our healthcare system without introducing a government healthcare insurance program. The panel members gave very informative, detailed answers to each question. Then a doctor in the audience asked a question.

"I am a doctor," he said, "and when I took the Hippocratic Oath, I swore to take care of everyone. Why are we saying we don't want to take care of the children who are on Medicaid? And why do doctors feel they have to make a gazillion dollars?"

One of the doctors on the panel took the microphone and addressed the man's question. "No one on this panel is saying they don't want to take care of children who are on Medicaid," he said, "I would never turn away a patient who needed medical care because they couldn't pay for it, and I don't know any doctor who would. It would be nice if Medicaid paid their bills once in a while, but that won't determine whether or not I treat my patients; it is just proof that a government-run system is faulty, impersonal, mismanaged, and slow. And as for doctors making gazillion dollars, I don't know what doctors you know but I am forty-seven years old and *still* paying off my student loans! Doctors don't make gazillion dollars. We're just trying to *make it*."

They *are* just trying to make it. Just like the rest of us. Some do better than others—just like the rest of us. These doctors have invested a lot of time and money into their careers. They have a *right* to see a return on that investment. That's what *we* would want. This has just become purely a matter of jealousy. The doctors have and we have not. And because we believe they have more, we think they should treat us out of the goodness of their hearts like they owe it to us to do so because of their Hippocratic Oath. But a doctor taking the Hippocratic Oath is *not* equivalent to a priest taking his vows. Doctors don't take a vow of poverty. They have families with children of their own, and they need to provide for them. They have to put food on the table too. They have a house payment and medical expenses, just like the rest of us. And they are (like the rest of us should be) planning for their future when they will no longer be able to work. If we deny doctors—or anyone, for that matter—the right to provide for themselves and their own families, their children will be on the government welfare rolls needing free healthcare, and they will need social security to survive in their old age. But I guess that would be fair, right? Can we not see how absurd this is?

One doctor on the panel said that if national healthcare passed, he would be forced into early retirement and have to close his doors, to which one woman responded, "What about your oath to take care of the children?"

"Ma'am," he said, "I can't help the children if I don't make enough money to pay my bills and keep the doors open."

I can't stand it when people pull our children into an argument like they use the race card. It's like they say "it's for the children" and we're all just supposed to jump on board because how could we not support the children? That's why election after election, people vote in favor of school levies (even though they already siphon 75 to 85 percent of our property taxes) because no one wants to be accused of not caring about the children. The whole reason I fight against these things is because I *do* care about children—especially my own. No government official could possibly care about what happens to my children more than I do. And the same thing applies to our own communities.

It is easy for members of Congress to say they want to help the needy and pass programs that make them feel good about being so "helpful," but how much help can they really be when they are so detached from those in need? Government compassion is an oxymoron. A *thing* cannot be compassionate because things don't have feelings—people do. And while the people supporting and voting for these programs often truly do have good intentions, they are way too far removed from those who need the program to be of any help to them.

Congress passes the programs and then sets up departments, divisions, and agencies to run them and hire people to fill them. There are thousands of bureaucrats, administrators, and government workers standing between Congress and the needy. Why would those people have compassion? It is just a job for them and they get paid the same amount of money whether they care or not. So why should they care? If you don't have anything to gain or lose, why would you bother making an effort? If a government hospital is going to get paid regardless of the care you receive, what kind of care do you think you will get? Just look at the government school system to answer *that* question.

Who is it that opens a soup kitchen? It's a person who has seen or experienced hunger and desires to help those who are hungry. The people who open battered women's shelters are often women who have been victims of abuse themselves. Homeless shelters are often opened by people who experienced or witnessed homelessness. Free clinics are often opened by doctors who want to help those who can't afford a doctor. Those are the programs that work because a community cares about the people in their community.

Community programs are born out of a local need and someone's sincere desire to meet that need. That kind of help comes from the heart, and more often than not, the people who run these programs work long hours for little pay—and in many cases for no pay at all—because they *believe* in what they are doing, and they *want* to be a part of it. You just can't get that from an unfeeling government with a bunch of uninterested workers. The government can't solve all our problems, and we shouldn't want them to. The more government gives us, the more they can take away from us. And they are always looking for that next "crisis" that will give them the ability to do just that.

In 1929, when the stock market crashed, the government jumped to our rescue. Their "help" led to a national depression that would have been short-lived had it not been for all the additional "help" the government gave us in the 1950s when they launched a "war on poverty." How well did that work out? From the Trail of Tears to government bailouts, anytime the government "helps," things get worse and we lose freedoms.

In September of 2008, a very unusual thing happened in the Ohio Valley. Hurricane Ike, after hitting land in the Gulf Coast, kept its momentum as it traveled north all the way to the Great Lakes . The usual rains Ohio receives from hurricanes were anticipated. What we did not anticipate, however, were hurricane-force winds that knocked down trees and power lines all over Ohio and Kentucky. Many families were without electricity for weeks. Our family was one of the lucky ones. Our power lines run underground, and we only lost electricity for a couple of hours.

The day after the storm, my husband and I stepped outside our front door to an unbelievable sight. Trees and limbs were knocked down all over our street. Some families lost roofs and awnings. We had lived in the Washington, D.C. area when Hurricane Isabel hit the Atlantic coast, so we knew what the aftermath of a hurricane looked like, but to see that kind of destruction in Dayton, Ohio, that morning was more than we ever could have imagined. I mean, we're in Ohio, for crying out loud! *You don't have hurricanes in Ohio!*

As the days passed, the local radio stations were very helpful in keeping up with the news of the day and the progress of the electric companies in restoring power. There were utility trucks everywhere, crews worked round the clock, and representatives from the electric companies gave updates on the radio frequently throughout the day. I was extremely impressed with how well the local companies handled the situation, considering they had never dealt with such a disaster before and had no idea they would ever have to. What I found surprising, however, were all the phone calls to the local radio stations from Dayton residents complaining that their electricity *still* wasn't back on.

There were calls from many disgruntled customers who felt the electric company wasn't doing a good enough job. There were even news reports of people driving by utility crews yelling obscenities and even throwing things because they didn't feel the crews were working fast enough. One woman even had the audacity to call in and complain because her cable was still out. "Really?" I thought. "There are people in Texas and Louisiana without homes and basic necessities, and you are complaining because you lost HBO?" Unbelievable. Within a week, there was a public outcry, "The government needs to do something about this! We *still* don't have electricity. What is the government going to do about it?"

They honestly thought the government *could* do something about it—like the mayor or the governor could wave some magic wand and suddenly everyone would have power. And I don't doubt that some self-serving politicians somewhere were willing to take advantage of the situation and use the public's outcry to usurp more power.

I was very impressed, however, when members of my city council did exactly the opposite and took time out of a city council meeting to thank all those who had worked so hard to restore power—and then asked the citizens to please exercise patience while they continued to do their job.

I was even more impressed when city council members encouraged the citizens to check on their neighbors and offer assistance as they were able. And the community came together and did just that. One woman even held a backyard barbecue and invited all her neighbors to come, so the food defrosting in her freezer didn't go to waste. It was just amazing to see the community come together—just like we should.

Sometime along the line, we've got to stop relying on the government to solve all our problems and start taking responsibility for ourselves. All these government programs may *sound* like good ideas, they may *seem* enticing and desirable, but they are only traps meant to slowly lure us into total submission. The healthcare debate is nothing more than another way for the government to control our lives—and us. If you want to know what all this is *really* about, just listen to what one of the monarchists says about their vision of the future of America. Roger Baldwin, the founder of the ACLU, stated, "I am for socialism, disarmament, and ultimately for abolishing the state itself. I seek social ownership of property, the abolition of the propertied class, and sole control by those who produce wealth. Communism is, of course, the goal."[3]

Is that our goal? Is having government-run healthcare worth the price of freedom? Is having government-run *anything* worth the price of freedom? For those of you who are still on the fence with that question, consider this: the IRS gives the government complete control over our paychecks and financial lives. They have the power to freeze our bank accounts, seize our assets, garnish our wages, take our property, and even put us in jail for not obeying *their* rules. Government officials have been known to use the IRS to perform extensive audits and relentless investigations to intimidate people they feel may be a threat to their power or agenda. Through the IRS, the government has the power to completely ruin a person's life. Do you really want the government to have that kind of power over your family's health? My answer is an emphatic *no!* When the government finally gets around to winning their "war on poverty," they can talk to me about my healthcare.

We need to ask ourselves, do we really want freedom? Really? Because if we do, then we need to be willing to say no. We need to look at all the things the government "gives us," from student loans to Medicare, and say, *I don't want it.* We have to be willing to make sacrifices, suffer losses, and be dedicated to taking care of ourselves. That is what it is going to take to be free—it is going to take millions of Americans waking up and asking not *how much I get from the government* but *how much I can provide for myself;* not what my country can do for me, but what I can do for my country. Only then will we be truly committed to freedom—when we are willing to the pay the cost of preserving it.

From Our Founders

I predict future happiness for Americans if they can prevent the government from wasting the labors of the people under the pretense of taking care of them.
~Thomas Jefferson

The jaws of power are always open to devour, and her arm is always stretched out, if possible, to destroy the freedom of thinking, speaking, and writing.
~John Adams

Can the liberties of a nation be thought secure, when we have removed their only firm basis, a conviction in the minds of the people that these liberties are the gift of God?
~Thomas Jefferson

If ye love wealth better than liberty, the tranquility of servitude better than the animating contest of freedom, go home from us in peace. We ask not your counsels or arms. Crouch down and lick the hands which feed you. May your chains set lightly upon you, and may posterity forget that ye were our countrymen.
~Samuel Adams

The natural progress of things is for liberty to yield and government to gain ground.
~Thomas Jefferson

I would rather be exposed to the inconveniences attending too much liberty than to those attending too small a degree of it.
~Thomas Jefferson

Government is instituted for the common good; for the protection, safety, prosperity, and happiness of the people; and not for profit, honor, or private interest of any one man, family, or class of men; therefore, the people alone have an incontestable, unalienable, and indefeasible right to institute government; and to reform, alter, or totally change the same, when their protection, safety, prosperity, and happiness require it.
~John Adams

I am for a government rigorously frugal and simple. Were we directed from Washington when to sow, when to reap, we should soon want bread.
~Thomas Jefferson

Yes, we did produce a near-perfect republic. But will they keep it? Or will they, in the enjoyment of plenty, lose the memory of freedom? Material abundance without character is the path of destruction.
~Thomas Jefferson

The spirit of resistance to government is so valuable on certain occasions, that I wish it to be always kept alive. It will often be exercised when wrong, but better so than not to be exercised at all. I like a little rebellion now and then.
~Thomas Jefferson

Other Notable Quotes

It would indeed be ironic if, in the name of national defense, we would sanction the subversion of one of those liberties which make the defense of our nation worthwhile.
~Earl Warren

Few men desire liberty; most men wish only for a just master.
~Sallust

The problem with socialism is that you eventually run out of other people's money.
~Margaret Thatcher

Don't expect to build up the weak by pulling down the strong.
~Calvin Coolidge

Suggested Books & Resources:
Glenn Beck's Common Sense by Glenn Beck
Common Sense by Thomas Paine
The Proper Role of Government by Ezra Taft Benson
The Law by Frederic Bastiat
Atlas Shrugged by Ayn Rand
Animal Farm by George Orwell
Road to Serfdom by F. A. Hayek
Discovery of Freedom by Rose Wilder Lane

YOUR VOICE COUNTS

In my many years I have come to a conclusion that one useless man is a shame, two is a law firm, and three or more is a congress.
—John Adams

After shouting at rallies, signing a myriad of ignored petitions, and flooding the phone lines of congress to no avail I am sure you are probably wondering about now how your voice could possibly count. Believe me, I totally relate to your frustration but I want to assure you that your voice *does* count. I think, however, we have learned by now that shouting louder and carrying bigger signs doesn't get us heard any more than we already are. So the answer, I believe, isn't to speak louder, but to speak *smarter*! And there is no place where our voice is heard louder in Congress than with our vote.

Elections matter! And every election—*every* election—no matter how small or great makes a major difference in the direction our Nation takes. If we want to have a say in that direction then we need to start taking elections seriously—and we need to stop buying into the deceptive tactics that keep us from having our voices heard.

Another popular deception is the "wasted vote". We have allowed ourselves to be limited to the idea that we only have two choices in elections. And we have been convinced that if we don't vote for one of those *two choices* we are *wasting* our vote. That mindset is the very thing that has progressively muted the power of our voice for decades. We have been led to believe if we don't vote the party candidate we are letting the other party win. Republicans have been especially convinced of this and fear mongered into voting for people they don't like so they make sure they don't get "the *other* guy". It is time we break through the walls others have placed around us and realize the *true* power of our voice.

In 2003 the people of California had a rare and unique opportunity to have their voices heard in a big way. It has become infamously known as the California Recall. That was a difficult year for Californians.

The residents of California were already burdened with outrageously high taxes and mounting state fees and had become extremely frustrated with the careless, reckless spending of the state government. The California economy had greatly weakened in a very short time but it was the energy crisis that became the final straw that fueled the recall. Almost overnight, California residents saw their electricity bills tripled in cost and California's economic crisis suddenly became very personal.

Angry and frustrated, the people of California blamed the government for the crisis citing mismanagement, lack of accountability, poor planning, and overspending. And so an angry electorate, with the help of the media and the support of several financial backers, launched a recall on Governor Gray Davis. The recall was successful and a special election was scheduled where three major candidates emerged—Tom McClintock, Cruz Bustamante, and Arnold Schwarzenegger.

I remember this time in history very well. I was enthralled with the whole process. It was a remarkable thing to witness the power of the people in action. As time passed, however, the people's power began to be limited—and at the hands of some of our own fellow conservatives. Cruz Bustamante ran as a Democrat and the other two candidates both ran as Republicans. As the election neared, people started to voice concern that there were *two* Republican candidates and suggested the one with the least chance of winning should get out of the race—as has become the unwritten law of Party Politics.

The media followed the polls religiously and consistently reported that Arnold Schwarzenegger had the best chance. Parading his Hollywood friends at campaign appearances became a standard strategy for Arnold Schwarzenegger. Many compared him to Ronald Reagan simply because they were both actors who entered politics—which was about all they had in common. But that wasn't enough for many voters and while Schwarzenegger talked a good talk, many California voters (and those of us who followed the election around the nation) didn't have a great deal of confidence in his ability and commitment to walk the walk.

Tom McClintock, on the other hand, had a proven track record of fiscal responsibility and accountability and seemed by far, the best candidate.

Had I lived in California he would have been my choice as I felt he was the best person to serve as governor of the state. But that was not in the cards. Despite the fact that Tom McClintock was by far, the more conservative, fiscally responsible candidate, and had the record to prove it, the California Republican Party embraced Arnold as "their guy" not because he was the best person for the job, but because he had the best chance of putting the Republicans back in the Governor's mansion.

I remember the enormous pressure people put on Tom McClintock to get out of the race during this time. Even the conservative media joined in. Shortly before the election national radio host, Sean Hannity interviewed Tom and spent most of the interview trying to convince Tom that it was in the best interest of the Republican Party to get out of the race stating that if he didn't he could split the vote and give the election to the Democrats. I have often wondered how many voters bought into this argument and decided to change their vote during that election for the "good of the party".

Despite all the mounting pressure, Tom McClintock courageously stood his ground and stayed in the race stating that there were too many people counting on him and he would not disappoint them simply for the sake of a party. Tom understood the importance of the electoral process and he respected the voice and will of the people. Would Tom McClintock have continued to fight for the people of California had he won the election? Who knows. Maybe he would have ended up becoming as corrupt as all the other politicians. Since he didn't win the election we will never know. But the point is, the people of California had the right to find out for themselves. *They* had the right to decide who they would vote for—not a party and not the media.

When a party limits our choices by forcing people out of the race and the media refuses to recognize them as "viable" candidates, they take our voice away. There were 1,161,287 Californians who would have lost their voice in the California recall if Tom had bowed out of the race. Whether we win or lose isn't near as important as whether or not we are heard. Sure we'd like our candidates to win. But more than anything we want a voice. For 1,161,287 California voters, Tom McClintock was their voice in that election and no party, nor media outlet, has a right to silence their voice.

As we all now know, Arnold Schwarzenegger won that election and became governor of California. But what has the recall, voters fought so hard for, really done for the people of California? What has having a Republican in the Governor's office really changed? Things have actually gotten worse. California is bankrupt. They are so bankrupt that they had to steal from the citizens. Instead of receiving tax refund checks from the state they received I Owe You letters. Can you believe that? I Owe You letters! I think the people of California should send Sacramento a letter of their own.

> Dear Sirs,
> This letter is to inform you that we will not be paying state income taxes next year. As for the I Owe You, we'll just call it even.
> Sincerely,
> The People of California

I wonder what would have happened if more people had voted for Tom McClintock in that special election. Would he have won? Probably not. Would his supporters have split the vote? Maybe. But at least they would have had the peace of mind to know they voted their conscience—to know they took a stand and didn't compromise their principles. Isn't that the kind of integrity we expect of our elected leaders? Shouldn't we demand the same integrity from ourselves?

Our vote is never "wasted" when we research the candidates and vote our conscience. If we stick to it and keep voting our conscience eventually the tide will turn and we will start winning elections, but if we keep buying the lie we are just digging the hole we are in even deeper. And really, how much worse could the people of California have done with a Democrat governor? Corruption is corruption no matter what Party name you wear and there is plenty of corruption going around in both parties.

A few years ago I sat in the office of a high-ranking member in the Ohio State Legislature who happened to be a Republican. The legislator was the chairman of a committee that was about to vote on a bill I was strongly opposed to. As I discussed all the negative aspects of the bill with the committee chairman he listened and nodded frequently.

"I know everything you're saying is true," he said, "but the committee is meeting this afternoon and the bill is going to pass."

I was stunned. "You know this bill is going to cost the taxpayers an enormous amount of money," I said, "and not accomplish any of the objectives you set out to address and you are *still* going to pass it?"

"That's right," he said, "because if we don't the media will massacre us and the Democrats are just waiting in the wings to say we don't care enough to pass this bill."

I was completely befuddled. What do you say to that? Finally I was able to compose myself enough to speak. "Are you telling me that you are going to spend millions of dollars of the taxpayer's money on a bill that will hurt Ohio families so you can save face in the media and keep the Republican majority in the statehouse?"

"Well," he countered, "that's not exactly how I'd put it."

"Well, Sir, that is exactly how I'd put it. And when the people of Ohio find out what you're doing they will never stand for it."

The legislator leaned back and chuckled under his breath. "The people of Ohio don't care," he said, "No one pays attention to anything that goes on up here."

"I'm paying attention," I said. "These people elected you to represent them. If you vote for this they won't re-elect you."

The legislator leaned forward on his desk. "Voters don't pay any attention until a month before an election and as you can see from the calendar, we have plenty of time before we have to worry about that."

True to his word the bill passed committee that afternoon and for weeks I watched as it went back and forth from the House and Senate committees and then in the fall of that year it hit both floors for a vote and passed, almost unanimously in both houses. That is what Party politics have done to our nation. Our elected leaders count on the fact that we are not paying attention. And even when we do get involved in something like opposing national healthcare, government bailouts, stimulus bills, or illegal immigration we have to yell at the top of our lungs just to be heard by our own representatives—the very people we elected speak for us.

Believe me, I understand your frustrations. I don't understand why the American people have to spend hours of our valuable time and hard earned money (what Congress leaves to us that is) to print flyers, make phone calls and start organizations just so we can be heard on Capitol Hill. We shouldn't have to spend all this time and money to combat tyranny and oppression. Our elected leaders are supposed to be doing that *for* us. That is what we elected them for. But unfortunately, they are the very ones who have become the tyrants.

I don't know if any of you have ever had a chance to walk through a congressional building, or even your statehouse, but if it is at all possible, I strongly encourage you to do so. There is nothing like walking through the halls of Congress to get a clear picture of why it is so hard for our voice to be heard. It doesn't matter which office building you visit. Any one will do. They're all the same. You don't even have to talk to anyone.

Just walk through the halls—not on a tour, on your own. Yes, it's legal! Just walk through the halls and observe. It will only take a few minutes for you to understand why so many people refer to the U.S. Capital as "the Beltway Bubble". That is exactly what it feels like—a whole other universe surrounded by an invisible dome. It's like watching ants.

My children and I visited our local science center a few years ago where they had a whole ant colony on display in a glass case. It was fascinating watching the ants marching to some silent drum walking in rows throughout the myriad of tunnels that made up their world. We watched the ants for over an hour going through the same tasks and walking the same paths. Nothing ever changed. They just kept doing the same things over and over again and didn't even seem to realize there was a whole world outside of their own.

The only ants that *did* seem to notice the world outside of their small mound of dirt were the ones that streamed back and forth, in search of food, through the long tube that led to the woods outside the science center. It was amazing. There in that little casing was an entire ant world. The ants were completely oblivious to the fact that they were only a very small part of a much bigger world just outside. They didn't even notice my son tapping on the glass. They just kept marching to that silent drum as if that little mound of dirt was all there was.

That is exactly how I felt walking through the halls of Congress. It's a whole little world of isolated halls and chambers—aides and interns marching back and forth, offices filled with little workers all doing their own thing while they carefully shield the members of Congress from the outside world like the ants protect their queen. And the only time anyone leaves the bubble is when they have to go out and get votes so they continue to survive in the bubble. Other than that, they just go on marching to their silent drum; having their little luncheons, working their little deals, playing with their little friends, and they don't even notice us when we tap on the glass.

The *state* legislative office buildings aren't much different. There are just fewer ants marching, a lot less European vacations, and it is a little easier to get through the protective shield. State office is like Minor League Baseball—training camp for the big leagues. And there are a lot of people joining the league in hopes of someday living in the bubble themselves.

Last year I visited Washington D.C. and spent three months trying to get appointments with my Senators and Congressman to discuss a bill. After three months I could only get one appointment with an actual member of Congress. The rest were with aides. And when I finally got to D.C. the one in-person appointment I had cancelled—even though I confirmed several times including the day before I arrived. It should not be this hard to meet with the people we elect to represent us. It should not be this hard to have our voice heard. We can't get Congress to build a fence on our borders but they've certainly been very successful in building an invisible fence around *themselves*.

As I walked through the congressional office buildings that day it was like a little kid who just disturbed an ant colony. I interrupted their silent drum and disrupted their rhythm. When I showed up for my appointments I felt like the woman who just walked in an exclusive men's cigar club and everyone was looking at me like "how dare you come in here". And the worst part is—not only are you treated that way but you have to go all the way to D.C. for it. Our representatives spend more time in foreign countries than they do their own districts. And we're paying for it. Not only that, we are paying for their entourage of gatekeepers whose job it is to keep us at bay.

There are more *non*-elected people running Washington than there are elected. Each Senator and Representative has a team of aides, staff, and interns that answer phones, open mail, schedule appointments, respond to emails, read and write bills, give advice, and meet with constituents. So what exactly do the Congressmen and Senators do you ask? Good question. The fact is, they have so many people working for them to do all things we elected *them* to do that they don't have to do anything at all. Basically, we pay them to live the carefree life of the rich and famous spending their days at luncheons, dinner parties, and cultural events where they are distinguished as "honorable", lavished with luxury, and given gifts like trips to Hawaii and European vacations, all funded by one special interest group or another, in hopes of winning a contract, bailing out their company, or getting their pet project funded.

Congress are the purse keepers and there are plenty of people pulling the purse strings willing to beg, borrow and bribe, their way to a piece of the American pie. So while we are angry with Congress for passing stimulus bills and bailouts the truth is, they aren't doing it at all—their aides are. While Congress is jet-setting around the world and taking their wives and children on Paris vacations (which we pay for), their little minions are back home writing bills, reading the bills up for vote, advising the Senator or Congressman on *how* to vote, and hanging out with all the other minions who are doing the same. All the members of Congress have to do is show up and vote. They don't even have to think. They have people for that too. It is the thousands of aides and staffers that run our government and write these bills not the people we elected. And we are footing the bill for the whole convoluted mess.

Larry Schweikart, a bestselling author and friend of mine suggested a great idea to remedy this situation. In a speech he gave at a Dayton Ohio Tea Party, July 3, 2009, Larry said,

> "We've got about 10,000 to 1 unelected representatives in Washington to every elected representative. Folks, those are the people who are really making your laws. You wonder why they don't read the bills, they don't even write the bills. These [unelected representatives] are the guys writing your bills. They're the ones passing all this ridiculous legislation, they do all the research, they do all the work and Senator Foghorn Leghorn shows up and signs his John Henry on the bill and pats himself on the back. And that ain't right. So here's how we can fix that. We need a Constitutional Amendment that limits the number of staffers for every Congressman and Senator to two! They can answer their own damn phones. They can talk to their own constituents. They can write their own letters and they can read their own bills!"

What a concept. Just having to read and write their own bills would slow Congress down so much it would take them years to push all this garbage through. And can you imagine what would happen if members of Congress suddenly had to answer their own phones, write their own letters and talk to their own constituents? They wouldn't have time to attend all those luncheons and dinner parties with special interest groups. They'd be too busy talking to us. We'd finally get our money's worth and save a bunch of money to boot, on all the aides and staffers we'd no longer be paying for. That ought to pop the D.C. bubble.

Bottom line is, it just doesn't matter which party you are anymore. Once elected to Congress you are admitted into that exclusive club, the shield goes up, and the door closes on the people that elected them. And once those doors close Congress is free to do whatever they want because they know we are too far away, and too busy with our own lives, taking care of our own families, to do anything about it. And so they take advantage of the trust we have placed in them and pass laws left and right giving themselves more power while whittling away at the very freedom we elected them to protect. Gideon J. Tucker couldn't have stated it more accurately when he said, "No man's life, liberty, or property are safe while the legislature is in session." [1]

It is time we started banging on those closed legislative doors and remind our elected leaders that we are here. It is time we break up their exclusive club. And it is time we stopped allowing the media to convince us that this is the way things are and the way they will always be. In America the people rule. We don't have to do it *their* way. We elect them to do it *our* way. It is time we started learning from the past instead of reliving it over and over again. If we want real change, if we really want our voice heard, we are going to have to start by pulling our support from an exclusive club of Party politics. I know for many of us that will be hard but it is a price we must be willing to pay if we want our voice heard.

When elections are limited to parties it seriously reduces our options and as voters become more and more frustrated with these limited options, we do the best we can to operate within the status quo—hoping our voice will eventually be heard. Under these conditions we have the three basic options. One is to just throw our hands in the air and ignore the whole mess saying we "can't stand politics"—the *bury your head in the sand* strategy. The second option is to continue to vote party lines hoping it will all work out in the end—the *playing craps* strategy. Maybe we'll get lucky and get a good candidate this time. Though we know the odds aren't good we play them anyway.

Then there's the third option—*playing musical parties*. When we are unhappy with the way things are going under one party, we vote for the other one. That happened in a big way in 1994 when Republicans were voted into the majority; and then again in 2006 when, after twelve years of doing the exact opposite of what they promised in 1994, the Republicans lost the majority to the Democrats. All of these options are counter-productive and none of them will give voters what we want—a voice.

In the last few elections voters have used *all* of the above options but in the 2006 and 2008 elections they favored the *playing musical parties* strategy hoping to change a system of corruption by voting *against* a party.

I remember the climate of the 2006 election very well. People were angry. They came to the polls not to vote for a candidate, but to vote *out* a party. Many voters came and voted Democrat strait down the ballot—not because they agreed with the Democrats but because they were fed up with Republicans and wanted to teach them a lesson. The American people felt no one was listening to them or representing their interests and they didn't know any other way to be heard. There were even talk radio hosts suggesting voters do that very thing. "If you don't like what Republicans are doing," they'd say, "then teach them a lesson and vote the whole lot of them out in the next election." And that is just what the people did. It was a bad year for Republicans. But the message voters wanted to send was *not* the message received by the Parties.

The Democrats decided the reason they won the majority was because Americans embraced their agenda (which includes higher taxes, more government, abortion on demand, and reducing the military). Not likely.

Republicans decided they lost because they weren't "moderate" enough and concluded they needed to move more toward the "middle" to gain their power back. The last thing the American people need is more fence riders who will sway whichever way the wind blows to secure their "career". But that is exactly what we got in 2008 when, after another dog and pony show primary (which is all they are anymore), Republicans were left with a moderate who consistently "crosses the aisle" and prides himself in ignoring the will of the people by being a "maverick".

After the Democrat three-ring circus finally ended (with several deals cut I'm sure) the American people were presented with two self-serving, mediocre candidates for the showcase showdown. And that's pretty much how I feel about the whole convoluted, color-coded process of party politics. And I for one am done playing this ridiculous game. It is high time we end this charade and stop allowing the media, an out of control Congress, and a bunch of interns looking to further their career in a system of corruption, to dictate how the electoral process is going to run. *We **don't** have to play by their rules.* There *is* a better way but that better way will mean thinking outside the "Party" box.

We have to stop supporting the parties. I know there are a lot of people who cringe when I say that but what has the two party system really done for us? Does it really matter anymore which party holds the majority in Congress to anyone but the Parties themselves? Does either of them represent us? Does either of them hear us?

I am tired of being ignored by those who have been elected to represent us. And I know I am not alone because if I were there would not be thousands of people all over the nation attending Tea Parties, going to town halls, and marching on DC trying to get Congress to listen to us. And while many people believe a change of party is the answer, I can assure you the corruption doesn't stop at party lines.

I remember watching C-SPAN during the Senate debates on the Stimulus Bill in February of 2009. I watched as Republican Congressman John Boehner gave the most powerful, riveting speech I have ever seen on the floor of Congress. He slammed the 670 page stimulus bill to the floor explaining how bad it was for the people of America. In the middle of cheering him on I suddenly stopped and realized this was the very same Congressman who spent weeks just four months earlier doing everything he could to convince Republican members of Congress to pass the TARP.

So I have to wonder, was he and all those other Republicans decrying the stimulus opposed to the bill because it is wrong or because it was introduced by a Democrat? Is it really the *amount* of perpetual debt being heaped on the people of this country or is the issue really whose name is on it?

And what about the Democrats? They spent eight years whining and caterwauling about the national debt and how President Bush was adding to it, but when President Obama introduced a $787 billion increase to the national debt that was okay because he's a Democrat? Where is the integrity here? Either something is wrong or it isn't.

The problems our country faces are not Democrat or Republican. The corruption crosses the isle and is deeply embedded at all levels of government. We cannot solve the problems facing our nation by playing party games. It is time we said enough is enough. We have tried the changing of the guard. It doesn't work. There is no longer any difference in the parties. They may look different on paper but in practice, they are virtually the same. And neither party is representing the American people.

President George Washington warned us of this very thing. He was almost prophetic in his farewell address when he warned, "[parties] serve to organize faction, to give it an artificial and extraordinary force; to put, in the place of the delegated will of the nation the will of a party".

Isn't that exactly what has happened? If a candidate runs under a certain party they feel they owe allegiance to that party. When a Republican President wants a bill passed, the Republican members of Congress are expected to fall in line and support it—even if their constituents don't. They are expected to be a "team player" and "support the party". Apparently that means "to heck with the people". A good example of this was when President Bush wanted his comprehensive immigration bill passed and *we the people* had to spend weeks deluging the phone lines of our Senators and Representatives just to get them to listen to us and it still almost passed.

But Republicans aren't the only ones pushing this required "allegiance". Democrats are just as guilty. There were plenty of Democrats who got a good talking to when they opposed a Democrat President's stimulus bill or when they dared oppose the National Healthcare plan. It's like they've formed camps. It never seems to matter *what* the bill or plan is being introduced, it only matters **who** is introducing it. If the Republicans introduce it the Democrats are opposed to it—even if it is in the best interest of the country. If the Democrats introduce it the Republicans are opposed to it—even if they passed a very similar bill just months before under a Republican President. The whole thing has become a joke, a game, and we are the ones losing.

President Washington clearly understood the dangers of party allegiance and felt it extremely important to repeatedly warn us against them. In his final address to a devoted nation he said,

> "Let me now…warn you in the most solemn manner against the baneful effects of the spirit of party… It serves always to distract the public councils and enfeeble the public administration. It agitates the community with ill-founded jealousies and false alarms, kindles the animosity of one part against another, foments occasionally riot and insurrection. It opens the door to foreign influence and corruption, which finds a facilitated access to the government itself through the channels of party passions. Thus the policy and the will of one country are subjected to the policy and will of another. [2]

This is happening right now. Our nation is trillions of dollars in debt and a large portion of that debt is owned by China. Do you not think that puts our country in a position where we are subjected to the policy of another country? And while the Democrats went crazy over this fact in the fall of 2008 when the Republicans were passing their $700 billion bailout bill, it didn't seem to bother them at all when they passed theirs in January of 2009 putting our country even deeper in debt to China.

If Congress were truly acting in the best interests of the nation and the American people they would realize the danger of another country holding this much leverage over our own. All China has to do is get mad at something we do and call in the debt and our economy collapses. Our nation is being held hostage by a communist country—who doesn't even like us—because the greedy, power-hungry men and women we elected to represent us wanted more money and power. Do you *feel* represented?

The people of America were seeking change in the 2008 election. We were promised accountability and transparency. We were told things would change with a new Party in power. Nothing has changed.

There *is* no accountability in Congress. There *is* no transparency. And the only way we are going to get it is to vote *both* parties out of power. It is time we stop voting based on a letter on a ballot and started voting our conscience. It is time we vote for people not parties and issues not politics. We don't need any more *politicians* in Washington or anywhere else in this country. We need *statesman*—men and women who understand the fundamental principles and guiding values this nation was founded on—men and women who have the courage to stand up for those principles no matter what the cost.

Elected office is not an occupation it is an act of service. Those who are elected are *servants of the people* not the other way around. They serve *us*. We the people are *their* boss. We hired them and we can fire them. And it is high time we did. We need an almost complete overhaul in Congress. We need to stop the trend of Senators 'til death. The longer they are in Washington the more corruptible they become and the more power they have to infect any new leadership we elect. Nothing will *change* as long Congress stays the same.

I know many people are suggesting that change will come with term limits but that is not the answer. Term limits may be used as a *part* of the solution but it is not ***the*** *solution*—we are! We are the only ones who can fix this mess. We need to stop legislating our responsibilities away and start taking responsibility for our own government. I live in a state with that thought term limits was the solution and I can assure you, it didn't stop the corruption, it just made it more creative.

We already have term limits in our nation. Every two years we get a chance to tell our representatives how we feel. We already *have* the power to limit their time in office. We need to use it! And we need to stop relying on the parties for our candidates. We need to seek out our own.

I know, I know, that brings us back to those *two* choices again. Well, there is something you can do about that to. You don't have to limit yourself to two choices. You have options. If you want to stick with the party route, fine. Then get involved in your Party committees and vote in the Primary elections. Research the candidates running and vote for the one that best represents you. You can still have a voice if you just can't seem to stomach leaving your Party, but if you're ready to take a *real* leap, that will lead to *real* change, you will need to open your mind to a whole new way of thinking where you stop buying into the notion that you are throwing your vote away if you don't support one of the two parties. You can stop voting the lesser of evils and vote your conscience. Maybe the Republican candidate *is* the best choice; maybe the Democrat is, but what about when neither of them is worth voting for?

Some have suggested the *third party* option is the answer, but I cannot advise strongly enough *against* this. Sweeping change is *not* the answer. Adding another party to the mix for the sake of voting the other two out will only add another color to the pallet. It will not stop the oppression.

Let's say, in our utter frustration and anger, we *do* go to the polls on Election Day and vote Third Party straight down the ballot. Do you really think that Third Party would be better than the other two? Maybe for a short time but in the long term the only change we would get is three parties acting like bickering children fighting for power instead of two. Not only that, we would lose good people in the mix. The number may be few, but there *are* good people serving in Congress. If we vote someone like Congressman Jim Jordan out of office just for the sake of change we would lose a good man and may end up with someone like Arlen Specter instead. It is not worth the trade. The answer is *not* to vote another Party into power hoping things will change this time. The answer is to vote **no** Party.

It is time we stopped taking the easy way out. We need to stop voting by letters like preschoolers color by numbers. Instead of looking at candidates by what Party they represent we need to start looking at the candidates themselves. It shouldn't matter what Party they are with, or whether they are with one at all. It should only matter who the candidate is and where he or she stands on the issues. And it shouldn't matter what color or sex they are.

I am not going to vote for a woman simply because she is a woman. I am not going to vote for a white man just because he is white. For me, elections have never been a matter of gender, religion, or race. I care about *who* the person is not *what* the person is—or what Party they are with. I care how they vote. I care about their character. John Adams once said, "Liberty cannot be preserved without a general knowledge among the people, who have…a right, an indisputable, unalienable, indefeasible, divine right to that most dreaded and envied kind of knowledge, I mean the characters and conduct of their rulers."

Despite what many elected officials seem to think, character *does* count—for me it counts even more than experience. Washington has shown us what "experience" provides and I am not impressed. In fact, in many cases I find the claim of "experience" more a detriment than an advantage.

I attended a town hall meeting a few months ago where a woman shared her passionate plea. "We need people with character who we can vote for," she said. "We need people who understand what it means to raise a family and support a home. We need people who know what it's like to try and run a small business, balance a checkbook, or live within a budget. We need people who know what it's like to work hard. We *need* people who will represent the middle class!"

To which I responded, "Then that, Ma'am, is who we need to be voting for."

"But where are they?" she asked. "Where can we find them?"

For all those of you out there, who like myself, have wondered that same thing, let me tell you where they are. **We are them**. If we want a candidate who represents the middle class then we need to vote for someone from the middle class. If we want someone who understands the challenges of small business ownership then we need to vote for someone who owns a small business. We are the very people we want in office so we should consider running ourselves. And when one of us does, we need to stand by them and not allow the media to convince us we shouldn't vote for them because they don't have "experience." We don't need the kind experience Washington offers. We don't need more people who know how to play the system. We need people who go against it. We don't need people who are experienced in status quo. We need people who will break free of it.

Just what kind of experience are you looking for? Do you want the person who has twelve years of experience recklessly spending taxpayer's money and creatively cooking the books, or someone who has twelve years of experience balancing the family checkbook and living within a budget? Do you want someone who was "groomed" for politics and learned how to manipulate the law, or do you want someone who came into public service out of a desire to serve and concern that the law remain just? It's really pretty simple when you think about it. We are more experienced than most of the people in Washington because we live in the real world, not an inflated bubble full of champagne and caviar. We know what experience really means because we *experience* it every day.

I want candidates who know that the issues we face are not left or right, Republican or Democrat—candidates who know and respect the American ideals that our Founding Families died for, and so many are still willing to give their lives to protect. I want candidates with integrity who will put principles and values before Party. I want candidates who have the courage to stand up and say, in all sincerity, "I owe my allegiance to NO Party! My allegiance lies with the people!"

We need leaders with integrity and moral character who are willing to sacrifice their lives, fortunes and sacred honor for the public good—men and women who are committed to fighting for a cause that is *greater* than themselves.

We need to refrain, however, from looking for that *perfect* candidate because they don't exist. And we need to stop lamenting that we do not have a Reagan to choose from. There will never be another Reagan because he was one of a kind. And we need to clear up the fallacy right here and now that President Reagan was perfect. No president, no candidate, is *ever* perfect. The reason we all loved Ronald Reagan so much was not because he introduced conservative ideas. His ideas were *not* new. Our Founding Fathers *built* this nation on them. What *was* new was that President Reagan had the courage, fortitude and tenacity to embrace those ideals, even when it wasn't popular; and fight for them, even when it meant going against the flow—or a Party.

We loved him because he took the time to reach out to the citizens of this country and remind us just how great those ideals are and what a remarkable privilege it is to be an American. I have been in the grassroots conservative movement for over ten years and I can tell you it is *that* kind of passion that excites the American people. The best thing about Ronald Reagan was that he was *not* an establishment candidate. He was the *people's* candidate. He didn't reach across the aisle; he stepped over it to reach the people. And that is what endeared us to him. The political establishment just caught the wave.

But it is not the establishment that knocks on hundreds of doors, leaves early from work to volunteer at phone banks, and spends hours in the rain on Election Day passing out voter guides. It is not the *establishment* that wins elections. It is the grass roots conservatives—the homemakers, homeschoolers, pro-lifers, fair-taxers, Tea Partiers, small business owners—the everyday, overtaxed, outspent, underappreciated passionate Americans just like you and me.

We will never agree with *everything* a candidate says or does. And they will make plenty of mistakes along the way—as do we all. Perfection will not exist until God reigns on this earth. We can't expect perfection, but we can choose the best of what there is. We don't need another Ronald Reagan. We just need someone who will embrace the same founding ideas *he* did and fight for them as *hard* as he did.

It is time we held Congress accountable to *we the people*. We can no longer tolerate a Congress that passes bills without reading them. We can no longer tolerate a Congress that disregards the Constitution and ignores the people.

Our financial system may collapse, the government may crumble but America never will because America is bigger than a government. It is American families united in purpose, filled with the spirit of Freedom. It is the spirit of the *people* that make America—the plane full of patriots that went down in a Pennsylvania field—the firefighters who walked into a crumbling building when everyone else was running out. The men and women sleeping in tents in 100 degree heat in Iraq and Afghanistan. It is the mothers' teaching their children, the small business owners fighting for their dream, and the children who place their hands over their hearts to pledge allegiance to the flag of the United States of America.

America isn't a President. It isn't Congress. It is us. It is *we the people*. We are the life blood of this nation and *we the people* will determine the future of it!

From Our Founders

Pray Heaven to bestow the best of blessing on this house, and on all that shall hereafter inhabit it. May none but honest and wise men ever rule under this roof!

~John Adams
(Written in a letter to his wife after moving into the White House)

Always vote for principle, though you may vote alone, and you may cherish the sweetest reflection that your vote is never lost.

~ John Quincy Adams

The natural cure for an ill-administration, in a popular or representative constitution, is a change of men.
~Alexander Hamilton

Because power corrupts, society's demands for moral authority and character increase as the importance of the position increases.
~John Adams

Were parties here divided merely by a greediness for office,…to take a part with either would be unworthy of a reasonable or moral man.
~Thomas Jefferson

If the citizens neglect their duty and place unprincipled men in office, the government will soon be corrupted; laws will be made not for the public good so much as for the selfish or local purposes
~Noah Webster

When a man assumes a public trust, he should consider himself as public property.
~Thomas Jefferson

What country can preserve its liberties, if its rulers are not warned from time to time that this people preserve the spirit of resistance?
~Thomas Jefferson

The two enemies of the people are criminals and government, so let us tie the second down with the chains of the Constitution so the second will not become the legalized version of the first.
~Thomas Jefferson

Other Notable Quotes

We, the people are the rightful masters of both Congress and the courts—not to overthrow the Constitution, but to overthrow men who pervert the Constitution.
~Abraham Lincoln

Kimberly Fletcher

In our land the people rule. The great truth cannot be too often repeated that this nation is exactly what the people make it. It is necessary to realize that our duties are personal.

~Calvin Coolidge

The purpose of a campaign is to send an intelligent and informed voter to the ballot box.

~Calvin Coolidge

Suggested Resources:
The Abigail Adams Project
Abigailadamsproject.org

RISE UP, YE WOMEN!

Tyranny, like hell, is not easily conquered; yet we have this consolation with us, that the harder the conflict, the more glorious the triumph.
~Thomas Paine

I would like to ask your indulgence while I take the time and space allotted in this chapter to address the women of faith who are reading this book. Since over 75 percent of the people of America define themselves as Christians, I felt it fitting to address the majority. Of course, all are welcome to read the contents of this chapter. But proceed at your own risk. God is mentioned here, the Bible is quoted, and Christian themes abound. It should be noted, however, that while the sources may be different, many religions (and I believe a vast majority of the American people) espouse many of the same values advocated in Christianity. And while the specific language in this chapter may be Christian in nature, the concepts outlined are universal. You can, of course, skip to the next chapter and just forget you ever stopped here. The choice is all yours.
Come on, you know you're curious.

About a year ago, I had a conversation with a friend from church. She had heard that I had started an organization called Homemakers for America and asked me what it was. So I shared our mission with her.

> Our mission is to foster an understanding, love, and respect for America's history and heritage, her founding principles and values, her legacy and destiny, and build a nation of informed citizens and devoted patriots one woman and one family at a time.

When my friend finished reading the mission statement, she said, "Oh, I didn't know it was political. I don't get involved in politics."

I was confused as to how she thought preserving freedom and building a nation of informed citizens was political, and she went on to explain that politics was too cynical and petty, full of mudslinging and accusations. "I just don't get involved in that," she said.

Again, I was confused because political mudslinging has nothing to do with the mission and purpose of Homemakers for America. As I conversed further with my friend, I realized that the reason she, like so many Christians, doesn't get involved in elections or public policy issues is because we are confusing civic responsibility with politics, and they are *not* the same thing.

Politics is a product of pride, worldliness, and a lust for power. That is why so many of us cringe when we hear the word "politician" and look down our noses on the profession as beneath us—and it is. But politics is not what I am addressing here—civic responsibility is, and there *is* a difference.

Civic responsibility is that duty which every American has as a citizen of this country, to respect the law, preserve the U.S. Constitution, be involved in our communities, safeguard the Republic, watch over our government, and seek out and elect good leaders to represent us. Politics is the result of what happens when not enough of us *fulfill* that duty.

So that leads us to the perpetrators of politics—the politicians!

A politician is a person who lusts for power, is obsessed with self-importance and motivated by greed. Politicians have been groomed in politics. They learn the artful craftiness of deceit, the clever tactics of scheming to get gain and win votes, and the cunning methods of distraction, distortion, denial, and blame-shifting. Politicians will say and do whatever it takes to keep and add to their power. They are motivated by self-preservation and personal gain, and put their own interests above the people they serve. Politicians will vote for anything they feel benefits them, regardless of how their constituents feel or whether or not it is in the best interest of the country. Politicians are self-serving individuals who hold little regard for God or country and feel no loyalty or affection for the people they serve. Not very Christ-like attributes, are they?

A statesman, on the other hand, is a person of integrity and high moral character, who possesses a strong desire to serve others, recognizes his or her imperfections and strives to overcome them to be the best person he or she can be. Statesmen have been trained in humanity. They learn the moral code of right and wrong, the positive attributes of honesty, humility, patriotism, accepting responsibility, and the selfless standards of love thy neighbor, the Golden Rule, and country before self.

Statesmen are people of faith who believe in a Supreme Being and a future state of rewards and punishments. They research issues carefully and do their best to vote in the best interest of the Republic and the people they represent—even if it means losing votes.

Statesmen cherish freedom and liberty, have a deep affection and concern for those they serve, and feel a profound sense of duty and loyalty to their country. They live their faith, reverence God, and respect the faith of others.

Perhaps you feel I am oversimplifying in my definitions. Perhaps you are thinking I am too harsh on politicians. That is possible. I am sure there are politicians who possess some of the characters of a statesman and I know there are statesmen who fall prey to politics, but we must ask ourselves, are we willing to settle for mediocre? Is 80 percent statesman good enough? Well, how do you feel about your husband or wife being 80 percent faithful? I want a husband who is 100 percent faithful, and I want my elected officials to be 100 percent for the Constitution and the Republic. It is important that we clearly understand the difference between civic responsibility and politics, because politics is what is tearing this country down, and we need a major infusion of civic responsibility to save it. Just look at all the issues that have been politicized today. Marriage has become a political issue. God has become a political issue. Even life is considered political. If Jesus were in America today, he would be considered the most political person on earth.

We have to separate civic duty from politics and politicians from statesmen, because if we don't, our vision will become blurry and we allow things like killing babies and homosexual marriage to turn into "freedom of choice" and "equality." We will allow "acceptance" to become synonymous with brotherly love. And sin will just become one of those things people do, like riding a bike or going to the grocery store.

Now that we have defined the differences in these two groups—politicians and statesmen—we need to ask ourselves, as Christians, which one of these groups deserves our time and attentions? The answer is both of them, but you need to see the big picture to understand why.

In February of 2005, Bill Maher, host of *Politically Incorrect,* appeared on *Scarborough Country* and stated the following:

> We are a nation that is unenlightened because of religion. I do believe that. I think that religion stops people from thinking. I think it justifies crazies. I think flying planes into a building was a faith-based initiative. I think religion is a neurological disorder. If you look at it logically, it's something that was drilled into your head when you were a small child. It certainly was drilled into mine at that age. And you really can't be responsible when you are a kid for what adults put into your head.[1]

There is so much in that short statement that sheds great light on what we are facing today in our nation. I am not going to analyze Mr. Maher's statement for you. But if you came away with the idea that he is calling you insane, brainwashed, illogical, and a general threat to our nation because you believe in God, you would be right.

There are a lot of people who are trying desperately to convince us there is no God and religion is either a ridiculous waste of time or an enemy to humanity—or both. Just look at all the people who are attacked for even mentioning the phrase "intelligent design." With so much scientific evidence pointing to an intelligent designer, why would we not be including it in science lessons? Why are scientists, teachers, and anyone else who even questions evolution attacked for going against the "establishment"? Aren't freedom of thought and freedom to express ideas what science is all about? Why is there such a monumental effort to suppress even the mere mention of the idea of an intelligent designer? And why is the theory of evolution presented as irrefutable fact when there is so much scientific evidence that questions the validity of it? Ben Stein sought out to find the answers to these very questions in his movie, *Expelled*. I cannot recommend strongly enough that you take the time to see this movie.

Expelled is a riveting documentary that interviews several qualified professionals on the matter of evolution versus intelligent design. The evolutionists and scientists in the movie were very open and honest about their ideas and feelings on the subject, even going so far as to state that it was their study of evolution that led them to atheism.

One of the evolutionists, Will Provine, who is a professor of biology at Cornell University, said that he was a Christian and had never heard anything about evolution because it was illegal to teach it in Tennessee when he was in school. Once he entered college, however, he found that his biology class taught nothing *but* evolution. When he questioned his professor as to why God was not mentioned in the material presented, his professor challenged him to study the class textbook and materials and see if he could find any evidence of an intelligent designer. Professor Provine took the challenge and stated that he searched through the book but could find no evidence whatsoever of an intelligent designer, and he immediately began to question the existence of deity.

Dr. Provine said, "First you give up the idea of deity. Then that there's life after death. When you give those two up the rest of it follows very easily. You give up the hope that there's an eminent morality and finally there's no human free will. If you believe in evolution you can't hope there would be any free will. There's no hope whatsoever of there being any deep meaning in human life. We live, we die, and we're gone."[2]

I cannot even imagine going through life that way. How very sad that man must be. But what is even worse is that this man is a professor of biology at a major university, using his position to promote atheism in the name of science and poisoning the minds of thousands of young, impressionable students with his anti-God bias. But Professor Provine isn't the only one trying to convince our children to deny God and give up religion. There is a whole army of people out there trying to win our children over to the dark side. Bill Maher is one of them, as you can tell from his own statement:

> When people say to me, "You hate America," I don't hate America. I love America. I am just embarrassed that it has been taken over by people like evangelicals, by people who do not believe in science and rationality. It is the twenty-first century. And I will tell you, my friend. The future does not belong to the evangelicals. The future does not belong to religion.[3]

So who does the future belong to then, you ask? According to one of the scientists in Ben Stein's movie, it belongs to science. This "enlightened" scientist said science would gradually replace religion, little by little, until religion doesn't affect our lives anymore. He compared religion to a hobby like knitting and said as scientific ideas are brought more and more into society, religion will eventually reach the level that it *should* be—just something fun that people get together and do on the weekend.

You may be thinking to yourself, these people must not understand the purpose of religion. They just must not understand that worshipping God is what makes us better people and gives us purpose in your lives. Oh, I assure you, they already know this. Evolutionists know the kind of influence religion and God have in our lives, and they don't like it. It is not enough for them to have their *own* beliefs; they want to force *us* into believing it too. That is why they are preaching evolution like a religion in our schools. Professor Provine clearly understands what religion is about when he preaches against it.

> No God, no life after death, no ultimate foundation for ethics, no ultimate meaning in life and no human free will. We're all deeply connected to an evolutionary perspective. You're here today and you're gone tomorrow and that's all there is to it.[4]

I know it is hard to understand how someone could be filled with so much emptiness, disdain, and contempt, but it does explain how people can so easily justify and promote the taking of human life. It does explain the thoughtless killing of millions of Jews. It does explain the cavalier approach to genocide. It does explain the calculated, systematic murder of thousands of innocent people simply for the purpose of "cleansing the race" of impurities and imperfections. And it does explain why millions of babies were murdered for convenience.

If there is no meaning in life, then life has no value. If there is no Supreme Being, then we feel justified in playing God. If there is no free will, we accept no responsibility for our actions. If there is no future state of rewards and punishments, then we have no reason to be decent. If there is no life after death, why would we care about anything but ourselves and how much power and wealth we can amass before we die? And why would we care how we got it or who we step on in the process? If there is nothing more than here and now, then *that* is what we live for. Life would be nothing more than a self-indulgent party—eat, drink, and be merry, for tomorrow we die. What would America be like then? Tragically, we are well on our way to finding out.

There is a new rage among Christians today; it is known as "all truth," and it is infecting our youth. I had a conversation with a young college student not too long ago who introduced me to this new fad. I invited the young woman—who was a faithful Christian—to Viva la Vita, the annual fundraiser for Dayton Right to Life.

"Oh, I don't get involved in politics," the young woman said when I invited her.

"This isn't politics," I said, "it is a wonderful night of entertainment where you can meet good people and support a great cause."

"Well," she said, "Right to Life is a political organization, and I don't support political organizations."

"Dayton Right to Life isn't a political organization," I explained. "It is a non-profit foundation dedicated to preserving life and helping young mothers who decide to keep their babies. Dayton Right to Life provides resources, services, and educational programs that teach people about what abortion is and the alternatives to having one."

"I know that's *your* truth," she said, "but I accept *all* truth."

"What are you talking about?" I asked.

"You believe that abortion is wrong, and that is *your* truth. Others believe that abortion is right, and that is *their* truth. I embrace *all* truth."

"What do you mean you embrace *all* truth?" I asked, a bit confused.

"I mean I respect your truth and I respect their truth."

"But what is *your* truth? What do *you* believe?"

"I believe in embracing all truth."

"So you don't believe in *anything?*"

"Sure I do. I believe in an individual's right to seek out and accept their own truth."

"And you don't have a position on which 'truth' is right. I mean, if someone tells you the grass is purple, are you going to accept that as truth?"

"I would accept it as *their* truth."

"But grass isn't purple, it's green! Are you saying that you would just accept grass is purple because someone said it was?"

"I would accept that they believed it."

"Beliefs and truth are not the same thing. Believing something doesn't make it true. The grass can't be green *and* purple. Either it is green or it is purple. They can't both be right."

"What if the person looking at the grass is color blind?"

"What?"

"What if the person sees grass as purple because they are color blind?"

"Then you, as the person who *isn't* color blind, have a responsibility to teach the color blind person that the grass is *green* and not purple, so he doesn't go through his whole life telling people grass is purple and looking like an idiot. Just because a blind person can't see the nose on their face doesn't mean it isn't there. Truth is not all-encompassing. *Everything* can't be true. The grass can't be green *and* purple. There can only be *one* truth."

"But whose truth?"

"What?"

"Who decides what the colors are? Who decides that grass is green? In Mexico, people say grass is *verde*. So should I tell them they are wrong because grass is green?"

"No, you just explain that it is a different word for the same the color. It doesn't change what grass looks like. Truth is not universal, but there are universal truths. Grass is grass whether you're in Mexico or America. It doesn't matter if you're in France, Germany, Japan, or Zimbabwe, grass still looks like grass. If you tried to tell a Mexican grass is *morado,* they'd think you were just as nutty as the American who says grass is purple. The words may be different, but it doesn't change the color. It doesn't change the fact that grass is green and there can only be one truth."

I could see the gears turning in the young woman's head, and I finally thought I was getting through to her, when she suddenly looked at me smiling and said, "That was a bad example."

"No," I said, "it was a great example. It shows how easily a person can be manipulated and deceived when they are blinded from truth. Just imagine how easy it would be to convince someone who was blind that grass is purple. Embracing all truth simply means that we are not willing to seek out what is true. Whether we are talking about grass or abortion, it is our responsibility to seek out the truth and then stand up for that truth. Both positions can't be right. They can't both be true. Either abortion is killing babies or it isn't. Either you believe in preserving life or you don't."

"I don't believe in taking sides," the woman answered. "I believe in respecting both sides."

At this point, my mind was immediately drawn to the Scripture in Revelation 3:16: "So then because thou art lukewarm, and neither cold nor hot, I will spew thee out of my mouth."

"You know," I said, "there is going to come a time when you are going to have to get off the fence and choose whether the grass is green or purple and whether killing babies is right or wrong. Someday, you're going to have to decide whether you believe in the preservation of life or the propagation of death."

"I don't get involved in political issues."

"Life isn't political," I said, "it's self-evident."

"I understand that's *your* truth," she said.

Ugh! By this time my head was spinning from all her circling around, and realizing we were at a stalemate, I just smiled, wished her a good day, and went home to ponder on the experience. What I witnessed that day was the result of a culture of tolerance convincing us that we need to move beyond right and wrong, beyond good and evil, and beyond truth and falsehood. If truth is universal and all-encompassing, then there is no truth. If there is no truth, then right and wrong becomes a matter of opinion and good and evil unnecessary extremes.

So if we are then moving to a world where we embrace all truth, do we excuse a man who murders an innocent little girl, dismembers her body, and carelessly discards her remains because *his* truth was that it was okay? I mean, if we are embracing all truth, then there is no right and wrong, so the murder and dismemberment of a little girl is no big deal, right? Before you pass that off as a ridiculously grotesque example because nothing like that would ever happen, let me remind you—it already is. Every time a doctor cuts a baby out of a mother's womb piece by piece and drops the severed pieces into a metal pan, he is murdering a little girl or a little boy. But we don't call that murder; we call it reproductive healthcare and declare it a woman's right.

So if the people who are for abortion think it is so right, then why do they keep introducing new words to make it sound less offensive? Why do they hide it behind closed doors so no one will see what it really is? Why do they refer to it as a "medical procedure" and disguise it as "reproductive healthcare"? Why do they call it "pro-choice," and not pro-abortion? Why do they call it "a woman's right" instead of a baby's death? If they're so proud of what they're doing, why don't they just call it what it is—killing babies? But I guess that's just *my* truth, and "enlightened" people embrace all truth, right?

This is why we need to stay alert and informed in politics—not because we need to sling mud and play petty games—but because we need to expose them. We need to know what politicians are doing so we can stay alert, think clearly, and be aware of deceptions. The Bible warns us of this. "But evil men and seducers shall wax worse and worse, deceiving, and being deceived."[5] "And Jesus answered and said unto them, Take heed that no man deceive you."[6]

There has never been a time when we needed a discerning mind more than we do now. Truth is being twisted, right and wrong are being redefined, and the people of America are being conspired against on a grand scale. This is not a conspiracy theory, it is conspiracy fact. It is the greatest conspiracy of all, because it is being orchestrated by the greatest conspirator of all.

We are in the midst of the greatest war the world has ever known. It started in the beginning of time, before we were even born. It began with the war in heaven (Revelation 12:7–11) when Satan declared war on the souls of men and Cain marked the battle lines when he drew the first blood. Throughout the history of mankind, we have seen the devastating effects of this war. There have been casualties. Prices have been paid, bargains made, and lots cast. Battles have come and gone, but the war rages on, and with each passing generation, it escalates and intensifies.

Our battles today aren't as complicated as Democrats vs. Republicans, liberals vs. conservatives, or Americans vs. terrorists. We are in a war of good versus evil, and it is simply a matter of who *is* and who *isn't* on the Lord's side.

Since Cain and Abel, every civilization, every culture, and every people has been fighting the same war. The names, faces, and battlegrounds have changed, but Satan has always been at the helm. Ephesians 6:12 tells us, "For we wrestle not against flesh and blood, but against principalities, against powers, against the rulers of the darkness of this world, against spiritual wickedness in high places."

Satan reigns supreme on this earth. His evil works are apparent in countries all over the world. But there is one glimmer of hope in this dark and dreary world: it is the glorious light of America! The United States of America is the emblem of freedom for the entire world. Good people all over the earth are praying that America stays strong and remains free, for we are their hope of a brighter day. People who live under constant violence, tyranny, and oppression look to America and have hope that if freedom can live on in America, then freedom is possible for them too.

It is the American spirit of freedom that causes people from nations all over the world to rise up and stand for freedom in their own lands. It is *our* banner of freedom that burns deep in the hearts of God's children everywhere and gives them the courage to carry on. It is *our* banner of freedom that supplies food, medicine, and necessities we take for granted to the impoverished of the world. It is our banner of freedom that, with an outpouring of love, spreads the light of Christ to God's children in every corner of the earth. As long as America remains free, there is hope, but if freedom is lost and the United States of America falls into oppression, tyranny, and want, then the last bastion of hope for the world is lost.

America is Satan's last battleground. Once we realize this, we can clearly see why it is so important to preserve freedom and liberty at all cost. And God is counting on us to do it. We cannot feed the world if our own cupboards are bare. We cannot provide clothes and medicine if the government has regulated healthcare and restricted our industries. We cannot share the light of Christ if the government strips us of our freedom to worship. Don't you understand, everything we do to give hope and provide support to the people of the world we can do because we are free. There is no country on earth that is more generous than the United States, because the light of Christ still burns bright here. We are not just a nation of plenty; we are a nation with a deep desire to share our plenty with others, and it is freedom that makes it all possible.

Preserving freedom isn't a matter of politics; it is a matter of national survival—both physical and spiritual—not just for us but for the world. In 1831, the famous French historian Alexis de Tocqueville said: "I sought for the greatness and genius of America in her commodious harbors and her ample rivers, and it was not there; in her fertile fields and boundless prairies, and it was not there; in her rich mines and her vast world of commerce, and it was not there. Not until I went to the churches of America and heard her pulpits aflame with righteousness did I understand the secret of her genius and power. America is great because she is good, and if America ever ceases to be good, America will cease to be great."[6]

And that is why God and religion are under attack in our nation—because Satan knows that is where America's greatness lies. He knows if he can harden the hearts of the people and turn them from God, then he destroys America. And since the greatness comes from our churches—from the belief in God and the desire to live a Christ-like life—it is there that he puts his focus. He is targeting the family—most especially the Christian family—and the Christian church as a whole. That is why Satan has worked so hard to blur our vision with his deceptive tactics, hoping that if he confuses the issues, we will walk away from the fight altogether. And his plan is working. But it is not too late to turn the tide. We need to stand up and rub the fog of deception from our eyes.

America is *God's* design. Liberty is *His* plan. The Bible tells us, "But whoso looketh into the perfect law of liberty, and continueth therein, he being not a forgetful hearer, but a doer of the work, this man shall be blessed in his deed.[7]

Freedom for all is *God's* banner. And He is counting on His people to hold it up and sustain it. "Therefore thus saith the Lord; Ye have not hearkened unto me, in proclaiming liberty, everyone to his brother, and every man to his neighbor: behold, I proclaim a liberty for you."[8]

God is the great builder. Satan is the great destroyer. And since God was at the very foundation of this nation, it only stands to reason that Satan will use all his powers to tear it down. Politics is just one of his tools. Politics has nothing to do with preserving liberty. Politics is confusing, and God is not a God of confusion. Politics breeds contention, and contention is of the devil. Politics is full of anger, and God is a God of love. Politics is man's way, but God is counting on us to introduce *His* way. He is counting on us to seek truth and have the courage to stand up for truth in all things. He is counting on us to think straight and use the spirit of discernment. He is counting on us to get involved and have our voice heard. He is counting on us to seek out, elect, and support statesmen. He is counting on us to preserve freedom and sustain the Republic. And He is counting on us to pray for guidance and direction as we do it.

Now that you see the big picture, it puts a whole new perspective on things, doesn't it? Do you realize now why it is so important that we get involved? Do you understand why it is so important that we pay attention to what is going on around us? This has nothing to do with the National Organization for Women, or the ACLU or ACORN, or any group or individual trying to destroy God, freedom, and family. No matter what we call them—monarchists, politicians, progressives, or feminists—they are all just pawns in a much greater scheme. They are Satan's antagonists, propelling *his* agenda forward and they don't even know it—because *they* have been deceived. They have fallen into the trap of politics and have become consumed with a lust for power that clouds their vision and turns them even further away from the light of Christ.

1 John 1:5 tells us that "God is light, and in him is no darkness." John 3:19-21 further tells us, "And this is the condemnation, that light is come into the world, and men loved darkness rather than light, because their deeds were evil. For every one that doeth evil hateth the light, neither cometh to the light, lest his deeds should be reproved. But he that doeth truth cometh to the light, that his deeds may be made manifest, that they are wrought in God."

This is not a war against people. This is a fight against Satan and all the powers of darkness. Once we recognize that, it changes everything, because we know something very important. Unlike the antagonists of the world, we already know who *wins* this war—and it isn't them! Truth will prevail and the "devil that deceiveth the world" will be cast into a lake of fire and brimstone. (Revelation 12:9, 20:10) Satan will get in his licks, and we may lose some battles, but it is God who wins this war!

Knowing we are on the winning team gives us a whole new perspective, and the picture doesn't look so bleak anymore. Suddenly, all those battles that seemed so massive and unwinnable look like little skirmishes. All those walls that seemed impenetrable come tumbling down, and all those people who made us so angry just don't bother us anymore. Try it out for yourself.

When you read what Bill Maher said about religion, it made you mad, didn't it? You got hot under the collar and started yelling at words on a page, right? Now that you see the big picture and you know you are on the winning team, go back and read what he said again. Suddenly, instead of wanting to scream at the book, you just roll your eyes and give a big "whatever!" And when you read Professor Provine's words of pain and emptiness, you ache for his soul. These are our brothers and sisters. They need our prayers, not our anger. But that doesn't mean we condone or excuse their actions. If they want to sin in private, that's fine; it's their choice. But when they make their sins public, throw them in our faces, and demand we accept and even embrace those sins, we must draw the line. And we absolutely *cannot* allow them to infect our children with their lies under the pretense of educating them. We can no longer allow our children to be proselytized in atheism camouflaged as science.

We need to realize what our children are being exposed to and prepare them to face it. Every day our children go out to battle in the midst of this terrible war. Are we sending them out armed for battle? We would not send our children out the door in winter without a coat, so why in heaven's name would we send them out to battle against the forces of darkness completely unprotected? They need the whole armor of God to protect them. We can't just shield our children from the world; we have to prepare them to face it.

We need to not just *teach* our children about God, we need to help them gain a testimony of Him. You will not always be there to carry them. They will have to stand on their own, and they need to know how. They can lean on your faith and testimony for a while, but eventually they will have to gain their own, because if they don't, they could be led astray, just like Professor Provine was. We need to pray with our children and teach them how to pray themselves, so when they need direction when we're not there, they will know how to get it. And—I cannot stress this enough—please don't isolate your children from politics.

It is not enough to say abortion is wrong. Our children need to know it for themselves. We need to teach our children what the pro-choice people are saying. Talk about it, discuss it, share the arguments of the other side. Be open and truthful with them, show them the facts, and use the Word of God. They will see the truth and come to a firm understanding of that truth on their own, because we have taken the time to teach them. And when someone comes along and uses the "woman's right" argument, they will immediately realize it for the lie it is. When someone tries to convince them it is "political," they will know that life is not political but self-evident. Shielding our children from the lies will only make it easier for them to be deceived. We cannot shield them from the lies; we need to expose the lies.

Knowing now how dangerously toxic evolution is to one's faith, why would you ever send your children out in the world to find out about it there? I have a lot of friends who teach creation science and refuse to even mention evolution to their children. May I remind you that the first time Professor Provine heard about evolution was in college? We can't assume that just teaching creation is going to be enough to thwart off the fiery darts of Satan's evolution scam. We need to refute evolution early; and if your children are attending public school, you can't do it early enough.

From the time our children were very young, we started refuting evolution. We started by joking about it. We had an old picture book about a bunch of monkeys in a zoo that always got into mischief, and I'd say, "You know something funny? There are people who think we used to be monkeys. Isn't that silly?" As they got older, the conversations become more in-depth. We read books, had discussions, and even did research projects. By the time our children were in fifth and sixth grade, they had disproven evolution so many times, there was no way anyone was going to convince them it was true. We don't need to shield our children from science; we just need to approach it with the right perspective.

I really like Ken Ham's perspective. Ken Ham is the president of Answers in Genesis. A few years ago, I had the privilege of hearing him speak. Ken said people of faith tend to use science to explain the Bible, but that we should do exactly the opposite. Instead of trying to fit the Bible into science, we should start with the Bible when studying science. Then Ken asked an interesting question of the audience: "How many of you believe kangaroos once inhabited Turkey?"

A couple of hands slowly crept up. Then Ken asked the audience how many of them believed that a man named Noah built an ark, filled it with animals, floated in the ark for forty days and forty nights, and then landed in Turkey. The audience started to chatter among themselves. Ken asked the question again. Every hand went up. Then he made this profound statement, "I don't know how kangaroos came to be only in Australia," he said, "but I know there was at least one time when kangaroos were in Turkey."

This is such a good analogy that I have used it over and over again in Sunday school classes and youth group meetings; and every time I get a real kick out of seeing that light bulb go off in people's heads.

Evolutionists use science to disprove God. They start with science and then try to see how God fits into *their* mold. The problem is their mold is inferior. God is the great designer. He *owns* the mold. We need to do just the opposite of what the scientists are doing—we need to start with God first and then study science as a way to discover what He already knows. And that's really all science is—*man's search for what God already knows.*

God warned us we would face an onslaught of deceitfulness in our day. The Bible states that we would be "tossed to and fro, and carried about with every wind of doctrine, by the sleight of men, and cunning craftiness, whereby they lie in wait to deceive …"[9] "And they will deceive everyone his neighbor, and will not speak the truth: they have taught their tongue to speak lies, and weary themselves to commit iniquity."[10] "For they that are such serve not our Lord Jesus Christ, but their own belly; and by good words and fair speeches deceive the hearts of the simple."[11] "But cursed be the deceiver."[12]

If we build a firm foundation in truth and light for our children—and have a firm foundation ourselves—we will be much more prepared to face whatever the antagonists throw at us. Armed with the shield of faith, the belt of truth, and the spirit of discernment, we are prepared to stand on the front lines of this war for the souls of men. Wherefore take unto you the whole armor of God, that ye may be able to withstand in the evil day[13]… that ye may be able to stand against the wiles of the devil.[14]

God knew the times we would live in. He knew what we would face, and He has not left us alone. In 2 Timothy chapter 3, Paul gives comfort to Timothy in a time of great persecution against the saints of God. Paul, who suffered immense persecutions, tells Timothy "all that will live godly in Christ Jesus shall suffer persecution."[15] Paul then speaks specifically of our day and gives guidance to both Timothy and us on how to endure the evil and persecutions of our day:

> This know also, that in the last days perilous times shall come. For men shall be lovers of their own selves, covetous, boasters, proud, blasphemers, disobedient to parents, unthankful, unholy, Without natural affection, trucebreakers, false accusers, incontinent, fierce, despisers of those that are good, Traitors, heady, high-minded, lovers of pleasures more than lovers of God; Having a form of godliness, but denying the power thereof: from such turn away. But continue thou in the things which thou hast learned and hast been assured of, knowing of whom thou hast learned them; from a child thou hast known the holy scriptures, which are able to make thee wise unto salvation through faith which is in Christ Jesus.[16]

I love the last part of that—continue in the things we have learned *knowing from whom we learned them.* We learned them from God. We learn truth from Him—not our pastor, priest, or teacher. Others can share with us what they have learned, and we can be inspired and motivated by them, but we still have to seek the Word for ourselves. We need to search the Scriptures ourselves and not rely solely on the interpretation of others. If we hang our faith and our whole belief system on what someone tells us the Bible says, then they can tell us anything and we will believe it.

It deeply saddens me to see what is happening in our churches. Satan's plan to attack the Church has been much too successful. Pastors have become slaves to the collection plate, fearing that if they speak too plainly or address certain issues, they may offend the congregation. Churches are becoming "inclusive," which is code for "we don't talk about sin here; we just have a good time." Isn't that what the evolutionists said their goal is—to put religion on the level where it belongs—just something we do on the weekend? Is that what we really want? What about teaching the Word of God? Unfortunately in many churches today, God's Word is often corrupted, and entire sections are just left out. New bibles are being printed eliminating whole passages of Scripture to make it less offensive to sinners. And many churches are using the pulpit to promote politics and preach bigotry and hate. This is not of God.

We need to remember that deception is all around us, and if we are not sure about the truth of something, we need to use the simple standard Paul shared with Timothy—remember where we learned these things. When we are faced with a spirit of contention, all we have to ask ourselves is—where does contention come from? Where does hate come from? Where does bigotry come from? Since none of those things come from God, then why would someone who claims to be serving God promote such things?

This is why it is so important that we build our relationship with God—seek out His words ourselves, pray to Him ourselves, build our own faith and not just rely on the words, prayers, and faith of others. This will give us the spirit of discernment and help us think straight—which is something we all desperately need to do.

Every one of us has the right to choose what we will believe and what we will do, but that choice is made based on our knowledge and understanding of things. That is why it is so important that we seek knowledge and understanding ourselves. I love what Benjamin Franklin said about this:

> We stand at the crossroads, each minute, each hour, each day, making choices. We choose the thoughts we allow ourselves to think, the passions we allow ourselves to feel, and the actions we allow ourselves to perform. Each choice is made in the context of whatever value system we've selected to govern our lives. In selecting that value system, we are, in a very real way, making the most important choice we will ever make.
>
> Those who believe there is one God who made all things and who governs the world by his Providence will make many choices different from those who do not. Those who hold in reverence that being who gave them life and worship Him through adoration, prayer, and thanksgiving will make many choices different from those who do not. Those who believe that mankind are all of a family and that the most acceptable service of God is doing good to man will make many choices different from those who do not. Those who believe in a future state in which all that is wrong here will be made right will make many choices different from those who do not. Those who subscribe to

> the morals of Jesus will make many choices different from those who do not.
>
> Since the foundation of all happiness is thinking rightly, and since correct action is dependent on correct opinion, we cannot be too careful in choosing the value system we allow to govern our thoughts and actions.
>
> And to know that God governs in the affairs of men, that he hears and answers prayers, and that he is a rewarder of them that diligently seek Him, is indeed, a powerful regulator of human conduct. [17]

I can think of no more powerful regulator of human conduct than that—which is, of course, why God and religion are being besieged so relentlessly. That is why the Church is so often used as a platform to promote politics and politicians, or on the flip side, why so many churches hide behind "politics" to keep from having to speak truth about things like life, liberty, and the preservation of marriage. Church is no place for politics, because that is not God's way, but it is the perfect place to teach and promote civic responsibility, because God's hand is all over that.

Remember, civic responsibility is that duty which every American has, as a citizen of this country, to respect the law, be involved in our communities, safeguard the Republic, watch over our government, and seek out and elect good leaders to represent us. As Christians, it is vital that we become actively involved in the electoral process. Please don't allow yourself to be deceived into believing that means joining politics. God doesn't want us to take part in mud-slinging, name-calling, and deceitful tactics. He wants us to go in and clean up the whole mess, and there is no better way to do that than to get rid of all the politicians running it.

We need to vote out the politicians and vote in statesmen. The Bible counsels us, "Moreover thou shalt provide out of all the people able men, such as fear God, men of truth, hating covetousness; and place such over them, to be rulers …"[18]

The Bible also warns what happens when we do not *follow* this counsel. "As a roaring lion, and a raging bear; so is a wicked ruler over the poor people."[19] "While they promise them liberty, they themselves are the servants of corruption …"[20] "When the righteous are in authority, the people rejoice: but when the wicked beareth rule, the people mourn."[21]

That is the difference between having politicians in government and having statesmen; and we're witnessing it today. So, instead of sitting on the sidelines saying, "I don't like politics," get in there and clean it up. I don't like them either. Together we can do it. But as we do, we need to remember that Satan is watching, and we must constantly be on our guard against his deceptive tactics.

The devil isn't going to just sit by and let us tear down his house of cards. When he sees us uniting, he is going to come after us in all his fury, using every weapon in his arsenal to stop us, and bigotry is one of his favorite weapons. Remember, the best way to defeat an enemy is to divide and conquer them, and Satan has been very successful at that—not just in the nation but in the church as well. I have sat in congregations and listened to the pastor preach against other religions. I have attended Bible classes that condemned other religions. I have been in church bookstores where they not only sell but promote books that attack other religions and malign and degrade the beliefs of others.

I have seen fellow Christians shun people of other faiths and sever friendships when they find out their friend is a member of what they feel is an "unacceptable" religion. Again, this is not of God. Anything that stimulates fear, breeds hate, or promotes bigotry is not of God. Jesus taught this principle when he told the story of the Samaritan. The story doesn't really hit us like it did the Jews of the time, because to us, *Samaritan* is just a word in the story, but what if we changed the word to one that we would understand? Since Mormons are one of the most widely recognized religions prejudiced against in America, let's use that word. Let's replace "Samaritan" with "Mormon." What if it was a Mormon who stopped and took care of the man on the side of the road and it was a Baptist and a born-again who passed him by? And then Jesus asks, "Which of these three, the Mormon, the Baptist, or the born-again was a neighbor unto him that fell among the thieves?"

If you got a bad taste in your mouth when you had to answer, "the Mormon," then you have just realized the same thing the Sadducees and Pharisees did—you have been infected with bigotry—and Jesus just called you to repentance. It doesn't matter how the bigotry got there. It only matters that it is there. And you need to decide, are you going to follow God or give in to Satan? What if instead of replacing the Samaritan in the story with a Mormon, we replace it with a Muslim, a Buddhist, or even an atheist? Does it change the message of the story in anyway? Does it really matter what religion the Samaritan was, or does it matter that he was the one who stopped and had true compassion for another?

Just imagine what would happen if we purged ourselves of our bigotry and hate and stood together as brothers and sisters for a common purpose without worrying about what color, race, or religion we are. Actually we don't have to imagine. We witnessed it firsthand with California's Proposition 8. Side by side, Californians stood together united in purpose to pass the California marriage amendment. There was a massive and intense effort to stop the proposition from passing, but people gathered and churches united—Catholic, Mormon, Baptist, Methodist—and it wasn't just Christians. Jews, Muslims, Buddhists, people from all faiths united for the same cause, and they didn't ask what religions were involved before they decided to join the fight. They just got in there, rolled up their sleeves, and fought for what they believed was right. People of faith from all over California stood together and because they did, a law banning homosexual marriage was passed—*in California!* If that isn't a miracle, I don't know what is. It is amazing what we can accomplish when we do it *together*.

Being united in purpose doesn't change who we are or what we believe as individuals. We don't have to agree with the personal beliefs of others to stand together and fight for a common cause. America is full of diversity. Our Constitution was constructed in the midst of it, and freedom of religion was the greatest gift we received from it. If we want the freedom to worship God as we choose, then we need to allow our brothers and sisters to do the same and not criticize, condemn, and attack them because their beliefs are different from ours. We don't have to agree with the beliefs of others, but we do have to respect their right to have them. As President Bush stated in his 2005 Inaugural Address, "Liberty for all does not mean independence from one another … we cannot carry the message of freedom and the baggage of bigotry at the same time."

The fact is, religion is one of the main things that unite us as Americans, just as it was in the days of our founding families. Of course, there were differences in specific theology and sects, but the basic foundational beliefs of our founding families were the same. Benjamin Franklin defined these shared beliefs as the fundamental points in all sound religion. He outlined these fundamental points in a letter to Ezra Stiles, the president of Yale University:

> Here is my creed. I believe in one God, the Creator of the universe. That he governs it by his Providence. That he

ought to be worshipped. That the most acceptable service we render to him is in doing good to his other children. That the soul of man is immortal, and will be treated with justice in another life respecting its conduct in this. These I take to the fundamental points in all sound religion.[22]

When you think of the major religions on Earth—Judaism, Hinduism, Islam, and Christianity with all its many sects, you realize they all adhere to these same fundamental principles. These fundamental beliefs unite us. I think we can all agree that, unless you are an atheist, Benjamin Franklin's creed is something we can all live by—and should. And if we all did, the world would be a much better place.

So let's stand together as children of God and work together as brothers and sisters to tear down the politics of corruption that fill our government, and let us restore the glorious Republic of freedom and liberty that God gave us. We *can* do it. I believe in miracles, after all, America is one *big* miracle. It was a miracle Columbus received the funding he needed to sail to a land he didn't even know existed. It was a miracle the Pilgrims survived the first winter. It was a miracle George Washington lived to lead the colonial army. It was a miracle we won the Revolutionary War. It was a miracle when fifty-six men met at Independence Hall in Philadelphia, and it was a miracle when they signed the Constitution of the United States.

Yes, I believe in miracles—especially the greatest miracle of all—Jesus Christ. As Christians, there is no greater contribution we can make in this war than to share the light of Christ. The virtue of the Word of God has a more powerful effect upon the minds of people than anything else. If you want to stop wars, teach people of Christ and they will want to lay down their weapons. No sword has the power to do that.

Former agriculture secretary Ezra Benson said, "The world would take people out of the slums. Christ takes the slums out of the people, and then they take themselves out of the slums. The world would mold men by changing their environment. Christ changes men, who then change their environment. The world would shape human behavior, but Christ can change human nature."[23]

That is a very powerful thing, and that is why Satan is so afraid of it. Nothing can instill goodness in a people more than a mighty change of heart. That is what will preserve our freedom. Do you remember the Cycle of Democracy chart I showed you? Well, I'd like to show you another chart. It is the cycle of apostasy from the book of Judges. I placed both charts side by side so you can see just how much God fits into this. When we spread the light of Christ, and people embrace it, they are drawn to goodness and that leads to freedom.

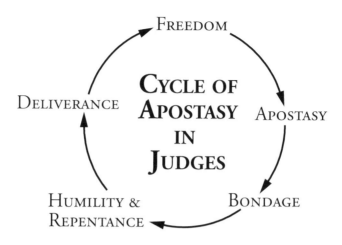

Of course, Satan will be there with all the powers of darkness to try to stop us, because he has too much to lose. As one religious leader said, "The fight against Satan and his forces is not a little skirmish with a half-willed antagonist, but a battle royal with an enemy so powerful, entrenched, and organized that we are likely to be vanquished if we are not strong, well trained, and watchful."[24]

Our nation is being attacked from all sides. We are in a hotbed of issues that confront us every day. Satan has used women to tear America down. God will use women to build her back up. We must have the courage to stand for what's right. *We must join this fight.*

We have the power to influence our nation for good. We must stop allowing the battle to rage on without us. We have the ability to counteract Satan's deceit with the strength and influence of truth. We can turn his corruption into virtue, his hatred into benevolence, and his darkness into light. He may have the power to bruise our heel, but we have the power to crush his head (Gen. 3:15).

No matter who you are, what you believe, or where you worship, if freedom is something you want to preserve, then let us join together. Our nation is at the crossroads, ladies, and we stand at the center of the conflict. Jezebel is taking down our beloved nation, and only Esther can save her. It is not by accident or some coincidence that you are in America. This was your destiny. God put you here for such a time as this. And when the battle seems too fierce and it feels like everything stands in your way, know that you are not alone. Be strong and of a good courage; be not afraid, neither be thou dismayed: for the Lord thy God is with thee whithersoever thou goest.[25]

Abraham Lincoln said, "It is my constant prayer that I and this nation should be on the Lord's side." This is my prayer as well. The battle lines are drawn. The war is raging on. It is time we put on the whole armor of God and stand on the front lines of freedom. Rise up, ye women, this *is* our fight. Be strong and of good courage—and do it![26]

From Our Founders

Of all the dispositions and habits which lead to political prosperity, religion and morality are indispensable supports. It is impossible to rightly govern the world without God and the Bible.
~George Washington

Your love of liberty—your respect for the laws—your habits of industry—and your practice of the moral and religious obligations, are the strongest claims to national and individual happiness.
~George Washington

It cannot be emphasized too strongly or too often that this great nation was founded, not by religionists, but by Christians; not on religions, but on the gospel of Jesus Christ! For this very reason, peoples of other faiths have been afforded asylum, prosperity, and freedom of worship here.

~Patrick Henry

The moral principles and precepts contained in the Scripture ought to form the basis of all our civil constitutions and laws. All the miseries and evil men suffer from vice, crime, ambition, injustice, oppression, slavery, and war, proceed from their despising or neglecting the precepts contained in the Bible.

~Noah Webster

Our ancestors established their system of government on morality and religious sentiment. Moral habits, they believed, cannot safely be trusted on any other foundation than religious principle, not any government secure which is not supported by moral habits.... Whatever makes men good Christians, makes them good citizens.

~Daniel Webster

Without morals a republic cannot subsist any length of time; they therefore who are decrying the Christian religion, whose morality is so sublime and pure [and] which insures to the good eternal happiness, are undermining the solid foundation of morals, the best security for the duration of free governments.

~ Charles Carroll

It is the duty of the clergy to accommodate their discourses to the times, to preach against such sins as are most prevalent, and recommend such virtues as are most wanted.

~John Adams

The legitimate powers of government extend to such acts as are only injurious to others. But it does me no injury for my neighbor to say there are twenty gods, or no God. It neither picks my pocket nor breaks my leg.

~Thomas Jefferson

The highest glory of the American Revolution was this; it connected in one indissoluble bond the principles of civil government with the principles of Christianity.

~John Quincy Adams

Is uniformity attainable? Millions of innocent men, women, and children, since the introduction of Christianity, have been burnt, tortured, fined, imprisoned; yet we have not advanced on inch towards uniformity. What has been the effect of coercion? To make one half the world fools, and the other half hypocrites.

~Thomas Jefferson

A patriot without religion in my estimation is as great a paradox as an honest Man without the fear of God. Is it possible that he whom no moral obligations bind, can have any real Good Will towards Men? Can he be a patriot who, by an openly vicious conduct, is undermining the very bonds of Society?....The Scriptures tell us "righteousness exalteth a Nation."

~Abigail Adams

The belief of a future state of rewards and punishments, the entertaining just ideas of the main attributes of the Supreme Being, and a firm persuasion that He superintends and will finally compensate every action in human life (all which are revealed in the doctrines of our Savior, Christ), these are the grand foundations of all judicial oaths, which call God to witness the truth of those facts which perhaps may be only known to Him and the party attesting; all moral evidences, therefore, all confidence in human veracity, must be weakened by apostasy, and overthrown by total infidelity.

~Sir William Blackstone

Moses lifting up his wand, and dividing the Red Sea, and Pharaoh in his chariot overwhelmed with the waters. This motto: "Rebellion to tyrants is obedience to God."

~Benjamin Franklin

I consider the doctrines of Jesus as delivered by himself to contain the outlines of the sublimest system of morality that has ever been taught but I hold in the most profound detestation and execration the corruptions of it which have been invented.

~Thomas Jefferson

Suggested Books & Resources:
Expelled: No Intelligence Allowed (DVD by Ben Stein)
Defeating the Totalitarian Lie: A Former Hitler Youth Warns America by Hilmar Von Campe
Icons of Evolution by Jonathan Wells
The Great Evolution Hoax by Randall Hedtke
Icons of Evolution, DVD
Unlocking the Mystery of Life, DVD by Illustra Media

ORDINARY WOMEN DOING EXTRAORDINARY THINGS

The price of freedom is eternal vigilance.
—Thomas Jefferson

In November of 2008, after three straight weeks of volunteering eight- to fourteen-hour days as the operational manager in a presidential campaign office in the battleground state of Ohio, I was asked what I was going to do when the election was over. There were several paid staff members in the office, as well as state campaign officials and various interns. They were each asked the same question and had just finished sharing their plans, goals, and aspirations.

Some would go on to work with Congress, some were moving on to other campaigns, some were being promoted to regional directors and state chairs, and others were going to full-time jobs on Capitol Hill or state legislative offices. They all seemed so excited to be moving forward in their political careers and looked to me with anxious anticipation, wondering where I would go and what I would do after the election. Just as I was asked the question, my five-year-old son came running in from the children's room we had set up in the back of the campaign office and jumped in my lap. "So, what are you going to do?" they asked again. I smiled at my little boy and answered, "I'm going home to be a mom."

I have never considered myself remarkable. I am just an ordinary woman. I don't have a college degree. I've never sat in an executive board room. I don't hold public office, and I've never been listed in *Forbes* magazine. I am not a member of the media. I am not a political pundit or a pollster. I am simply an American woman—a wife and mother—

living every day for my home, my family, my faith, and my freedom. I am no different than any other everyday, hard-working, freedom-loving American, just trying to do the best I can to provide for my family and my future. I am not paid to predict elections. I am just one of the millions of Americans who determines them with my vote. But in the last few years, I have learned just what that means. I have learned the power of being an American.

I know you have learned a lot of things in this book. And maybe you are thinking, "*I* can't do anything to make a difference. I am just ordinary." But that is what heroes are—just ordinary people doing extraordinary things without even realizing how extraordinary they are. Stories of these people fill the pages of our history—like a young peasant girl named Joan who simply answered a call. Do you think Joan of Arc had any idea that one small act of courage would turn into an epic adventure that would bring England to its knees and immortalize her name? No, she had no idea. She was just standing up for what she knew was right. What made her a hero was that she had the courage to do it.

Americans have courage coursing through their veins. It is in our blood. It is the product of a free people. We don't have to live a life of servitude or go on a quest to be a hero. We can do it right in our own homes, in our own communities—within the sphere of our own influence. We don't need to go to Washington D.C. to influence our nation. We can do it in our own backyard. And we don't have to sacrifice our families to do it. All you have to do is be you.

The most effective way to make a difference is by getting involved in things that affect you or your own family, and the most productive way is in your own community. I know national politics can seem exciting, but the reason why our nation has fallen into such tyranny is because the people of America keep looking to Washington, D.C. to address our issues and problems, when we should be looking at our own City Hall.

Most of the programs, departments, and policies of our federal government are not only unconstitutional, they are ineffective and fruitless. The federal government cannot possibly address local issues on a national level, because each community has its own set of unique circumstances. What works for New York City will not work for Tuscaloosa and vice versa. If we are unhappy with the performance of our children's schools, we need to go to the local school board, *not* Congress. The further away we go from the problems we face in our community, the less say we have in how to address them. If we don't like the way sex education is being taught in our children's school, then we need to stop looking to Congress and start attending our local school board meetings. If we don't like the fact that our property taxes keep increasing, don't write to your congressman, attend your city council meetings and tell the mayor.

A system of government that is of the people, by the people, and for the people can only work when that government is where we can reach it. Government is supposed to be close to the people. And it is. The problem is, we keep running to Washington, D.C. and our state houses to address things that we should be addressing in our towns and counties. It is easy to blame the president of the United States when we are unhappy about something. He is an easy target. But it isn't the president of the United States who determines whether or not your local library will have filters on their computers or whether or not your town has an efficient 911 service. If we the people are going to rule in America, we are going to have to start in our own communities. If we want to stop government oppression, we are going to have to start in our own back yards. And it isn't that hard. Oppression doesn't start in Washington. It is all around us.

In May of 2004, our family moved from Fredericksburg, Virginia, to a small town just north of Dayton, Ohio. My husband's mother had gone to Mongolia to serve a Christian mission and she had given us her motor home to sell while she was away. We parked it in the yard right next to the side of our house and then started unpacking our boxes.

A couple of weeks later, while still settling in, we received a letter in the mail from the city we live in. The letter stated that our motor home was violating a city code and would have to be moved. The city code stated that all vehicles, such as motor homes and recreational vehicles, had to be parked behind the foundation line of the house. Ours protruded by six inches. My husband and I just rolled our eyes and then took down the fence in our back yard and drove the motor home back behind the foundation line. Two months later, we sold the motor home and replaced the fence.

A few weeks later, we received another letter in the mail from the city with a code violation. The letter stated that there had been trash in our side yard for over two weeks and we needed to remove it.

I just looked at the letter, wondering what the heck the city was talking about, and assumed they just accidently sent it to the wrong address. Still, I walked around the house to see if there was some debris that fell out of trashcans that I may have missed. There was nothing. So I promptly dismissed the whole issue.

A couple weeks later, we received yet another letter in the mail from the city. This time the code violation was our car. Since my husband is an active-duty member in the air force, our state of residence is Tennessee, and that is where we register all our vehicles. After we moved to Ohio, the registration on one of our cars needed to be renewed, so we sent in the necessary paperwork to do so. There was a mix-up in the move, however, and the registration was sent to our old address. While we waited for the registration to be re-mailed, the tags on our car expired, so we just parked the car in the driveway until the paperwork came back. According to the city's code violation officer, having a car parked in our driveway with expired tags was a violation of city code.

The day after I received the letter from the city, I contacted the city administration building and explained the situation. The lady I spoke with said, "No problem, I'll let the code enforcement officer know." A few days later, we received another letter in the mail from the city reminding us of the trash that was still in our yard, the car that had to be removed, and added a new violation to the list: the weeds on the side of our house were too high. By this time, I was starting to get pretty irritated. Still I checked the side of our house for the elusive "trash" the letter kept referring to and then looked for the "weeds." Still no trash. I did notice a few weeds growing in and around our yucca plants, so I pulled them and then rolled my eyes as I walked back in the house and dismissed the issue once again.

By this time, the town's "code enforcement officer" had become a frequent conversation at the dinner table. She had also become a frequent topic of conversation among many of our neighbors, and we affectionately began referring to her as the "Neighborhood Nazi." Apparently we weren't the only ones in our neighborhood she was harassing. Then one day we all received the city newsletter in the mail. On the second page was an article stating that the city recently voted to promote the city's code enforcement officer from a part-time to a full-time position because "the violations are too numerous" and they apparently felt the citizens of our community needed full-time harassment instead of just part-time. *Man,* I thought, *I sure wish I'd been at the city council meeting where that decision was made.*

A week later, I drove into the driveway after returning from taking our younger children to the local library, when my son Jordan met me at the door. He said the Neighborhood Nazi had come to our house while I was gone and dropped off a pink slip of paper. "Oh," I said, "so now we've upgraded to in-person harassment." Jordan handed me the pink piece of paper, which stated if we did not remove our car within three days, our violation would be taken to court. "Well, bring it on!" I said to myself. Then Jordan told me that when the code enforcement officer came by, she said she would have just dropped the note on our door but she couldn't see the back yard due to the privacy fence and wanted permission to go in the back yard and "inspect" it.

"Did you let her in?" I asked Jordan.

"No way," he said. "I've heard you talking enough about the Neighborhood Nazi in the last couple of months to know you'd have my hide if I let her in. I told her she would have to come back when you were home."

"Good boy!" I said. "I've raised you right." I then called a family meeting and sat all the children down in the living room, where we spent a half an hour going over our constitutional rights and discussing when it is and isn't appropriate to let someone into our house, just in case something like this happened again and one of the other children was to answer the door. I made sure the children understood they are never to let anyone in the house when their father and I were not home, even the police—unless they have a legal warrant signed by a judge. After ensuring they all understood, I sent them out to play. An hour later, the doorbell rang. It was the Neighborhood Nazi. I opened the door, smiling.

"Hello," I said, determined to be civil. She seemed like a nice enough lady. She was shorter than me by a few inches and a bit heavier, but other than that, she didn't seem much different than me. She looked like any other person you would see in the neighborhood.

"Hello," she said, "I am the city code enforcement officer."

"Yes," I said, "I know who you are."

"Oh, well I came by earlier and dropped off a note with your son."

"I know," I said, "he gave it to me."

"Oh, good. Well, when I came by earlier, I told your son I needed to inspect your backyard, but he said I would have to come back when you were home."

"Yes, that's because he is a responsible young man and knows better than to let strangers in the house."

"Yes, well, I have come back to inspect the yard. I would have already done it, but I can't see over the privacy fence, so I'll need permission to go through your back gate so I can see the backyard."

I couldn't believe she was actually saying this with a straight face. I mean, Jordan told me that's why she came by, but to hear it with my own ears was unbelievable.

"No," I said.

"What?" she asked, surprised.

"I said no. I am not giving you permission to go into my back yard."

"But I can't inspect the back yard without going in it."

"You can't inspect my yard at all. This is my private property and you have no authority to *inspect* anything. You have no authority to even step on my property unless I give it to you, and I don't."

The woman was floored. I guess she'd never come in contact with anyone who knew their rights before. She fumbled with the papers in her hands for a moment and then said, "Well, there is the matter of your car."

"I've already explained the situation with the car," I said. "I am not moving my car. It is going to stay right here."

"It is a code violation. Your tags are expired."

I then went on, again, to explain why the tags were expired. "There is nothing wrong with our car," I said. "It is in perfect working order. It isn't on blocks; it isn't a hazard or a danger to anyone. It is simply sitting in our driveway until the registration comes in the mail."

"Well, you can't leave it the driveway," she said.

"I'm not moving my car."

"You know," she said, "you could make the whole thing go away if you just park your car in the garage."

"I can't fit my car in the garage; we still have boxes everywhere, and …" The neighborhood Nazi walked around to the front of the driveway as I was talking.

"Sure you can," she said, walking into my garage. "Just put that there and move those things over here, and you'll have plenty of room to park your car in the garage."

"I don't think you understand," I said, "I'm *not* parking my car in the garage. This is *my* property and *my* driveway, and I am *not* going to rearrange my entire garage to fit my car in just to appease you."

"Well, if you don't move the car, we'll have to send the case to the courts."

"Fine," I said, "send it to the courts. Waste the taxpayers' money. It won't change a thing."

"Well, then I'll have to report this to the law director!"

"Go ahead," I said, "tell the law director. His name isn't on the deed to my house. He doesn't make my payments, and neither do you or the city council. When the city starts making my house payments, they can decide whether or not my car is parked in the garage. Until that time, my car will remain in my driveway."

The Neighborhood Nazi was beside herself. None of her threats had their intended effect. I would not be intimidated. There was nothing she could say that *would* intimidate me, because I knew my rights and I knew she was stepping all over them. The Neighborhood Nazi started writing something on her notepad and then mustered a smile. "Well," she said, "there are these other infractions. Like the trash. Would you like me to go over these things with you?"

"Yes," I said, "as a matter of fact, I would. I would really like you to show me the trash that you say has been in my yard for the last three months."

"Okay," she said in an almost giddy tone, as if she were finally getting somewhere with me. "Sure, it's right over here."

I followed her to the side of the house and watched as she pointed to the ground. "There it is," she said. I looked at the ground beneath my feet and stared in befuddlement.

"A gum wrapper!" I said in disbelief.

"Yes," she said, "it's been there for months." I couldn't believe it. I mean, you just can't make this stuff up. Who needs fantasy and fiction when real life is this entertaining?

"You spent the money for a stamp and made a special trip out here for a gum wrapper?" I said incredulously.

"And then there are the weeds," she said, walking up to the back fence as if completely oblivious to anything I was saying. "These weeds are out of control."

"Those are yucca plants," I said.

"No, here," she said, reaching and pointing into the plant. "You see, right here, behind these …"

By that time, I had had it with this nut job. The entertainment factor was over. "Lady," I said, "I don't know who the heck you think you are, but this isn't communist China, and I've had about enough of this. The whole reason we moved into this neighborhood instead of all the others we looked at is because this neighborhood doesn't have a homeowners association, and I won't live in a communist commune where I have to pay for the *'privilege'* of having people tell me when to mow my lawn and what color to paint my shutters. And I'm certainly not going to allow the City of Clayton to do it. I don't pay property taxes to have some flunky, who has to prove a full-time position is worth taxpayer dollars, to come snooping around my house, looking for gum wrappers, elusive weeds, and telling me where to park my car."

"I'm the city's code enforcement officer," the woman said, backing out of the yard toward the driveway.

"Those are just words on a business card," I retorted. "What you *are* is a menace to freedom and a thorn in the side of this city, and you have harassed the citizens of this neighborhood for quite long enough. There will be no more *'inspecting'* of my property today or any other day. If you want to drive by and look at my house and front yard, fine, it is a public street, but you step one foot on my property again and I'll have you arrested for trespassing. And you can tell that to the law director."

The woman stormed off to her car and drove away in a huff—no doubt to file a complete report on my insolence. This is what happens when you give a person a title and a little authority. Some people handle it better than others. This woman let the idea of power go right to her head—which is the only place it will do her any good. I know my rights, and I know neither she nor the city has any power over me that I don't give them, and I will not authorize the government to harass me or my neighbors.

Around the same time that I received my visit from our Neighborhood Nazi, the Supreme Court was making their landmark decision on property rights—the one where they said the government could take your land to build a shopping mall. As I thought about the events of that day, I realized just how much our local communities impact major decisions like that.

While the Neighborhood Nazi and I were sharing pleasantries that day, she was telling me how much she loved her job. "You must get yelled at a lot," I said.

"Oh, yes," she answered, "but I thrive on it."

She *thrives* on it? She seemed almost giddy as she went on to tell me how important her job is to our city. She said she runs the hotline where residents can call and report "violations" on their neighbors. They don't even have to leave their names. They just call and complain and the Neighborhood Nazi goes out and investigates. She seemed to take great pleasure in snooping around the houses of the citizens of our city and harassing them using her self-important title and assumed power.

So as I listened to all the people up in arms over the Supreme Court decision, I just thought to myself, *now that it affects you personally, you're suddenly upset about it.* But where were all those people when their neighbors' rights were being violated by town governments all over America for the sake of our property values? Where were they when the guy down the street was cited for having his grass too high or when the farmer down the road was told he couldn't build houses on his property? Rights aren't something we can regulate when it suits us. Either we believe in property rights or we don't. Either we respect free speech or we don't. Either we are a free country or we are not.

When we legislate our neighbors' rights away, we are legislating our own rights away as well. And then, before you know it, your city council has the power to take your house away to build a shopping mall—"for the good of the community."

All of these things were running through my head as I thought about my visit with the Neighborhood Nazi that day. And I decided if property rights were going to be protected, then someone was going to have to stand up for them. So, that night I wrote a letter to my city council. The next day, I made a copy of the letter for each member of the city council and then hand-delivered them to each of their houses. The following day was our city council meeting, and I made sure to attend. When it came time for visitors' comments, I stood at the podium and outlined all the grievances I had with the Neighborhood Nazi and how absurd all her "violations" were. As I was speaking, the city manager became very and angry broke in. "Madam Mayor," he said, "I am not going to sit by while this woman, who has been a problem for some time with repeated violations, attacks my employees and slings these insults."

I assume that at this point, the city manager and council members figured I would just apologize and slink back to my seat, but they obviously had no idea who they were dealing with. "Excuse me, Mr. Manager," I said, "but you seem to be under the mistaken impression that you *have* employees. You don't have any employees; the people of this city do. They are *our* employees, and so are *you,* for that matter. We are the ones that hire you. *You work for us. We* pay your salaries and I, for one, am no longer going to pay for harassment. And I know a lot of other citizens in this town who feel exactly the same way."

Sudden applause erupted from the council chambers from the citizens in attendance at the meeting. The city manager was stunned, and the council members were speechless. Finally the mayor spoke. "I think it would be a good idea if we set a meeting with Mrs. Fletcher, me, and the city manager to discuss this."

"That is a fine idea, Madam Mayor," I said, "but I would like my representative on the council to attend as well. And my husband will also be there."

A few days later, my husband and I walked into the city administration building to meet with the mayor, our council member, and the city administrator. I introduced everyone to my husband, exchanged a few pleasantries, and then we got down to business. The city manager began by presenting a thirty-page dossier that itemized, by date, all our "violations" to the city code as he began to read them one by one. I am sure he and the Neighborhood Nazi spent a great deal of time putting this little package of nonsense together, but in the end it was a complete waste of time, because he didn't even get through the first page.

My husband sat and quietly listened all the way through to violation number five before he put an abrupt end to the whole ridiculous fistful of fabrications. "This is absolute garbage!" he said. "There is not one thing on that paper that has any validity whatsoever. Is it your habitual policy to just make this stuff up?"

The city manager was obviously shocked by my husband's sudden outburst. He sheepishly tucked his lengthy "report" away, and my husband and I completely ignored him as we spent the next twenty minutes speaking with the mayor and our council member, addressing the issue with truth and common sense. In the end, the Neighborhood Nazi was told to back off her power trip, and the mayor instructed the city manager that the code enforcement officer was simply to enforce the code and that she was not to harass us or the citizens of Clayton anymore. And that is the last we heard from the Neighborhood Nazi.

Now, I will be honest. Had I not been directly affected by the issue of property rights, I would have never gotten involved in it at all, but that is the point. We need to get involved in the things that *we* are passionate about—the things that *we* are closest to. That is what will make the greatest difference. I was just one person who stood up for my own rights, but the citizens of the whole town benefitted from it. You may not think your little community is that important in the grand scheme of things, but it is the most important place to get involved, because that is where we have the most impact, and it is where all our future state and national leaders come from. We can't stop oppression in Washington, D.C., until we address the oppression in our own cities and counties. You never know when something you do will make a difference.

A few years ago, Rush Limbaugh was lamenting on his radio show about some of the codes and regulations passed by his local city, and then he said, "Well, you can't fight City Hall." I about came unglued. I couldn't believe he just announced that poppycock on the national airwaves. You certainly *can* fight City Hall, and I've proved it over and over again. But you *can't* fight City Hall if you don't show up to your city council meetings to have your voice heard—or even find out what it is you're fighting for. And you're not going to win any battles if you don't get involved in your local elections.

You need to know the people who represent you in your community. Just about every city, borough, county, and parish has a Web site now. You can get on your local community's Web site and find out who the city council members are and when and where they meet. Most school boards have the same information through your local school district's Web site. You would be surprised what a difference it can make when you take the time to get involved in your community and take part in your local elections.

I am not saying you need to devote your life to a candidate or convert your home into campaign office; I am just saying that when, on that rare occasion, we meet a candidate for elected office who truly impresses us, it is our duty to stand behind that person. Just making a few phone calls or stuffing a few envelopes is a huge help to any candidate. And don't think you have to know anything about politics to get involved. There are plenty of people who have been doing this for years who can guide you. It is as simple as asking, "What can I do to help?" And then you do what you can when you can. That's it. It's the Minuteman Factor.

When our founding families fought for their independence, they didn't have a standing army of professional soldiers. They were farmers and storekeepers fighting for their freedom, their homes, and their families. When the battle cry was sounded, the farmers put down their pitchforks, pulled their muskets from beneath their floorboards, and joined the fight. And when the battle was over, they went back home and plowed their fields, waiting until the next time the alarm was sounded. That's what we need today—a patriot's taskforce—ordinary people who are willing to stand at the ready to be called in time of need to make phone calls, knock on doors, or pass out voter guides on Election Day.

You don't have to give up your life and work 24/7 to make a difference—you just need to be willing to be at the ready and accept the call. Just do what you feel comfortable doing. If you don't feel comfortable making phone calls, then stuff envelopes or pass out voter guides instead. And you don't have to say yes every time you're asked either. If you can't help when you're called, that's fine, because there are plenty of others who can, and the next time one of them isn't able to help, you will be. It is just as simple as that—each one of us doing our small part to get good people elected to represent us, and it is worth a little bit of our time.

One of the greatest rewards of getting involved, aside from helping to get good people elected to office, is realizing that you aren't alone. You will meet so many remarkable people who share your love for this nation, and you would be amazed at how much fun you can have stuffing envelopes. You can make a difference, and you don't have to sacrifice your family to do it. In fact, family is oftentimes the reason why we get involved in the first place.

A few years ago, I met a woman at my church who told me how her mother, Betty, became involved more than twenty years ago. In the 1970s and '80s, there was a strong movement to bring sex education to the classroom in public schools. I remember that time very well. My mother attended several school and parent organization meetings to fight that battle. Some states and school districts moved faster than others in their effort to infiltrate and saturate our schools with sex.

Back when the movement started, the classes were easy to identify and students could opt out of them with parent's permission. Back then, parents had to be notified when these classes were coming to their school, and the personal views of the students and parents were at least attempted to be respected. Today, graphic sexual content is everywhere in our schools, parents' concerns are dismissed, and there is nothing to notify parents of, because it is commonplace—and because they don't want the parents to know.

In the late '70s and early '80s, the sexual education movement was moving like a bulldozer through our schools, often steered by homosexual activist groups. For them, meddling parents were just in the way. Betty was one of those parents. The first time the issue came up was when Betty received a notice that her children's school was going to start sex education classes in kindergarten. She and her husband decided to deal with the problem by moving away from it. They moved their family from Phoenix to Scottsdale, hoping to shield their children from the offensive curriculum. This was not a movement that you could escape, however, and just a few years after they moved, it caught up with them.

Betty and her husband received notice in the mail that her children's school had decided to implement a new sexual education curriculum. After looking into the curriculum, Betty found the curriculum to be very explicit and included photos of young boys and girls together in a bathtub with no clothes on, and the older grades' curriculum included graphic discussions about oral sex and masturbation. The curriculum also discussed homosexuality in detail and offered it as an acceptable option. The curriculum, in progressive stages of content, was intended for students from kindergarten through twelfth grade. Betty suddenly realized that running away from the problem was not going to solve it, so she decided to face it head on.

Betty had no idea that taking a stand would spark a six-year battle with a massive team of lawyers and homosexual lobbyists. Betty and several other mothers stood in the battle, continuing to fight for their children as the battle went from school district to county and all the way to the governor's office. Then, just when the war seemed lost, Betty and her little group of mothers, with the aid of some lawyer friends, found a section in Arizona state law that stated sex education was to be *limited* and *must be abstinence-based*. Finally, after six years, the law was on their side and they won.

The offensive curriculum was pulled from the schools. The school district, however, still felt they had to have a sexual education program, so Betty took the offensive curriculum the school district had purchased and completely rewrote it to fit within the law so that abstinence was the focus, consequences were discussed, and the parents were respected. That is what happens when just one woman stands up and speaks out. And when each of us does our small part, we add to the large picture like joining pieces in a puzzle of liberty. Each of us holds a piece in the puzzle, and each of us adds to it—simply by adding our own little contribution, because it is by small and simple things that great things come to pass. There is no better example of this than the story of one of my heroes, Olga T. Weber.

Olga Weber was an Ohio homemaker who, in 1951, became very concerned that American citizens were taking their freedoms too much for granted. After reflecting on the matter Olga decided she needed to do something to remind the people of America just how important freedom is. She began distributing copies of the Constitution, the Bill of Rights, flag booklets, and other patriotic leaflets to the local schools, churches, and libraries. Then, in 1952, Olga decided it would be a good idea to establish a Constitution Day to commemorate the signing of the Constitution of the United States. Olga met with Mayor Gerald Romary and members of the Louisville, Ohio, city council and shared her idea with them.

On September 17, 1952, Mayor Romary declared the day as Constitution Day in the city of Louisville. It was such a success that Olga decided to approach members of the Ohio General Assembly and ask that Ohio make a statewide designation for Constitution Day. The general assembly thought it a fine idea, and Constitution Day was signed into law by Governor Frank J. Lausche. Olga's efforts didn't end there, however. She had one more stop—the United States Congress.

In August of 1953, Olga urged the United States Senate to pass a resolution designating September 17–23 as Constitution Week. The Senate and House approved her request, and it was signed into law by President Dwight D. Eisenhower. Today, Constitution Week is nationally recognized, and children all over America celebrate it in their classrooms. The city of Louisville is now known as Constitution Town, and for over fifty years they have been faithfully celebrating Constitution Week in grand fair—and all because of an Ohio homemaker named Olga Weber.

I know you are all busy with your homes and your families. I know how hard you work and the long hours you keep, but I also know how desperately you want to be heard. I know how much freedom means to you and how badly you want to do everything you can to preserve it for your children. I know how deeply you ache for your country and mourn the loss of the society that once supported families, reverenced God, and cherished freedom. I know you long to have those days back, and I know that's why you feel such a need to get involved. And yet you wonder what you can possibly do to make a difference. Well, I want you to know that you can.

I have seen miracles performed by God through the hands of good women, and I am inspired by their good works every day.

I was very moved by the labors of love that I witnessed from the women who came and volunteered their time at the Huber Heights Victory Center in the November 2008 election. I have worked on a lot of campaigns, but what I saw at that center—the passion for the purpose, the dedication to the work, and the undying commitment to the preservation of our nation—was something I just haven't seen on any other campaign. The women who came and volunteered hours upon hours of their time at that center came not because they believed in a party, but because they were devoted to America and they believed in a woman named Sarah Palin.

I wonder if Sarah will ever know how much good she did for this country simply by having the courage to join the fight. Despite the outcome, what she did for this nation in that short time that she was willing to propel herself and her family in the national spotlight was phenomenal. She had a major impact on so many of us. As an American woman and mother, I finally had someone who represented *me*—one of the real women of America, instead of the feminists who continue to insist upon speaking for us.

Every day at the Victory Center held a little miracle that inspired me. I was able to meet so many amazing people—mothers who came into the center with their nursing babies; the woman who came in every day for six to eight hours, calling volunteers to fill the phone bank; the young mother, seven months pregnant, who came in every day with her three little children to walk neighborhoods and make phone calls. She and her children almost single-handedly walked every neighborhood in Huber Heights. It was truly freedom in action.

The whole experience is one I will treasure forever. But when the election was over and the offices were cleared, we hugged each other with tear-filled eyes and said our good-byes. Then we closed the door, holding tight to cherished memories, and went back home to be moms—until the next time we are called to arms.

I have met so many remarkable people in the last ten years as I have served on elections and become involved in my communities. I have learned so much and had so many amazing experiences. And I often think of my friend Herb, who started it all when he invited me to a town hall meeting in Fredericksburg, Virginia, all those years ago. So today, I am inviting you to a town hall meeting. I am inviting you to join the front lines of freedom.

Betty, Olga, Sarah, and all those women at the center were just ordinary women, but look at the extraordinary things they did. Don't ever sell yourself short. It isn't extraordinary people who make this world better. It's ordinary people like you and me who stand up for what's right and do extraordinary things without even meaning to. And you know what? That's what makes you extraordinary!

So stand up on the front lines of freedom and engage in the Battle of Liberty. It is time we remove the shackles that bind us. No longer can we be slaves to ignorance. No longer can we allow ourselves to be divided by income, race, religion, or political party. No longer will we the people be held subservient to an oppressive, tyrannical band of government monarchists who have no respect for our Republic and are hell-bent on destroying our liberty and tearing down the American family.

This is our Independence Day. Independence from ignorance, tyranny, and an oppressive Congress, and it all starts here, with us. We must educate ourselves, inspire our children, and influence within our sphere of influence. That is how we will save our beloved America; that is how we will preserve our liberty—one person and one family at a time.

From Our Founders

I have no fear that the result of our experiment will be that men may be trusted to govern themselves without a master.
~Thomas Jefferson

The time is now near at hand which must probably determine whether Americans are to be freemen or slaves; whether they are to have any property they can call their own; whether their houses and farms are to be pillaged and destroyed, and themselves consigned to a state of wretchedness from which no human efforts will deliver them. The fate of unborn millions will now depend on God, on the courage and conduct of this army. Our cruel and unrelenting enemy leaves us only the choice of brave resistance, or the most abject submission. We have, therefore, to resolve to conquer or die.
~George Washington; 1776

Good government generally begins in the family, and if the moral character of a people once degenerate, their political character must soon follow.
~Elias Boudinot

These are the times that try men's souls. The summer soldier and the sunshine patriot will, in this crisis, shrink from the service of their country; but he that stands it now, deserves the love and thanks of man and woman.
~Thomas Paine

Every government degenerates when trusted to the rulers of the people alone. The people themselves, therefore, are its only safe depositories.
~Thomas Jefferson

On matters of style, swim with the current, on matters of principle, stand like a rock.
~Thomas Jefferson

He that would make his own liberty secure must guard even his enemy from oppression; for it he violates this duty, he establishes a precedent that will reach himself.
~Thomas Paine

But a Constitution of Government once changed from Freedom, can never be restored. Liberty, once lost, is lost forever.
~John Adams

THE ANGELS BEHIND IT ALL

One person can make a difference and every person should try.
—John F. Kennedy

I hope you now know just how important you are as women. I hope I have been able to give you a glimpse of your incredible worth and influence. I know it's hard to think about that when you're running through your busy day. I know there are times when life seems overwhelming, the dishes are piling up, and your schedule is mounting. I know there are times when you feel inadequate, ineffective, and unappreciated. But I also know the countless hours you selflessly dedicate to your family, your home, and your community. And I know *that it doesn't go unnoticed.*

I know this because one morning a few years ago, I woke up and found an e-mail on my computer from my seventeen-year-old daughter. The previous day had been very challenging, and Cassie noticed I was obviously frustrated.

"What's wrong?" she asked.

"I feel like I'm letting the women of America down. It just doesn't seem like I'm doing enough. I'm not able to accomplish everything I want to."

There have been many times when I have felt overwhelmed or discouraged since forming Homemakers for America. I have seen miraculous things happen, but I have also faced great challenges. It takes an enormous amount of time and effort to build up and run a national organization. But life must carry on as well. And I have done my best to balance it all.

In the last ten years, I have given birth to our youngest two children; moved twice; run for public office; worked feverishly on elections, various campaigns, and community projects; organized a neighborhood watch group; volunteered at church; helped organize the Dayton Tea Party Events; spoken at various church and community functions; served on various community groups and civic organizations; started a national organization; and written a book—all while caring for our home and family and homeschooling our children. No, I'm *not* Superwoman—far from it. I haven't done it all at once. I do what I can when I can, and sometimes take-out is the weeklong special, but everything always seems to fall in place somehow. My family has been right there with me through it all. I have a very supportive husband, and even our extended family has played a significant role, but it has been my daughter Cassie who has been my closest friend and supporter through it all.

Cassie is an amazing young lady. She has lifted my spirits on numerous occasions. But the gift she gave me that cool fall morning in 2005 will be something I will cherish for the rest of my life. The night before, Cassie listened intently as I shared my concerns and frustrations with her; then she smiled and hugged me and assured me that she knew, somehow, everything would be all right.

I started Homemakers for America to inspire the women of our nation and help them realize just how desperately important they are in the grand scheme of things. But it was my daughter who reminded me. The morning after I poured my heart out to her, I opened my e-mail, and found this:

> The Angel Behind it All
> To my mom (from Cassie Fletcher)
>
> For thousands of years humans have inhabited this earth, living and moving through life to the best of their abilities. Most were content with the simple life they led, but few knew that *they* were made for greater things—things which were to change the world, by people who were simply doing what was right.
>
> From the humble and meek do powerful things arise; through the divine influence of God are those miracle workers chosen, by the hands of our Father they are molded, and from the lips of those He has chosen spill his holy works.

> In early October of 2004, the Lord sought out the next earthly angel he needed to fulfill his next great work. From his hands to her heart were the words given, and through her love and devotion she has begun the mission she has been assigned. From her heart, to her mind, to her fingers have flown the words that have given hope to those of this nation that need it the most; those of us who have been taught to disbelieve our true worth—Homemakers.
>
> We have been led away by the words of those who would see our homes fail, and many of us have taken to the bait without a fight. Still, there are those who have remained hopeful, faithful that we would not be forsaken. And we have not been.
>
> We have received an angel—an angel who works so hard to see that we feel our true worth. It does not matter if we work outside of our homes or within. She has placed herself on the front line for each and every one of us, and I will be right there with her. From the very first step to the very last blow, I will see to it that I will be holding her hand—the hand of the angel behind it all.

Just when it seems all is in vain, your own child reminds you just what an influence you are! Remember the words of Benjamin Rush? "The women of America have at last become principals in the glorious American controversy. Their opinions alone and their transcendent influence in society and families must lead us on to success and victory." As it was true then, so it is today.

Abigail Adams, and so many courageous women like her, stood alongside their husbands in creating this great nation. Today, the women lead out, carrying the light of liberty and the beacon of truth. *We* are the hope of America. We hold the future in *our* hands. Tomorrow's leaders are in *our* care. What we teach them, and what we know ourselves, will make all the difference. In the impassioned words of Patrick Henry, "We are not weak if we make a proper use of those means which the God of Nature has placed in our power…The battle is not to the strong alone; it is to the vigilant, the active, the brave." It is to you! The future of America is on *our* hands.

So go out and conquer, ladies! This is *your* day. All is not in vain. Your children are watching. Your family is watching. And God is waiting. There is hope for America. And you are the angels behind it all!

May God bless you as you continue to seek for truth and knowledge; and may He, through your dedicated efforts to preserve freedom and liberty, continue to bless America.

Appendix

Patriot's Reading List

This eclectic list of literature, documents, and biographies is sure to inspire a nation of patriots and promote a foundation of liberty. This reading list is full of books and resources that will help all who read them gain a deeper understanding of our nation's history and heritage as well as the principles of liberty and values of character that have kept America free for more than two hundred years. While learning our history and the principles of liberty our nation was founded on is important, it is equally important to understand those forces and philosophies that are a direct threat to freedom and liberty. For this reason, I have not only included the Declaration of Independence and the Constitution of the United States in the list, but I also included the *Communist Manifesto, Mein Kampf,* and other similar writings.

A Patriot's History of the United States by Larry Schweikart and Michael Allen
A Thomas Jefferson Education by Oliver DeMille
America: The Last Best Hope Volumes I & II by William J. Bennett
America's God and Country by William J. Federer
American Minute by William J. Federer
Animal Farm by George Orwell
Atlas Shrugged by Ayn Rand
Betrayed by the Bench by John A. Stormer
Common Sense by Thomas Paine
Declaration of Independence
Defeating the Totalitarian Lie by Hilmar von Campe
Endangered Speeches by William J. Federer
Fahrenheit 451 by Ray Bradbury
Four Trojan Horses of Humanism by Harry Con
From Sea to Shining Sea by Peter Marshall and David Manuel
Glenn Beck's Common Sense by Glenn Beck
Great Women in American History by Rebecca Price Janney
John Adams by David McCullough
Light and the Glory, The by Peter Marshall & David Manuel
Lives of the Signers (reprint of 1848 text) by Wallbuilder Press 1995)
Making of America, The by W. Cleon Skousen
Mein Kampf by Adolf Hitler
New Deal or Raw Deal by Burton W. Folsom

Our Country's Founders by William J. Bennett
Our Town by Thornton Wilder
Patriots in Petticoats by Patricia Edwards Clyne and Richard Lebenson
Prelude to Glory (nine-volume set) by Ron Carter
Rise to Rebellion by Jeff Shaara
Sounding Forth the Trumpet by Peter Marshall and David Manuel
The 5000 Year Leap: A Miracle that Changed the World by W. Cleon Skousen
The American Patriot's Almanac: Daily Readings on America by William J. Bennett and John Cribb
The Communist Manifesto and other Revolutionary Writings edited by Bob Blaisdell
The Federalist Papers edited by Clinton Rossiter
The Interesting History of Income Tax by William J. Federer
The Law by Frederic Bastiat
The Naked Capitalist by W. Cleon Skousen
The Naked Communist by W. Cleon Skousen
The Proper Role of Government by Ezra Taft Benson
The *Real Benjamin Franklin* by Andrew M. Allison
The *Real George Washington* by Parry, Allison, Skousen
The *Real Thomas Jefferson* Andrew M. Allison
Three Secular Reasons Why America Should Be Under God by William J. Federer
Tragedy of American Compassion, The by Marvin Olasky
United States Constitution
Unlikely Heroes by Ron Carter
When Queens Ride By by Agnes Slight Turnbull
Wives of the Signers (Reprint) by Walbuilders
Women Patriots of the American Revolution by Charles E. Claghorn
1776 by David McCullough
1984 by George Orwell

Little Patriots Reading List: *(Great family books to read aloud and picture books for young ones)*

If every American read this list of books and shared them with their children, freedom and liberty would be secured for generations to come. I love these books. The best way to learn about history is through historical fiction, exciting biographies, and moving narratives. They're all here. Dive in and enjoy! You are in for an unforgettable experience.

A Child's History of the World by Virgil M. Hillyer
A Is for Abigail: An Almanac of Amazing American Women by Lynne Cheney and Robin Preiss Glasser
A Lion to Guard Us by Clyde Robert Bulla
A More Perfect Union by Betsy and Guilio Maestro
Across Five Aprils by Irene Hunt
Advice to the Young by Noah Webster
America: A Patriotic Primer by Lynne Cheney and Robin Preiss Glasser
American History Stories You Never Read in School but Should Have (Volumes 1 & 2) by Mara L. Pratt
Amos Fortune: Free Man by Elizabeth Yates
Are You Liberal? Conservative? or Confused? by Richard J. Maybury
Ben and Me by Robert Lawson
Benjamin Franklin You Know What to Say by Lloyd Uglow
Betsy Ross and the Silver Thimble by Stephanie Greene and Diana Magnuson
Buffalo Bill by Ingri Parim D'aulaire
By the Great Horn Spoon by Sid Fleischman
Caddie Woodlawn by Carol Ryrie Brink
Calico Captive by Elizabeth George Speare
Carry On, Mr. Bowditch by Jean Lee Latham
Colonial Days: Discover the Past with Fun Projects, Games, Activities, and Recipes (American Kids in History Series) by David C. King
Columbus by Ingri Parim D'aulaire
A Connecticut Yankee in King Arthur's Court by Mark Twain
Constitution Translated for Kids by Cathy Travis
Crossing the Delaware by Louise Peacock
Fine Print: A Story About Johann Gutenberg by Joann Johansen Burch
George Washington by James Cross Giblin
Give Me Liberty: The Story of the Declaration of Independence by Russell Freedman
Gulliver's Travels by Jonathan Swift

Heidi by Johanna Spyri
Hittite Warrior by Joanne Williamson
Impossible Journey by Gloria Whelan
In Freedom's Cause by G. A. Henty
Joan of Arc by Diane Stanley
Johnny Appleseed by Reeve Lindbergh and Kathy Jakobsen Hallquist
Kidnapped by Robert Louis Stevenson
Little Women by Louisa May Alcott and Susan Straight
Men of Iron by Howard Pyle
Mr. Revere and I by Robert Lawson
Night Journeys by Avi
O Pioneers by Willa Cather
Our 50 States: A Family Adventure Across America by Lynne Cheney and Robin Preiss Glasser
Pass the Quill, I'll Write a Draft, A story of Thomas Jefferson by Robert Quackenbush
Paul Revere's Ride by Henry Wadsworth Longfellow, illustrated by Ted Rand
The Red Badge of Courage by Stephen Crane
Sign of the Beaver by Elizabeth George Speare
Sojourner Truth: Ain't I a Woman?
Son of Charlemagne by Barbara Willard
Squanto and the Miracle of the First Thanksgiving by Eric Metaxas and Shannon Stirnweis
Squanto: Friend of the Pilgrims by Clyde Robert Bulla and Peter Buchard
Stories of the Pilgrims by Margaret B Pumphrey
Story of the World (multi book set) by Susan Wise Bauer
The 13 colonies by Gail Sakurai
The 4th of July Story by Alice Dalgliesh
The Adventures of Huckleberry Finn by Mark Twain
The Amazing Life of Benjamin Franklin by James Cross Giblin
The American Revolution for Kids: A History with 21 Activities by Janis Herbert
The Apple and the Arrow by Mary and Conrad Buff
The Arrow Over the Door by Joseph Bruchac and James Watling
The Bald Eagle's View of American History by C. h. Colman and Joanne H. Friar
The Black Arrow by Robert Louis Stevenson
The Book of Virtues by William J. Bennett

The Bronze Bow by Elizabeth George Speare
The Bullet Proof George Washington (Wallbuilders)
The Children's Book of America by William J. Bennett and Michael Hague
The Children's Book of Heroes by Amy Hill, William J. Bennett, and Michael Hague
The Children's Treasury of Virtues by William J. Bennett and Michael Hague
The Chronicles of Narnia by C.S. Lewis
The Courage of Sarah Noble by Alice Dalgliesh and Leonard Weisgard
The Declaration of Independence (Cornerstones of Freedom) by R. Conrad Stein
The Declaration of Independence: the words that made America by Sam Fink
The Door in the Wall by Marguerite De Angeli
The Giver by Lois Lowry
The Golden Goblet by Eloise Jarvis McGraw
The Hiding Place by Corrie Ten Boom
The Journey of the One and Only Declaration of Independence by Judith St. George and Will Hillenbrand
The Land of Fair Play by Geoffrey Parsons
The Light and the Glory for Children by Peter Marshall & David Manuel
A Time for Freedom by Lynne Cheney
The Man Who Would Not Be King (Wallbuilders)
The Matchlock Gun by Walter D. Edmonds
The Pearl by John Steinbeck
The Scarlet Pimpernel by Emmuska Orczy
The Spirit of America by William J. Bennett
The Star Spangled Banner (a Scholastic book)
The Witch of Blackbird Pond by Elizabeth George Speare
Theras and His Town by Caroline Dale Snedeker
Thomas Jefferson by Cheryl Harness
Trumpet of the Swan by E.B. White
Twice Freed by Patricia St. John
Uncle Tom's Cabin by Harriett Beecher Stowe
We Came Through Ellis Island: the Immigrant Adventures of Emma Markowitz
We the Kids: The Preamble to the Constitution of the United States by David Catrow
We the People: The Story of Our Constitution by Lynne Cheney and Greg Harlin
What's the Big Idea, Ben Franklin by Jean Fritz and Margot Tomes
Whatever Happened to Justice by Richard J. Maybury

Whatever Happened to Penny Candy by Richard J. Maybury
When Mr. Jefferson Came to Philadelphia by Ann Turner and Mark Hess
When Washington Crossed the Delaware: A Wintertime Story for Young Patriots by Lynne Cheney and Peter M. Fiore
With Lee in Virginia by G. A. Henty and Gordon Browne
Woodrow the White House Mouse by Cheryl Shaw Barnes
Yankee Doodle America by Wendell Minor

Book Series—
American Girl Book Series
Boxcar Children Book Series
Childhood Lives of Famous Americans Book Series
Dear America Book Series
If You Lived … (Book Series)
Little House on the Prairie Book Series
My America Book Series
Royal Diaries Book Series
Prelude to Glory Book Series
Story of the World Series by Susan Wise Bauer
Tales from Shakespeare Series by Eric Kincaid

Libraries of Hope *www.librariesofhope.org*
Libraries of Hope is a non-profit foundation that has an inspiring collection of history stories from the golden age of literature—late 1800s and early 1900s, when authors wrote to instill patriotism, inspire faith, and promote strong character. Libraries of Hope has gathered many of these stories and reproduced in their Forgotten Classics Library. Their Freedom Series is a must-have for every American patriot and their family.

Yesterday's Classics *www.yesterdaysclassics.com*
Yesterday's Classics republishes classic books for children in high-quality paperback editions. These books, first published in the golden age of children's literature from 1880 and 1920 and long out of print, are reprinted in modern, easy-to-read type for today's readers. I highly recommend these remarkable classics in historic literature.

ADDITIONAL RESOURCES
Great States Jr. (board game)
Hooray for the USA (craft book)

Mad Dash—3 Minutes Across America (board game)
Take Your Hat off When the Flag Goes By by Janeen Brady (book and audio tape)
Snapshots Across America (board game)
Little Hands Celebrate America (craft book)
I Love America Books 1 and 2 by Julianne Kimber
The Family Guide to Classic Movies by J.S. Ringler
Learning with the Movies: A Guide for Education and Fun by Beth Holland
Let the Author's Speak: A Guide to Worthy Books Based on Historical Setting by Carolyn Hatcher
Turning Back the Pages of Time—A Guide to American History Through Literature by Kathy Keller

MOVIES
A More Perfect Union (1989)
Animated Hero Classics by NEST Entertainment
Ben and Me (1953, animated film)
Braveheart (1995)
Gettysburg (1993)
Gods and Generals (2003)
Into the Arms of Strangers: Stories of the Kinder transport (2000)
Johnny Tremaine (1957)
Mr. Smith Goes to Washington (1939)
My Side of the Mountain (1962)
Red Dawn (1984)
Sarah Plain and Tall (1990)
The Alamo (1960)
The Hiding Place (1975)
The Man Without a Country (1973)
The Patriot (2000)

Online Sources for Great Books & Resources
Love to Learn *www.lovetolearn.net*
Classic Books *www.classicbooks.com*
Yesterday's Classics *www.yesterdaysclassics.com*
The National Center for Constitutional Studies *www.nccs.net*
Wallbuilders *http://www.wallbuilders.com*
ABEKA History Books *https://www.abeka.com*

ABOUT THE AUTHOR

Kimberly Fletcher is the president and founder of Homemakers for America—a national, non-profit organization, specifically designed for women and their families, dedicated to the education and preservation of America's history, heritage and legacy.

Kimberly is the wife of a United States Air Force officer and the mother of 8 children.

On September 11, 2001, Kimberly's life was turned upside down when a 757 flew into the United States Pentagon where her husband was stationed. Later that day, when her husband returned home safely, Kimberly determined that she would do everything in her power to ensure that her children remained free. This determination led her to an intense study of American history and public policy and a desire to become actively involved in government and politics.

Kimberly has made it her personal mission to educate and inspire the women of America on America's history and heritage and empower them to take an active role in their homes, communities and the nation to ensure that the legacy of freedom our Founders left us continues on to the next generation and for generations to come.

In 2004 Kimberly founded Homemakers for America in the living room of her friend's home with a group of 26 women. In just 6 months, through grassroots efforts, the organization grew from 26 members in Dayton Ohio to a National membership in all 50 states.

Kimberly is an experienced grassroots activist who has volunteered thousands of hours of her time with several local, state, and national, candidate and public policy campaigns. She has helped to organize and is the former Vice President of the Dayton Tea Party (the fourth largest in the nation) and has volunteered with three presidential candidates—including serving as the operations manager of a victory center in Dayton Ohio in the 2008 election.

As an author, columnist and public speaker, Kimberly has been heard on numerous regional and national TV and radio programs including the Sean Hannity Show and her articles have appeared in several print and on-line publications including American Thinker and Worldnetdaily. Kimberly and her husband Derek live in Dayton Ohio with their children. Her husband recently returned from serving a tour of duty in Iraq.

ENDNOTES

Two Sides of Women
1. Capital Research Center, 2002, Guide to Feminist Organizations, p. 14, Kimberly Shuld.
2. What I Know for Sure, O, *The Oprah Magazine*, 66.

A Woman's Influence
1. Ex-NFL star Tillman makes 'ultimate sacrifice', NBC, MSNBC and news services, Updated: 3:39 a.m. ET April 26, 2004.
2. Ibid.
3. Legal Defense and Education Fund, Women's ENews on July 11, 2001.
4. *Wives of the Signers,* Forward.
5. Ibid.
6. Ibid.
7. Ibid.
8. *Great Women in American History,* Rebecca Price Janney, Horizon Books, 245–253.
9. Ibid.
10. Ibid.
11. Ibid.
12. Ibid.
13. Ibid.
14. Ibid.
15. *Wives of the Signers,* 106.
16. *Wives of the Signers,* 69.
17. *Wives of the Signers,* 72.
18. Ibid.
19. *Patriots in Petticoats,* Patricia Edwards Clyne, 8.
20. *Patriots in Petticoats,* Patricia Edwards Clyne, 66.

21. *Wives of the Signers,* 95.
22. *Wives of the Signers,* 119–126.
23. Ibid.
24. *Wives of the Signers,* 170.
25. F.M. Bareham, *A Mother's Love* by Benjamin Devey, 2004.
26. John W. Whitehead, *The Stealing of America,* 1983.

Lest We Forget
1. Introduction, NOW Web site, *www.now.org.*
2. "High Court's Philosophy Imperils Women's Rights" July 11, 2001 by Isabelle Katz Pinzler, *Women's Enews.*
3. C. Bradley Thompson, *The Strange Career of American History, 1995.*
4. Ibid.
5. Ibid.
6. Data taken from *World* magazine, January 29, 2005, p. 23.
7. *American History Stories You Never Read in School,* by Mara Louise Pratt, 52.

White Wigs and Fat Cats
1. NOW Web site, Introduction, *www.now.org.*
2. Ibid.
3. Abigail Adams, letter to John Adams, March 31, 1776.
4. John Adams, letter to Abigail Adams, April 14, 1776.
5. *Newsweek,* May 23, 2005, 38, 43.
6. *America's God and Country,* William Federer, 636.
7. Ibid.
8. *America's God and Country,* William Federer, 636, 637.
9. *American History Stories,* Mara Louise Pratt, 89.
10. *America's God and Country,* William Federer, 640.
11. Ibid
12. Ibid.
13. Federer, 641.
14. Federer, 644.
15. *Lives of the Signers,* Wallbuilder Press, 96.
16. *Lives of the Signers,* 97, reprint of 1848 publication by Wallbuilder Press, 1995.

God Is too Controversial
1. The address of the Danbury Baptists Association in the state of Connecticut, assembled October 7, 1801. To Thomas Jefferson, Esq., President of the United States of America.

2. Thomas Jefferson, letter to a Committee of the Danbury Baptist Association, Connecticut, January 1, 1802.
3. John Adams, Thoughts on Government, 1776.
4. Ronald Reagan at the Alfred M. Landon Lecture Series, 1982.
5. Watts, Pauline Moffatt, "Prophecy and Discovery: On Spiritual Origins Christopher Columbus's Enterprise of the Indies." *American Historical Review* (Feb. 1985), p. 95.
6. Ferdinand Columbus. *The Life of Admiral Christopher Columbus by His Son Ferdinand Coumbus.* New Brusnwick, N.J.: Rutgers University Press, 1959, p. 8.
7. Ibid.
8. *America's God and Country,* 639.
9. *America's God and Country,* 640.
10. *America's God and Country,* 646.
11. *America's God and Country,*643.
12. *America's God and Country,* 646.
13. George Washington, as quoted by Gouverneur Morris in Farrand's Records of the Federal Convention of 1787, March 25, 1787.
14. *In God We Trust,* edited by Norman Cousins, p. 42.
15. George Washington, Resignation Address, Annapolis, December 23, 1783.

Warmongers
1. Ronald Reagan, at Brandenburg Gate West Berlin, Germany, June 12, 1987.
2. Open letter to President Bush, March 7, 2003, NOW Web site.
3. *American History Stories You Never Read in School,* by Mara Louise Pratt, p. 86.
4. Open letter to President Bush, March 7, 2003, NOW Web site.
5. "Bush Protesting Mom Calls for 'Israel Out of Palestine'; Vows Not to Pay Taxes," Drudge Report, August 14, 2005.
6. Ibid.
7. *The Arizona Republic.* "A Wake-Up Call from Luke's Jets." Letters to the Editor. June 23, 2005.
8. *The Arizona Republic.* "Flyby Honored Fallen Comrade." Letters to the Editor. June 28, 2005.
9. George Washington, Farewell Address, September 19, 1796.
10. Senator Durbin, speech on Senate floor, June 14, 2005.
11. "Military Brass Hit Kennedy for Saying War Is a 'Quaqmire' *The Washington Times* Published: Jun 24, 2005 Author: Rowan Scarborough.
12. Ibid.
13. Ibid .
14. Ibid.
15. Ibid.

16. James Madison, Federalist No. 41, January 1788.
17. Copyright by Charles M. Province, *http://www.pattonhq.com*, cmprovince@gmail.com.

Is There Truth Out There?
1. Misery Index, US unemployment rate chart, *http://www.miseryindex.us/urbymonth.asp.*
2. *September 29, 2008*, Bush Administration Adds $4 Trillion to National Debt, Mark Knoller.
3. Martin Gottlieb: Dayton Tea Party seemed aimed at few by Martin Gottlieb, April 15, 2009.

Fort Knox
1. Thomas Jefferson, letter to Spencer Roane, March 9, 1821.
2. Thomas Jefferson, First Inaugural Address, March 4, 1801.
3. June 29, 2008, Interview with Farrah Gray—Author, Philanthropist and Real Estate Entrepreneur by Clayton Perry.
4. *5000 Year Leap: A Miracle that Changed the World,* 21.
5. James Madison, speech in the House of Representatives, January 10, 1794.
6. Words from the inaugural address of President John F. Kennedy, delivered in 1961.
7. Thomas Jefferson, letter to Thomas Cooper, November 29, 1802.
8. Thomas Jefferson, Note in Destutt de Tracy, 1816.
9. "Not Yours to Give," originally published in *The Life of Colonel David Crockett,* by Edward Sylvester Ellis.
10. Ibid.
11. Ibid.
12. Ibid.
13. Ibid.
14. Ibid.
15. Ibid.
16. Ibid.
17. Ibid.
18. Ibid.
19. Ibid.
20. Ibid.

Stimulating Facts
1. Henry Grady Weaver, *The Mainspring of Human Progress,* p. 40-1; P.P.N.S., p. 313
2. Elmer T. Peterson. "This is the Hard Core of Freedom," *Daily Oklahoman*, 9 December 1951, p. 12A.

3. From the Harvard Class Book of 1935, entitled "Thirty Years Later," spotlighting Baldwin's class of 1905 on its thirtieth anniversary, as quoted in a 1997 Insight on the News article.

Your Voice Counts
1. Gideon J. Tucker in *Final Accounting in the Estate of A. B.* (1866).
2. President George Washington Farewell Address, 1796.

Rise Up, Ye Women
1. "Bill Maher: Christians have neurological disorder," *Worldnetdaily*, February 18, 2005.
2. *Ben Stein, Expelled: No Intelligence Allowed,* Premise Media Corporation, 2008.
3. "Bill Maher: Christians have neurological disorder," *Worldnetdaily*, February 18, 2005.
4. *Ben Stein, Expelled: No Intelligence Allowed,* Premise Media Corporation, 2008.
5. KJV, 2 Timothy 3:13.
6. Quote attributed to Alexis de Tocqueville (1805–1859).
7. KJV, James 1:25.
8. KJV, Jeremiah 34:17.
9. KJV, Ephesians. 4: 14.
10. KJV, Jeremiah 9:5.
11. KJV, Romans 16:18.
12. KJV, Malachi 1:14.
13. Ephesians 6:13.
14. Ephesians 6: 11.
15. 2 Timothy 3:12.
16. 2 Timothy 3:1–5, 14, 15.
17. *Benjamin Franklin's The Art of Virtue*, ed. George L. Rogers (1996), 88–90.
18. Exodus 18:21.
19. Proverbs 28:15.
20. 2 Peter 2:19.
21. Proverbs 29:2.
22. Smyth, *The Writings of Benjamin Franklin*, 10:84.
23. Ezra Taft Benson, "Born of God," *Ensign*, July 1989, 2.
24. "Chapter 10: Fortifying Ourselves against Evil Influences," *Teachings of Presidents of the Church: Spencer W. Kimball*, (2006), 102–13.
25. Joshua 1:9.
26. 1 Chronicles 28:20.

Made in the USA
San Bernardino, CA
13 October 2014